THERE'S TREASURE EVERYWHERE

Other Books by Bill Watterson

Calvin and Hobbes
Something Under the Bed Is Drooling
Yukon Ho!
Weirdos from Another Planet
The Revenge of the Baby-Sat
Scientific Progress Goes "Boink"
Attack of the Deranged Mutant Killer Monster Snow Goons
The Days Are Just Packed
Homicidal Psycho Jungle Cat

Treasury Collections

The Essential Calvin and Hobbes
The Calvin and Hobbes Lazy Sunday Book
The Authoritative Calvin and Hobbes
The Indispensable Calvin and Hobbes
The Calvin and Hobbes Tenth Anniversary Book

THERE'S TREASURE EVERYWHERE

A Calvin and Hobbes Collection by Bill Watterson

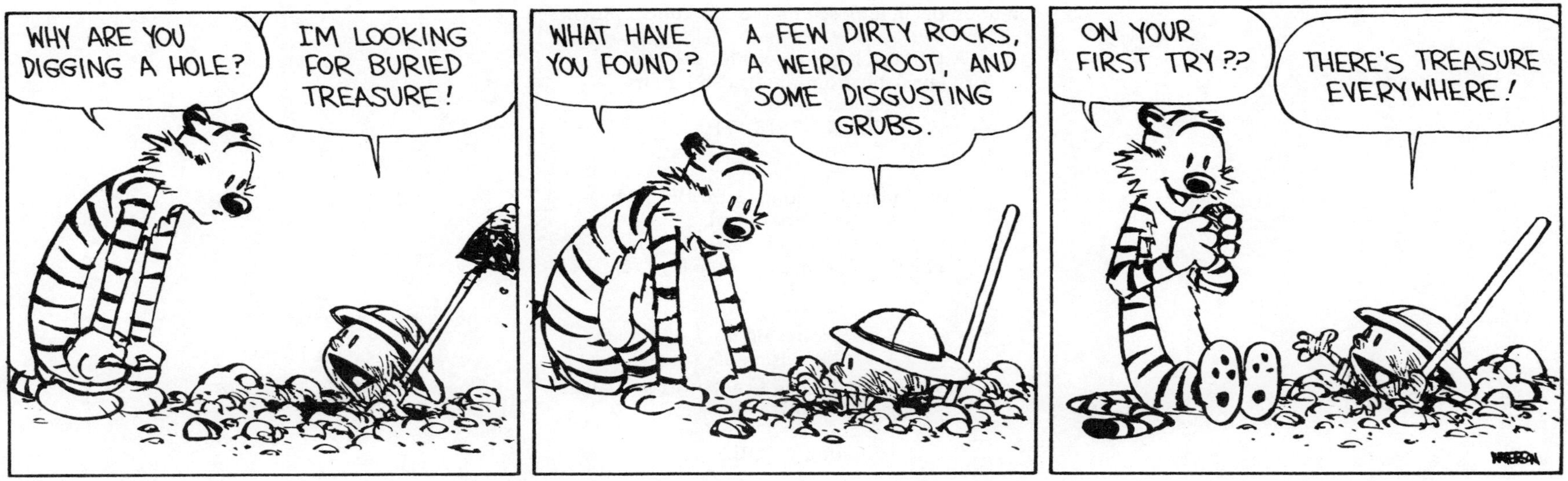
WHY ARE YOU DIGGING A HOLE?
I'M LOOKING FOR BURIED TREASURE!
WHAT HAVE YOU FOUND?
A FEW DIRTY ROCKS, A WEIRD ROOT, AND SOME DISGUSTING GRUBS.
ON YOUR FIRST TRY??
THERE'S TREASURE EVERYWHERE!

WARNER BOOKS

A *Warner* Book

First published in Great Britain
by Warner Books in 1996

There's Treasure Everywhere copyright © 1996 by Bill Watterson
Distributed internationally by Universal Press Syndicate.
All rights reserved.

Calvin and Hobbes is a cartoon feature created by Bill Watterson,
syndicated internationally by Universal Press Syndicate and
There's Treasure Everywhere was first published in the United
States by Andrews and McMeel.

The moral right of the author has been asserted.

A CIP catalogue record for this book is
available from the British Library

ISBN 0 7515 1719 4

Printed and bound in Great Britain by
BPC Books Ltd.
A member of
The British Printing Company Ltd.

Warner Books
A Division of
Little, Brown and Company (UK)
Brettenham House
Lancaster Place
London WC2E 7EN

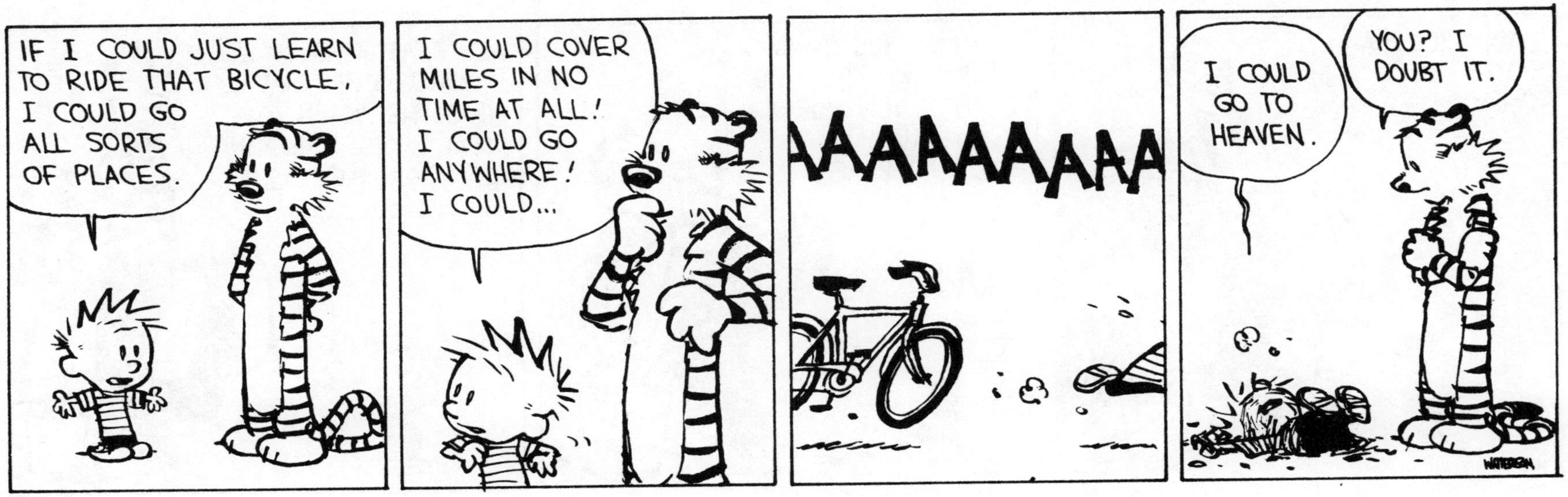
IF I COULD JUST LEARN TO RIDE THAT BICYCLE, I COULD GO ALL SORTS OF PLACES.
I COULD COVER MILES IN NO TIME AT ALL! I COULD GO ANYWHERE! I COULD...
AAAAAAAAAA
I COULD GO TO HEAVEN.
YOU? I DOUBT IT.

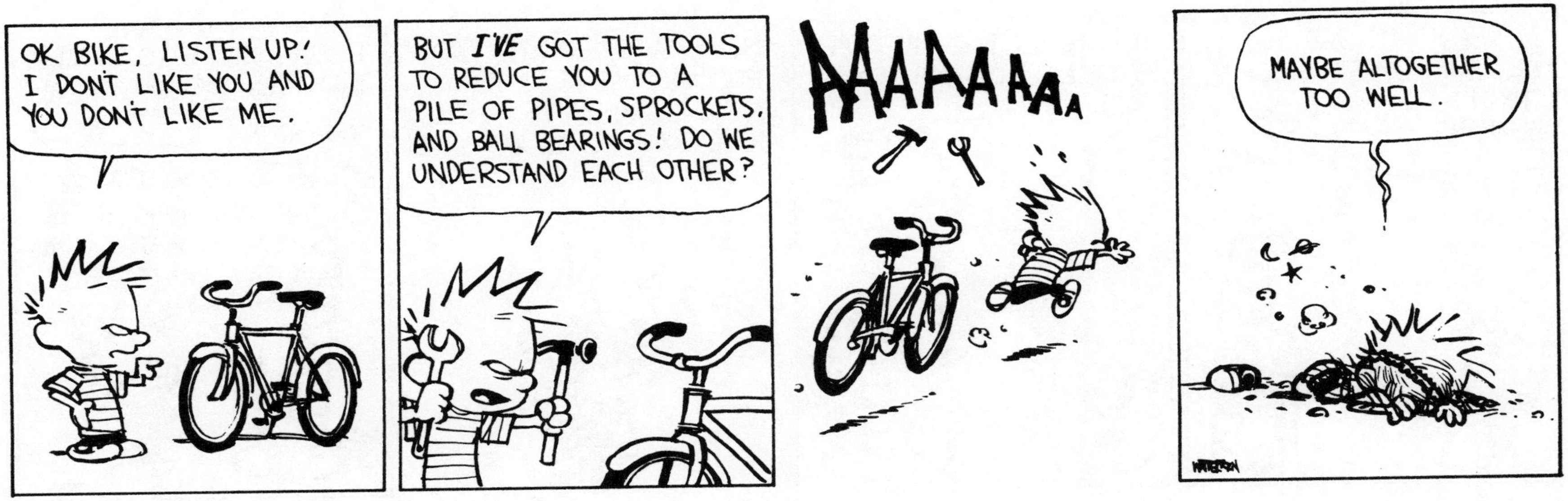
OK BIKE, LISTEN UP! I DON'T LIKE YOU AND YOU DON'T LIKE ME.
BUT *I'VE* GOT THE TOOLS TO REDUCE YOU TO A PILE OF PIPES, SPROCKETS, AND BALL BEARINGS! DO WE UNDERSTAND EACH OTHER?
AAAAAAAA
MAYBE ALTOGETHER TOO WELL.

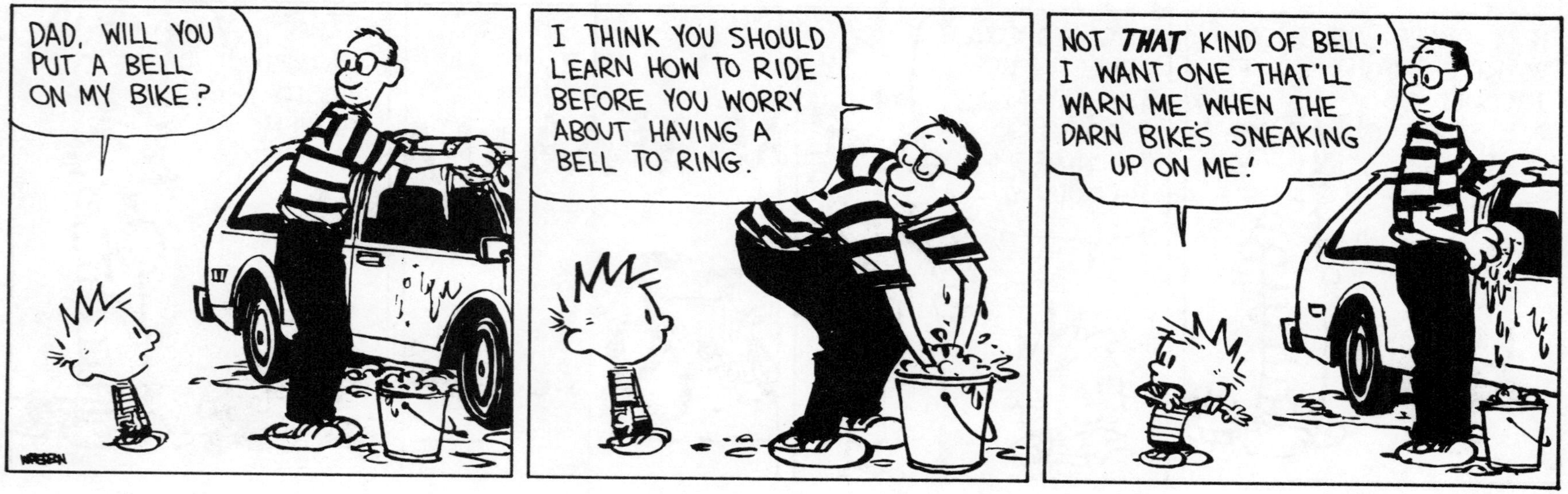
DAD, WILL YOU PUT A BELL ON MY BIKE?
I THINK YOU SHOULD LEARN HOW TO RIDE BEFORE YOU WORRY ABOUT HAVING A BELL TO RING.
NOT **THAT** KIND OF BELL! I WANT ONE THAT'LL WARN ME WHEN THE DARN BIKE'S SNEAKING UP ON ME!

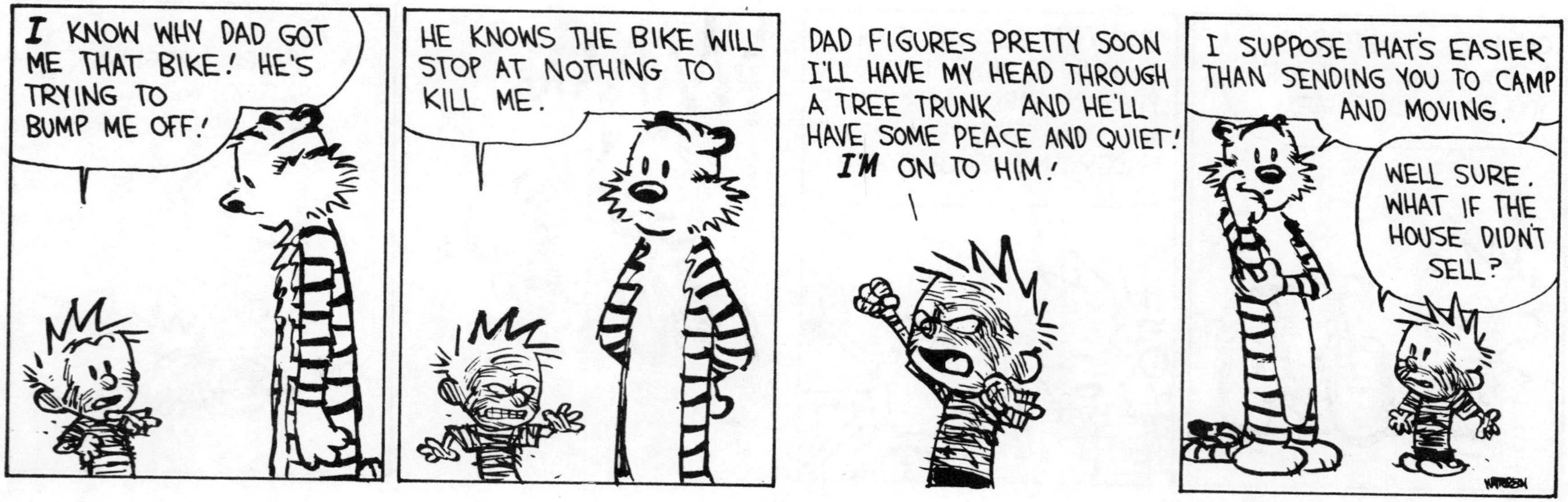
I KNOW WHY DAD GOT ME THAT BIKE! HE'S TRYING TO BUMP ME OFF!
HE KNOWS THE BIKE WILL STOP AT NOTHING TO KILL ME.
DAD FIGURES PRETTY SOON I'LL HAVE MY HEAD THROUGH A TREE TRUNK AND HE'LL HAVE SOME PEACE AND QUIET! **I'M** ON TO HIM!
I SUPPOSE THAT'S EASIER THAN SENDING YOU TO CAMP AND MOVING.
WELL SURE. WHAT IF THE HOUSE DIDN'T SELL?

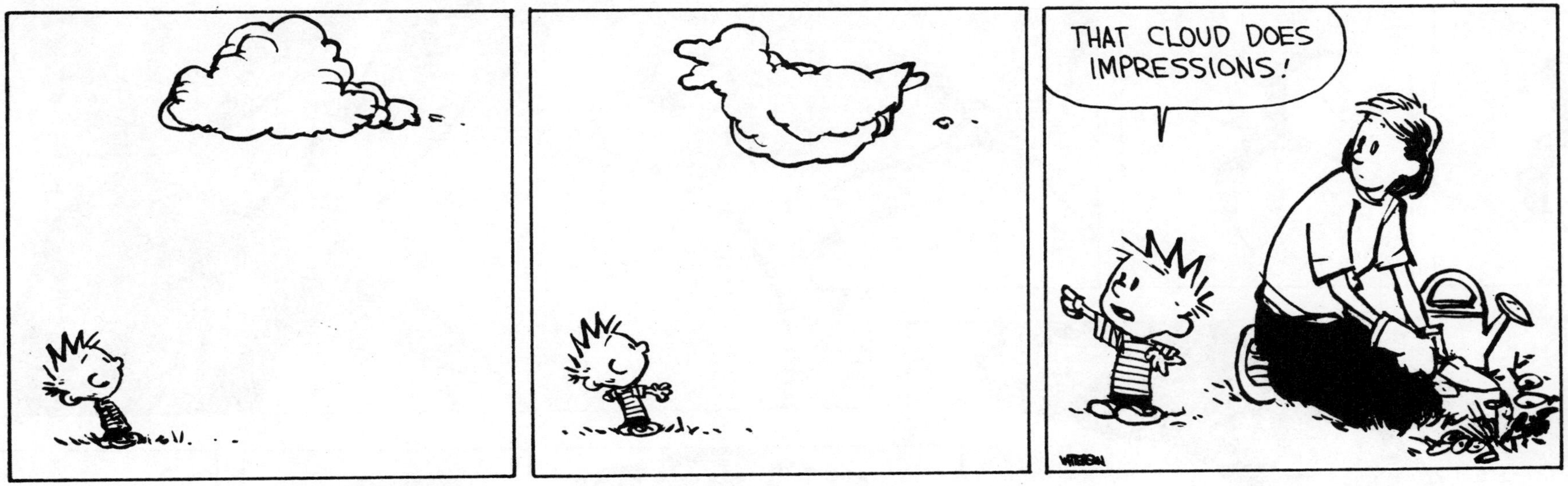
THAT CLOUD DOES IMPRESSIONS!

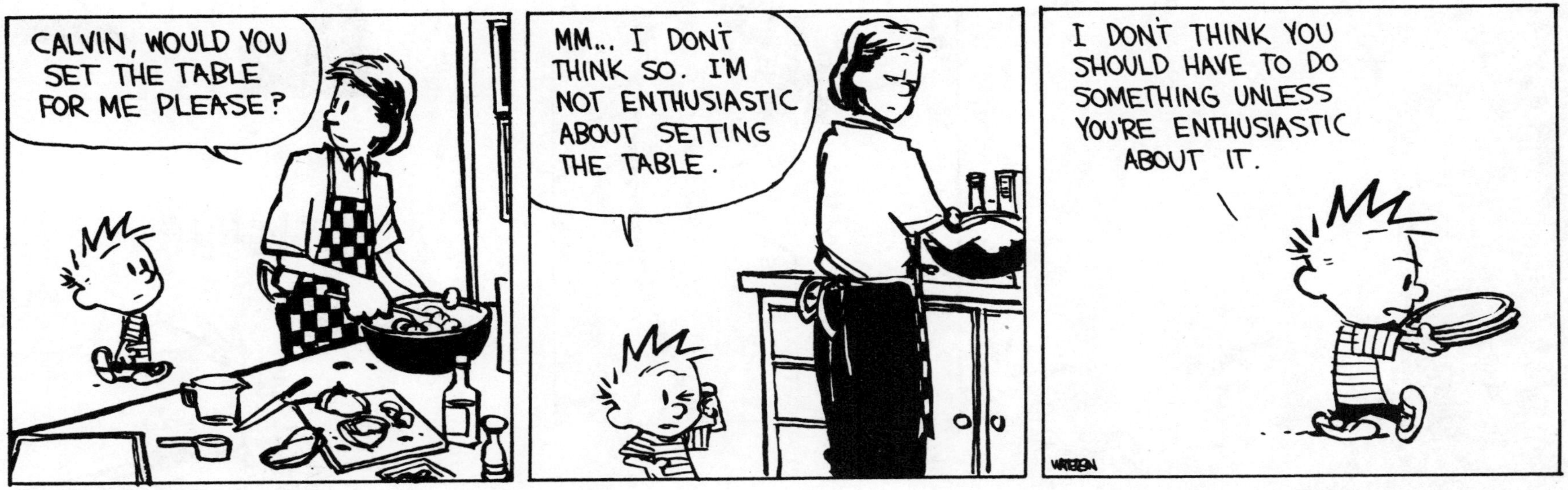
CALVIN, WOULD YOU SET THE TABLE FOR ME PLEASE?
MM... I DON'T THINK SO. I'M NOT ENTHUSIASTIC ABOUT SETTING THE TABLE.
I DON'T THINK YOU SHOULD HAVE TO DO SOMETHING UNLESS YOU'RE ENTHUSIASTIC ABOUT IT.

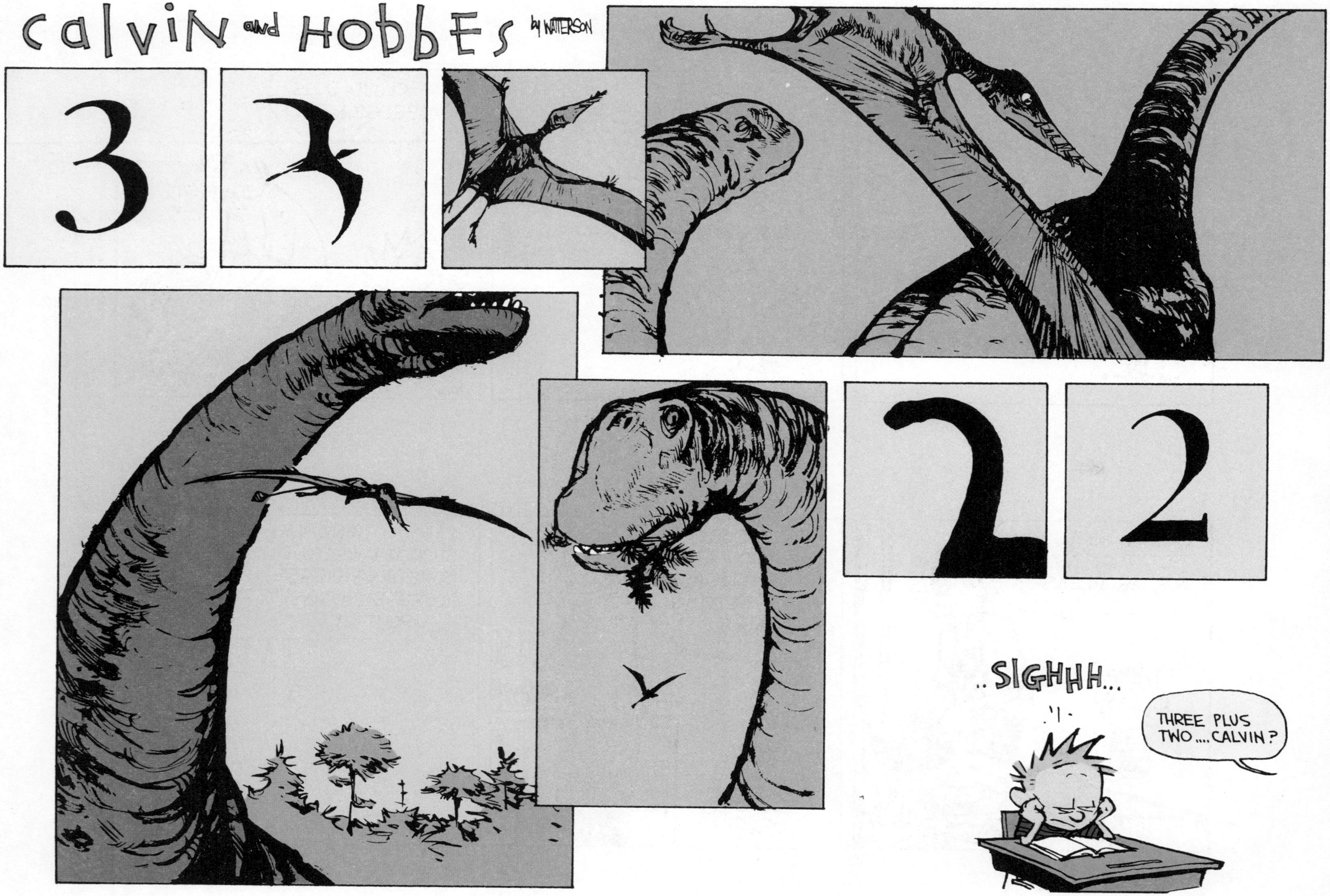
Calvin and HOBBES by WATTERSON
3
3
2
2
..SIGHHH...
THREE PLUS TWO....CALVIN?

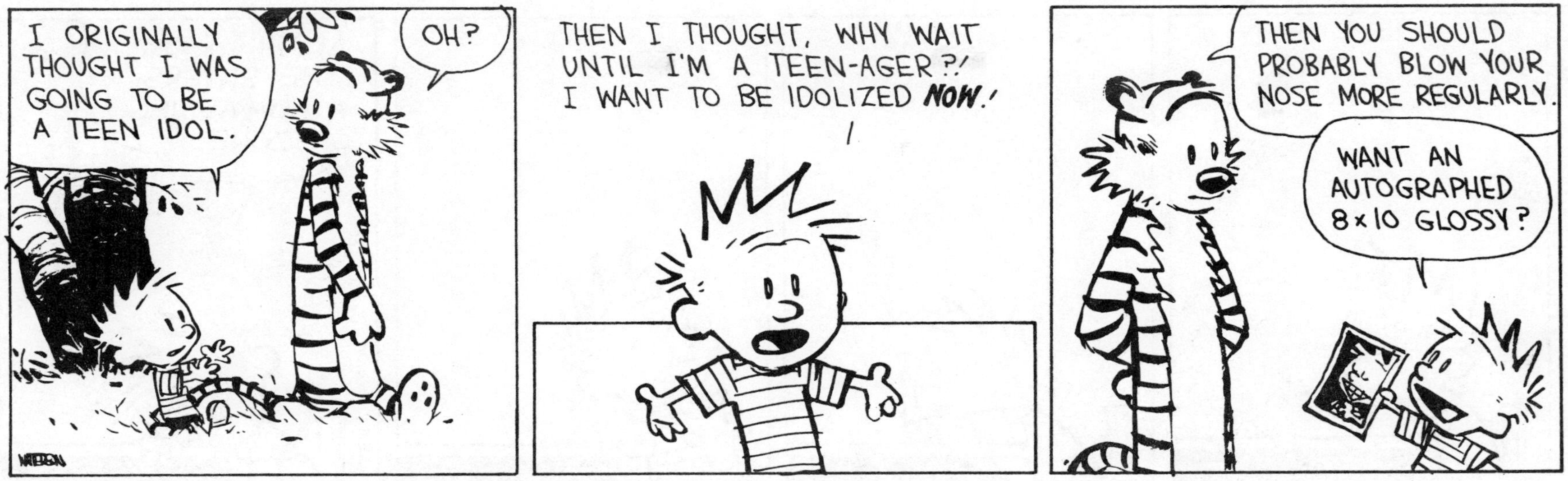
I ORIGINALLY THOUGHT I WAS GOING TO BE A TEEN IDOL.
OH?
THEN I THOUGHT, WHY WAIT UNTIL I'M A TEEN-AGER?! I WANT TO BE IDOLIZED **NOW**!
THEN YOU SHOULD PROBABLY BLOW YOUR NOSE MORE REGULARLY.
WANT AN AUTOGRAPHED 8×10 GLOSSY?

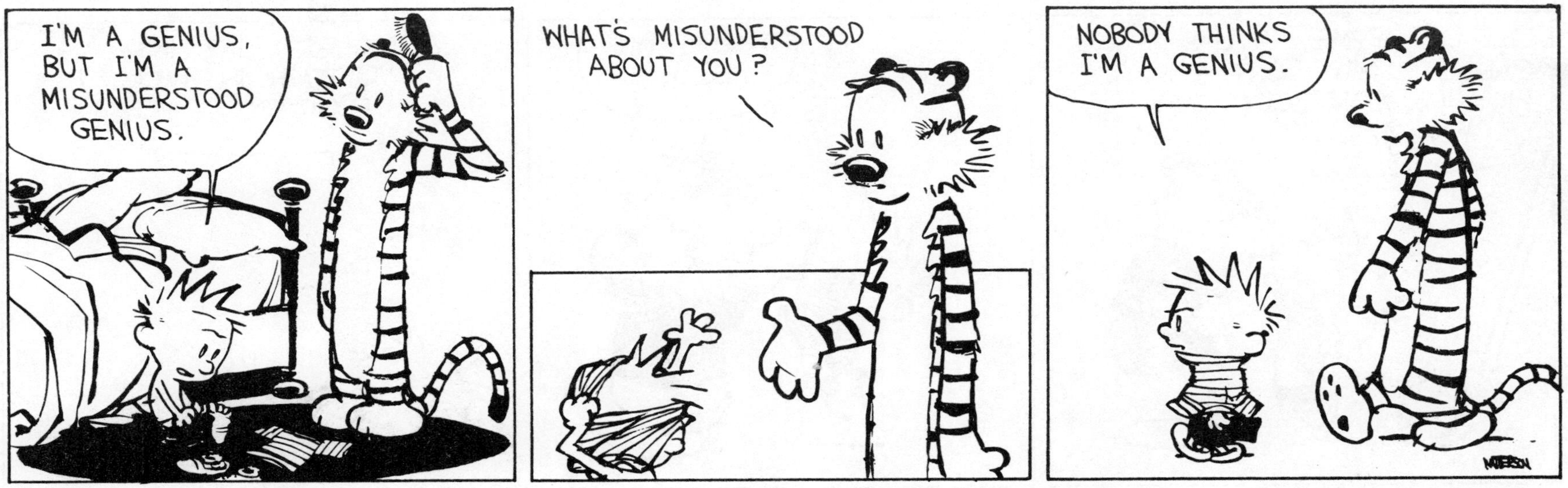
I'M A GENIUS, BUT I'M A MISUNDERSTOOD GENIUS.
WHAT'S MISUNDERSTOOD ABOUT YOU?
NOBODY THINKS I'M A GENIUS.

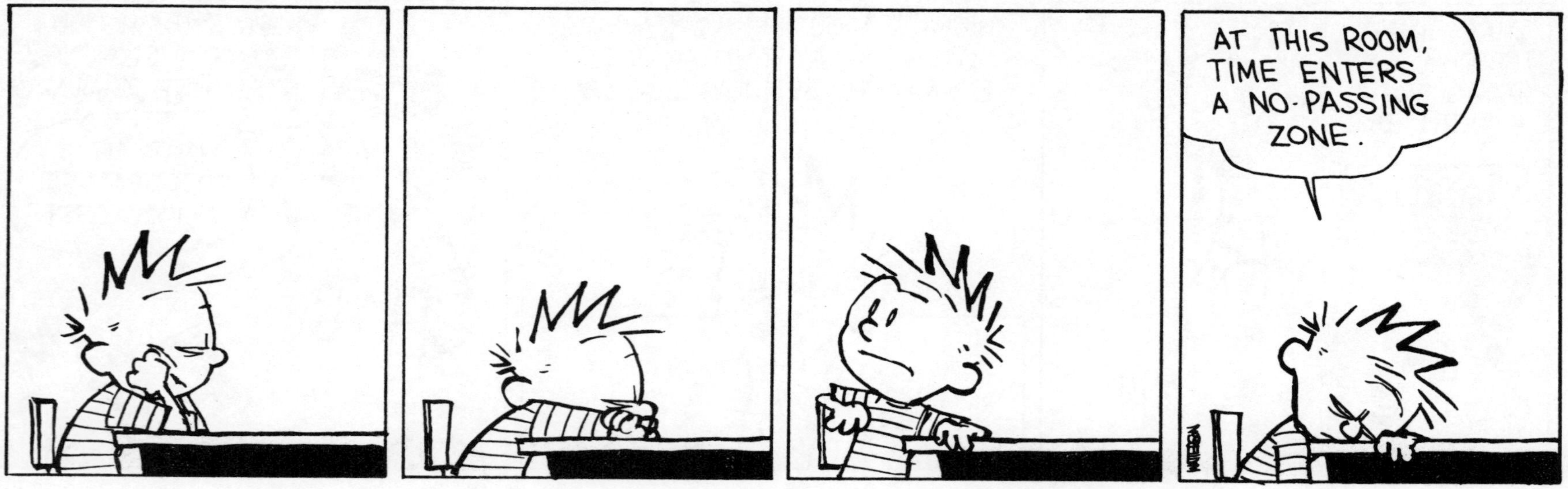
AT THIS ROOM, TIME ENTERS A NO-PASSING ZONE.

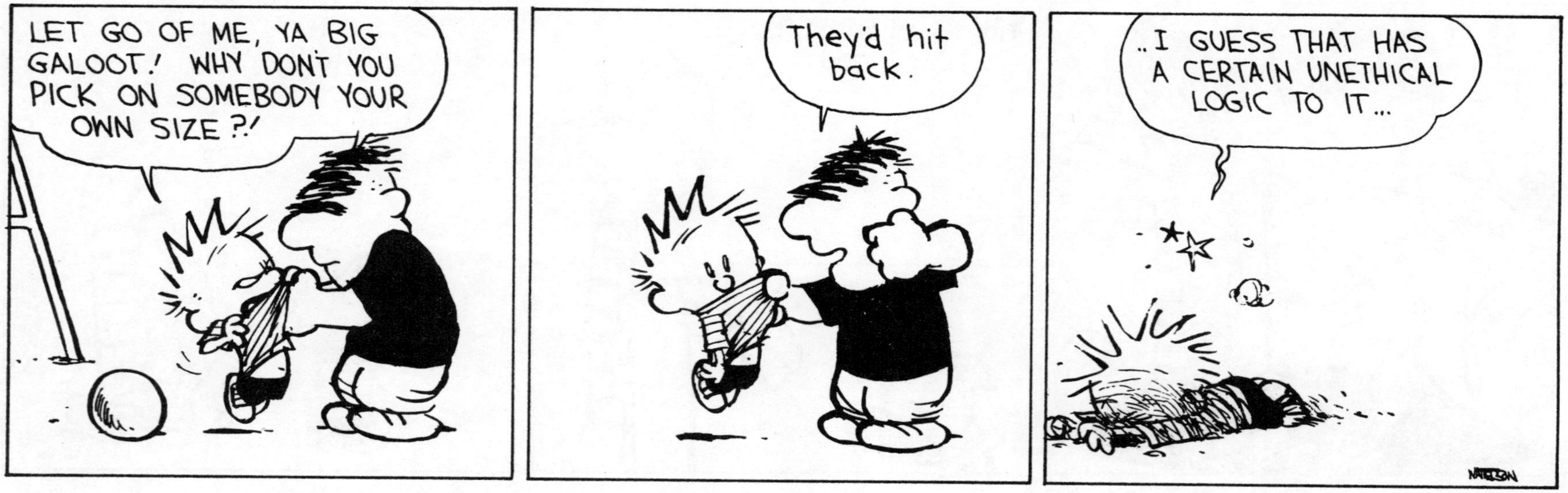
LET GO OF ME, YA BIG GALOOT! WHY DON'T YOU PICK ON SOMEBODY YOUR OWN SIZE?!
They'd hit back.
..I GUESS THAT HAS A CERTAIN UNETHICAL LOGIC TO IT...

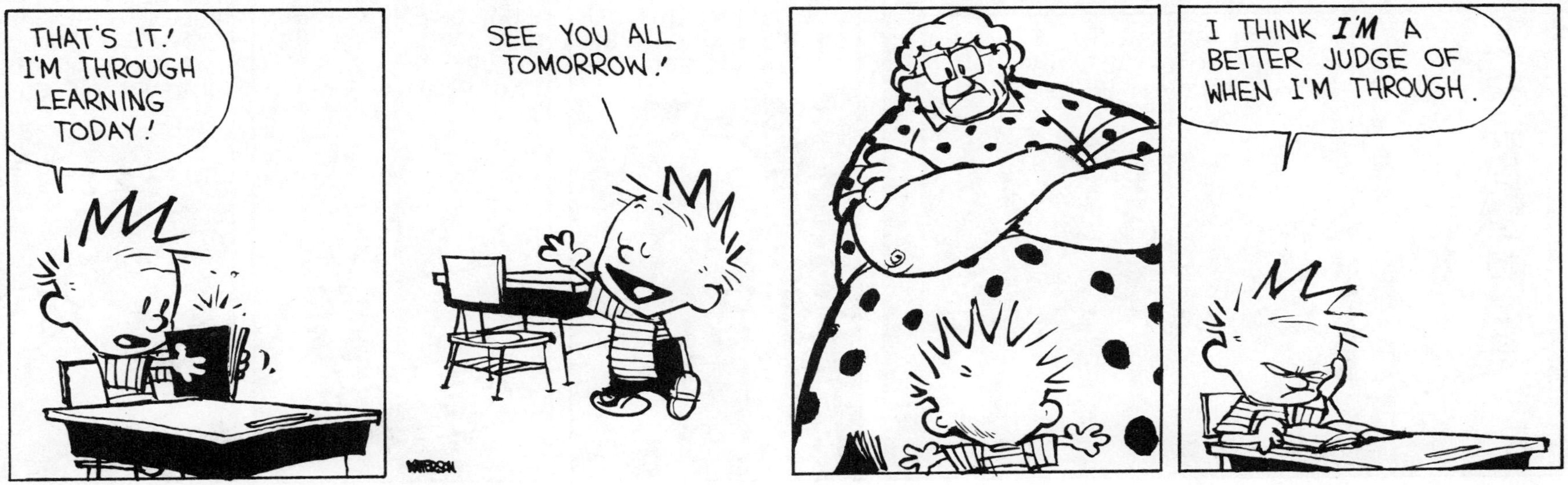
THAT'S IT! I'M THROUGH LEARNING TODAY!
SEE YOU ALL TOMORROW!
I THINK I'M A BETTER JUDGE OF WHEN I'M THROUGH.

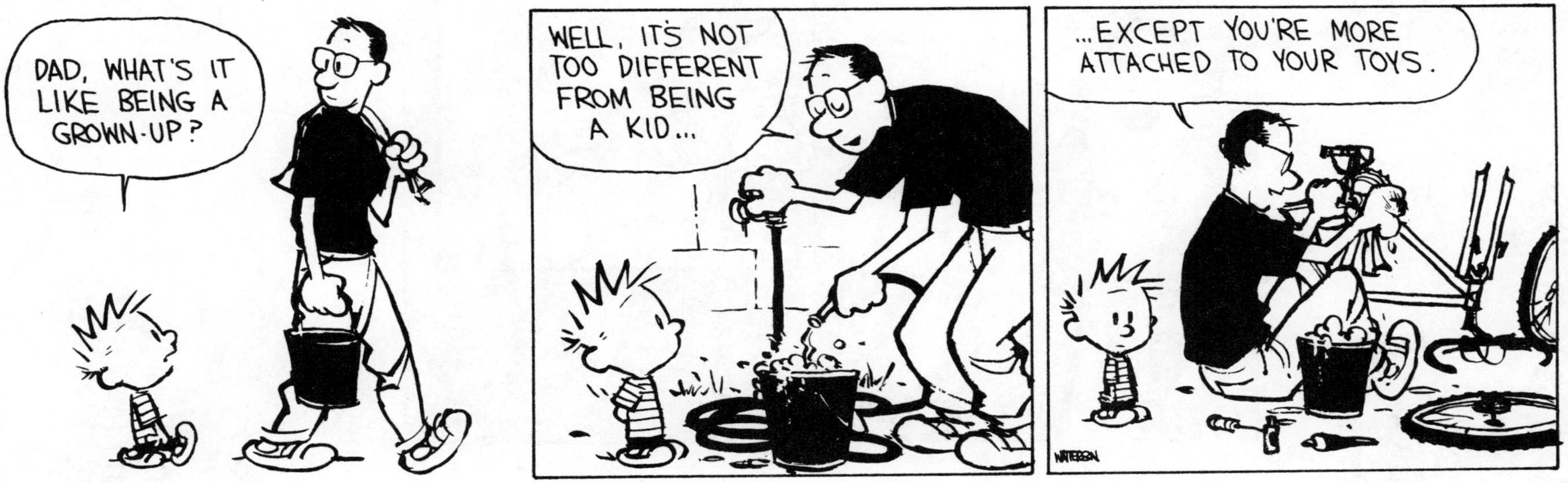
DAD, WHAT'S IT LIKE BEING A GROWN-UP?
WELL, IT'S NOT TOO DIFFERENT FROM BEING A KID...
...EXCEPT YOU'RE MORE ATTACHED TO YOUR TOYS.

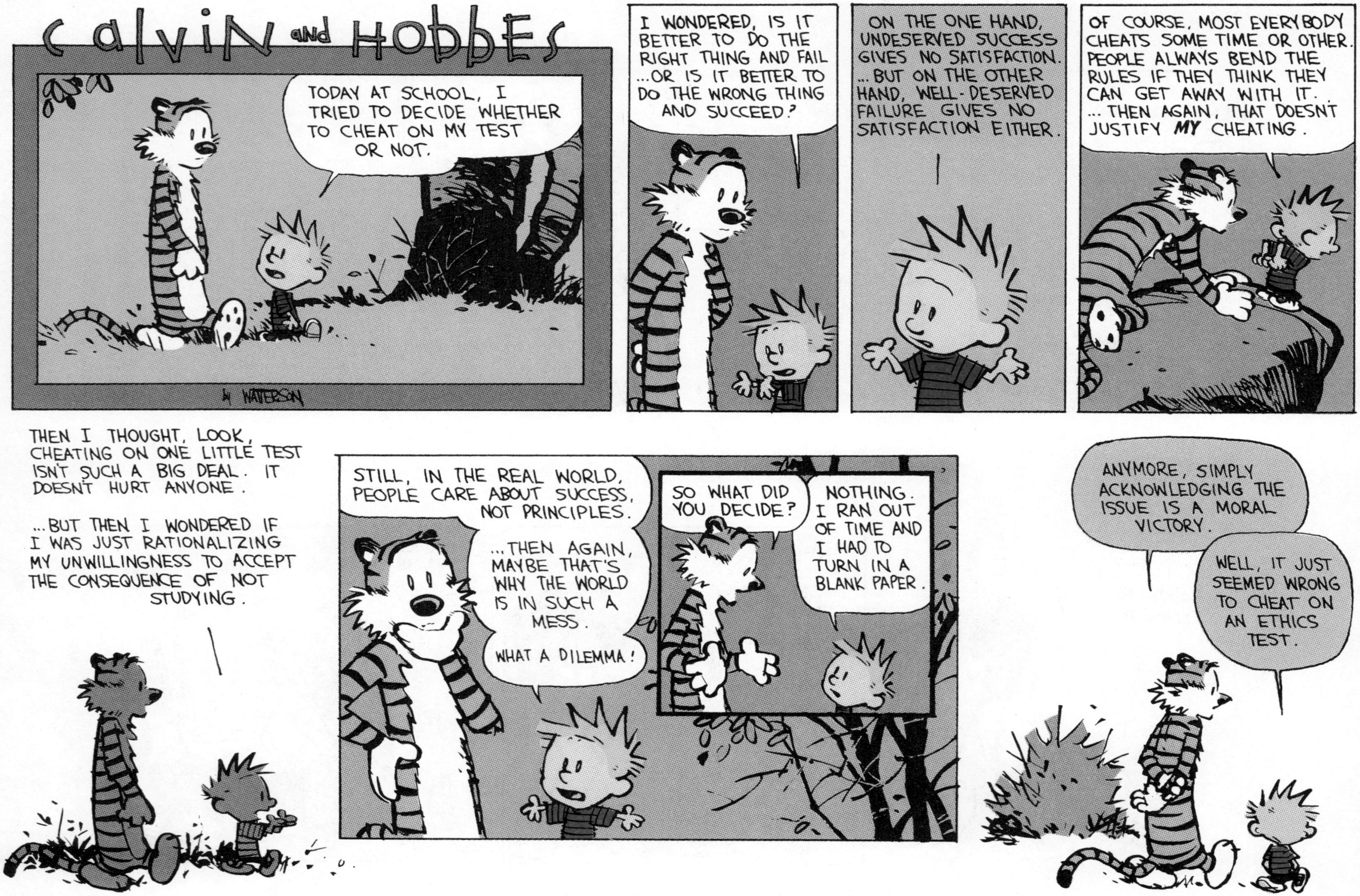
Calvin and Hobbes
by WATTERSON
TODAY AT SCHOOL, I TRIED TO DECIDE WHETHER TO CHEAT ON MY TEST OR NOT.
I WONDERED, IS IT BETTER TO DO THE RIGHT THING AND FAIL ...OR IS IT BETTER TO DO THE WRONG THING AND SUCCEED?
ON THE ONE HAND, UNDESERVED SUCCESS GIVES NO SATISFACTION. ...BUT ON THE OTHER HAND, WELL-DESERVED FAILURE GIVES NO SATISFACTION EITHER.
OF COURSE, MOST EVERYBODY CHEATS SOME TIME OR OTHER. PEOPLE ALWAYS BEND THE RULES IF THEY THINK THEY CAN GET AWAY WITH IT. ... THEN AGAIN, THAT DOESN'T JUSTIFY MY CHEATING.
THEN I THOUGHT, LOOK, CHEATING ON ONE LITTLE TEST ISN'T SUCH A BIG DEAL. IT DOESN'T HURT ANYONE.
...BUT THEN I WONDERED IF I WAS JUST RATIONALIZING MY UNWILLINGNESS TO ACCEPT THE CONSEQUENCE OF NOT STUDYING.
STILL, IN THE REAL WORLD, PEOPLE CARE ABOUT SUCCESS, NOT PRINCIPLES.
...THEN AGAIN, MAYBE THAT'S WHY THE WORLD IS IN SUCH A MESS.
WHAT A DILEMMA!
SO WHAT DID YOU DECIDE?
NOTHING. I RAN OUT OF TIME AND I HAD TO TURN IN A BLANK PAPER.
ANYMORE, SIMPLY ACKNOWLEDGING THE ISSUE IS A MORAL VICTORY.
WELL, IT JUST SEEMED WRONG TO CHEAT ON AN ETHICS TEST.

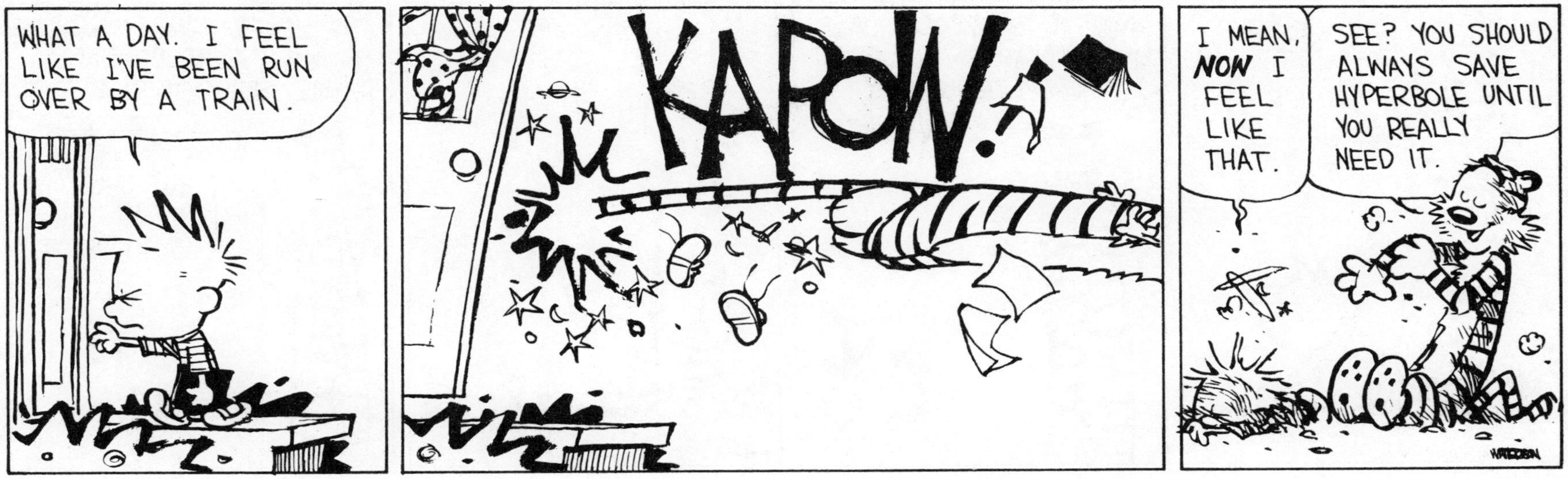
WHAT A DAY. I FEEL LIKE I'VE BEEN RUN OVER BY A TRAIN.
KAPOW!
I MEAN, NOW I FEEL LIKE THAT.
SEE? YOU SHOULD ALWAYS SAVE HYPERBOLE UNTIL YOU REALLY NEED IT.
WATTERSON

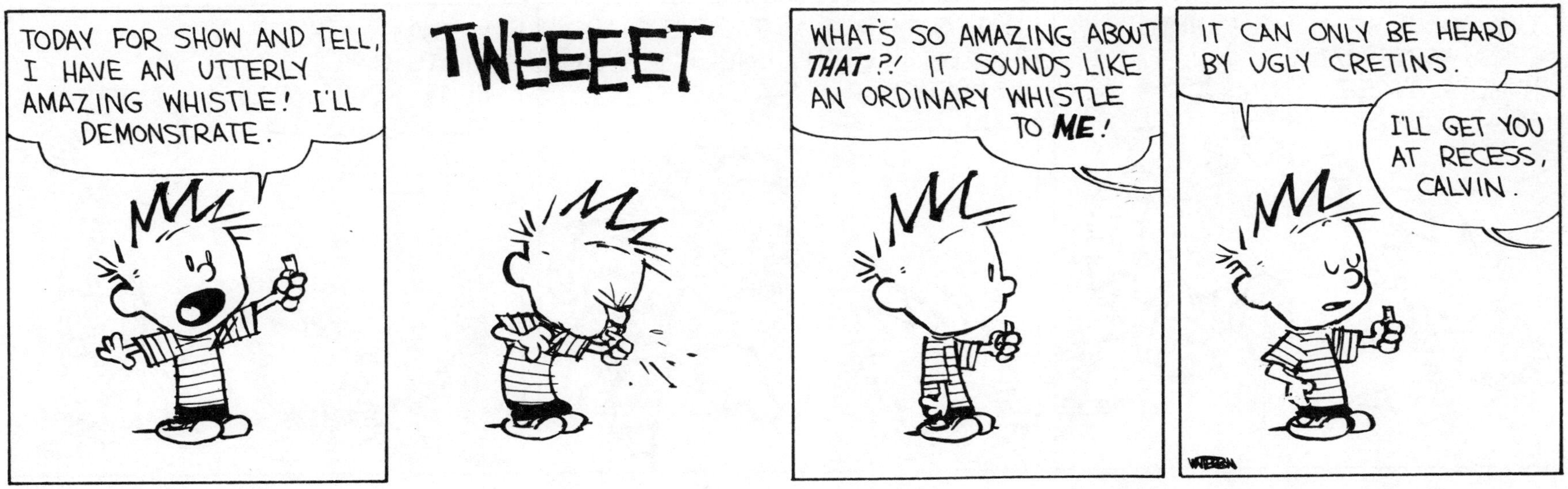
TODAY FOR SHOW AND TELL, I HAVE AN UTTERLY AMAZING WHISTLE! I'LL DEMONSTRATE.
TWEEEEET
WHAT'S SO AMAZING ABOUT THAT?! IT SOUNDS LIKE AN ORDINARY WHISTLE TO ME!
IT CAN ONLY BE HEARD BY UGLY CRETINS.
I'LL GET YOU AT RECESS, CALVIN.
WATTERSON

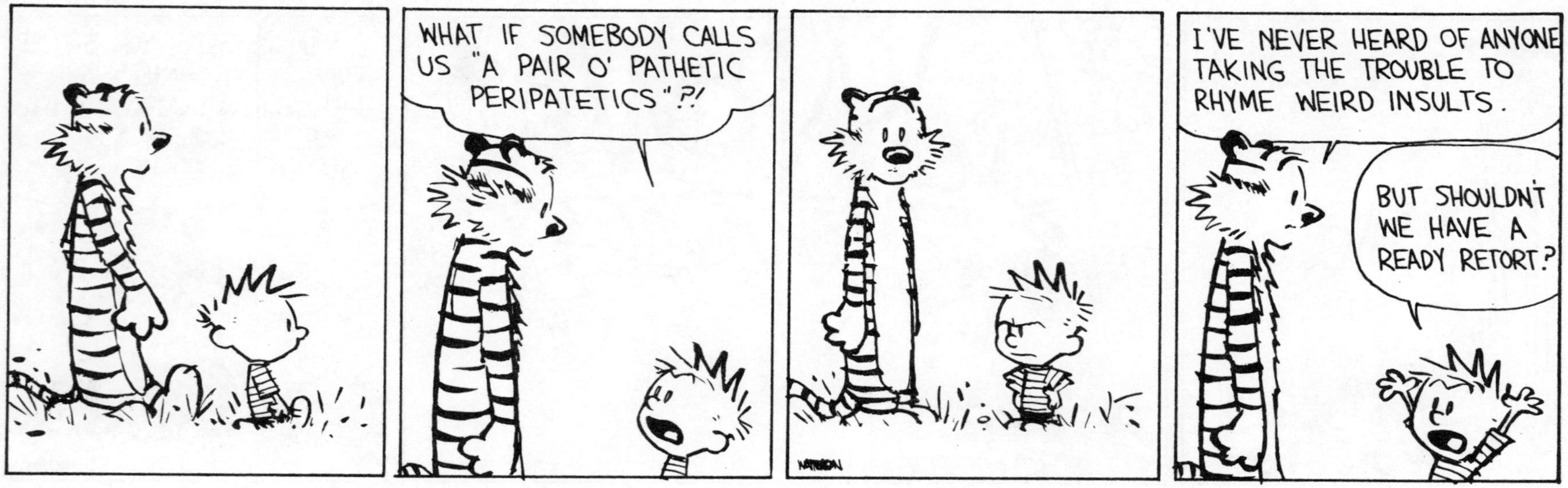
WHAT IF SOMEBODY CALLS US "A PAIR O' PATHETIC PERIPATETICS"?!
I'VE NEVER HEARD OF ANYONE TAKING THE TROUBLE TO RHYME WEIRD INSULTS.
BUT SHOULDN'T WE HAVE A READY RETORT?

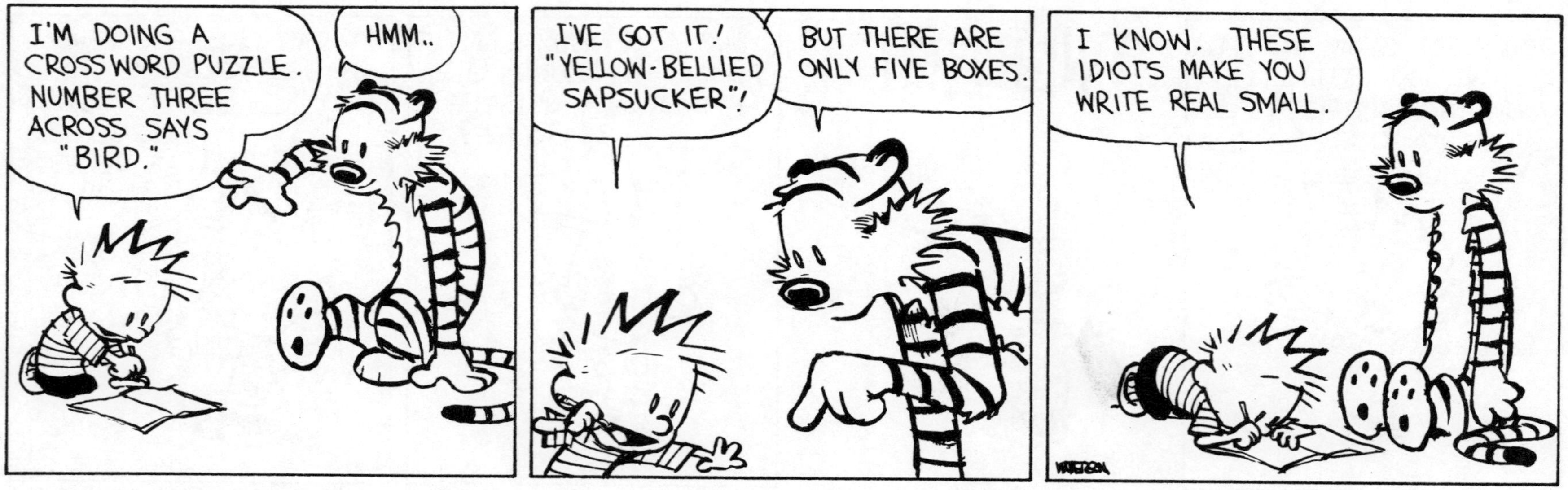
I'M DOING A CROSSWORD PUZZLE. NUMBER THREE ACROSS SAYS "BIRD."
HMM..
I'VE GOT IT! "YELLOW-BELLIED SAPSUCKER"!
BUT THERE ARE ONLY FIVE BOXES.
I KNOW. THESE IDIOTS MAKE YOU WRITE REAL SMALL.

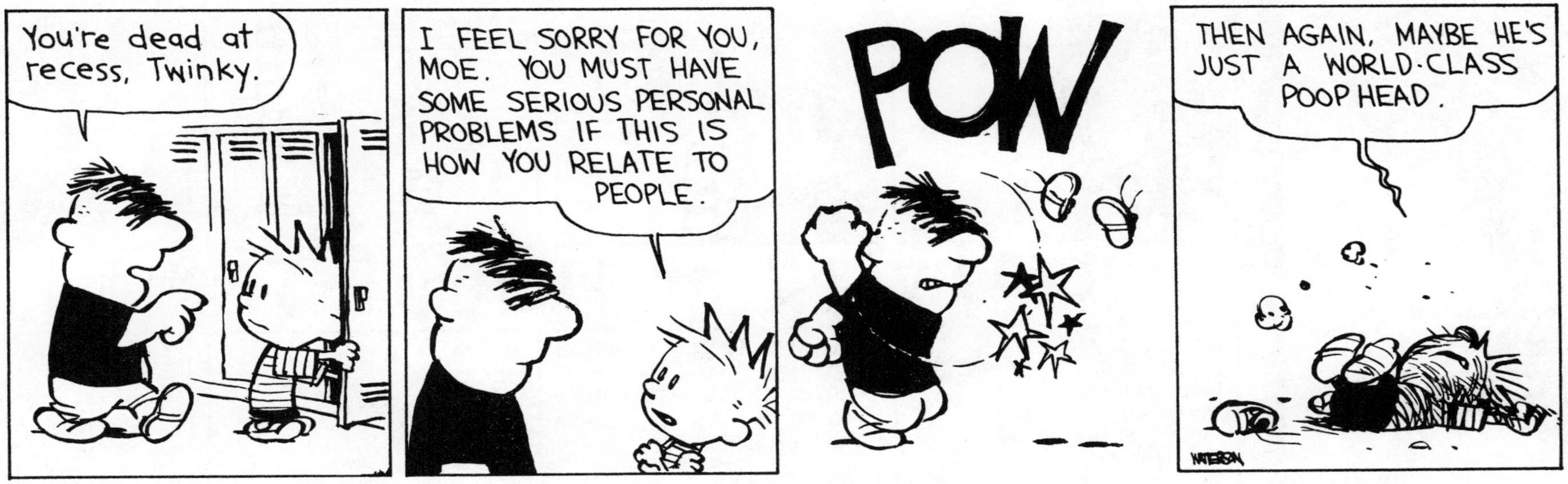
You're dead at recess, Twinky.
I FEEL SORRY FOR YOU, MOE. YOU MUST HAVE SOME SERIOUS PERSONAL PROBLEMS IF THIS IS HOW YOU RELATE TO PEOPLE.
POW
THEN AGAIN, MAYBE HE'S JUST A WORLD-CLASS POOP HEAD.

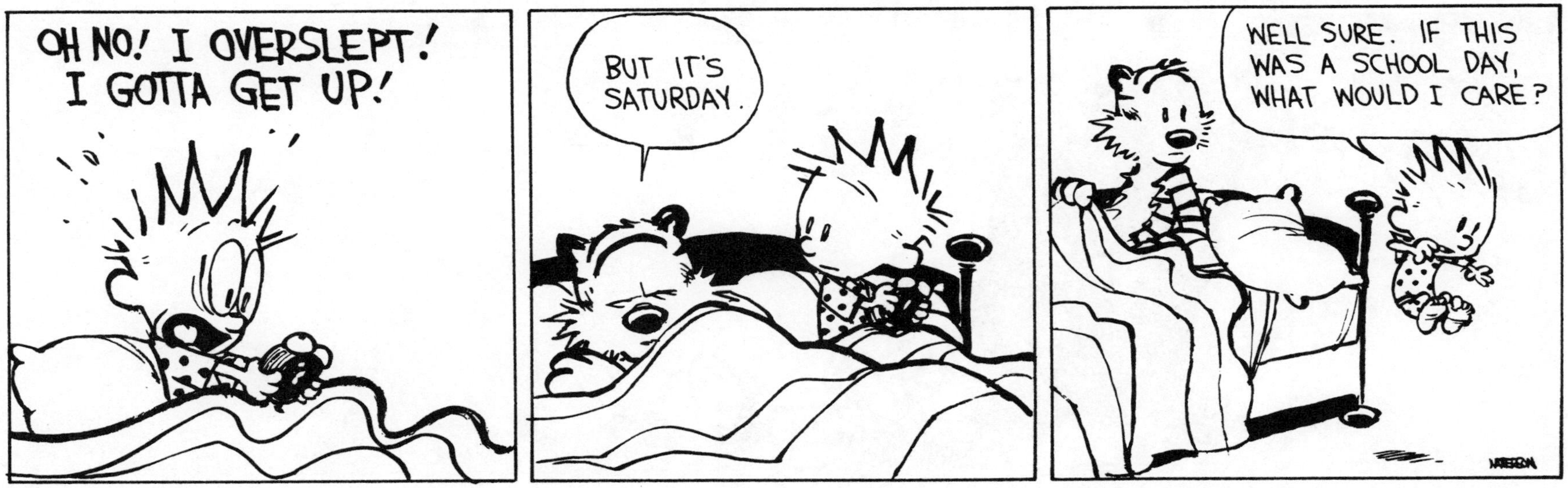
OH NO! I OVERSLEPT! I GOTTA GET UP!
BUT IT'S SATURDAY.
WELL SURE. IF THIS WAS A SCHOOL DAY, WHAT WOULD I CARE?

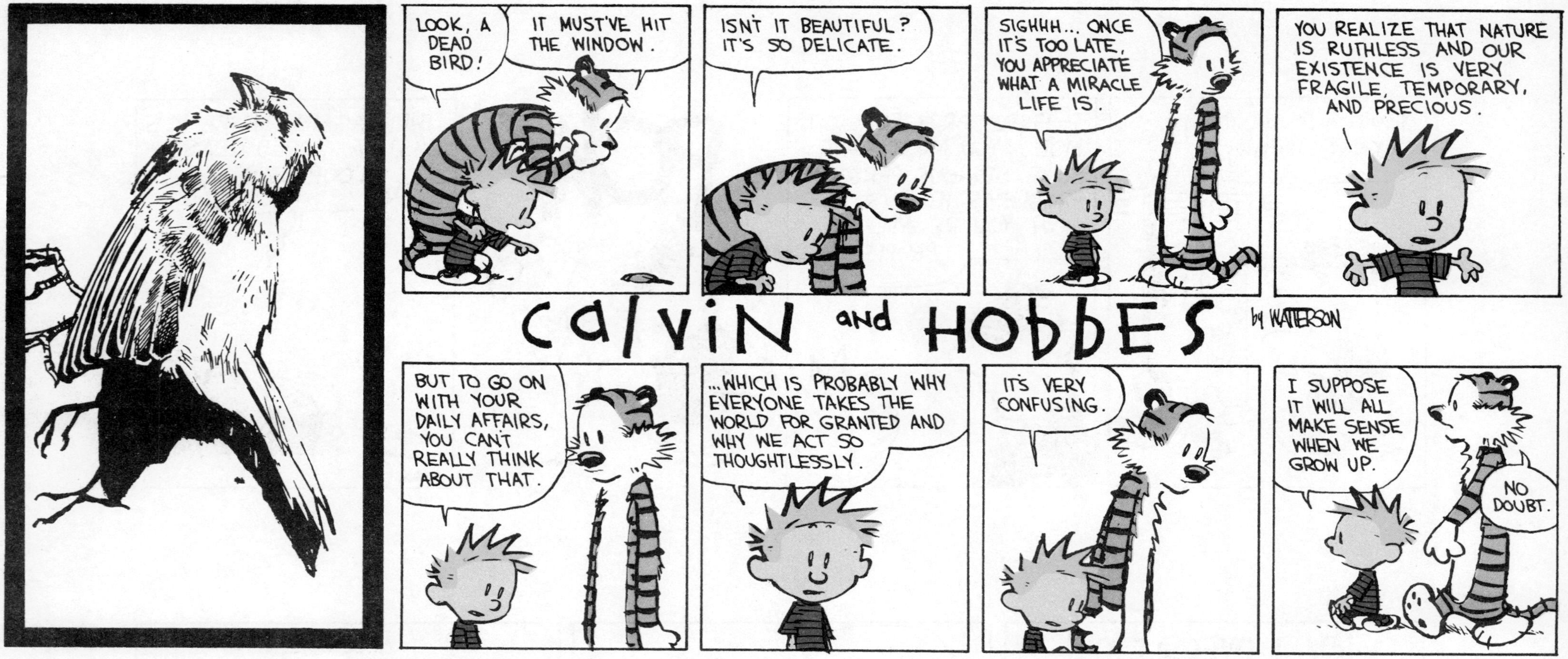
LOOK, A DEAD BIRD!
IT MUST'VE HIT THE WINDOW.
ISN'T IT BEAUTIFUL? IT'S SO DELICATE.
SIGHHH... ONCE IT'S TOO LATE, YOU APPRECIATE WHAT A MIRACLE LIFE IS.
YOU REALIZE THAT NATURE IS RUTHLESS AND OUR EXISTENCE IS VERY FRAGILE, TEMPORARY, AND PRECIOUS.
Calvin and HOBBES
by WATTERSON
BUT TO GO ON WITH YOUR DAILY AFFAIRS, YOU CAN'T REALLY THINK ABOUT THAT.
...WHICH IS PROBABLY WHY EVERYONE TAKES THE WORLD FOR GRANTED AND WHY WE ACT SO THOUGHTLESSLY.
IT'S VERY CONFUSING.
I SUPPOSE IT WILL ALL MAKE SENSE WHEN WE GROW UP.
NO DOUBT.

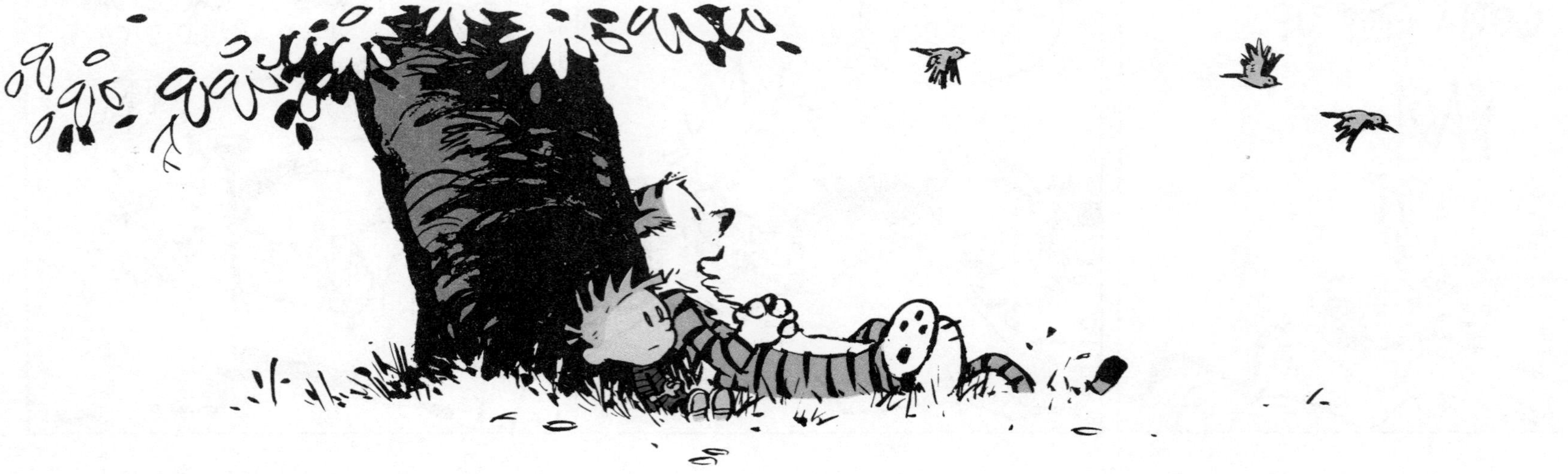

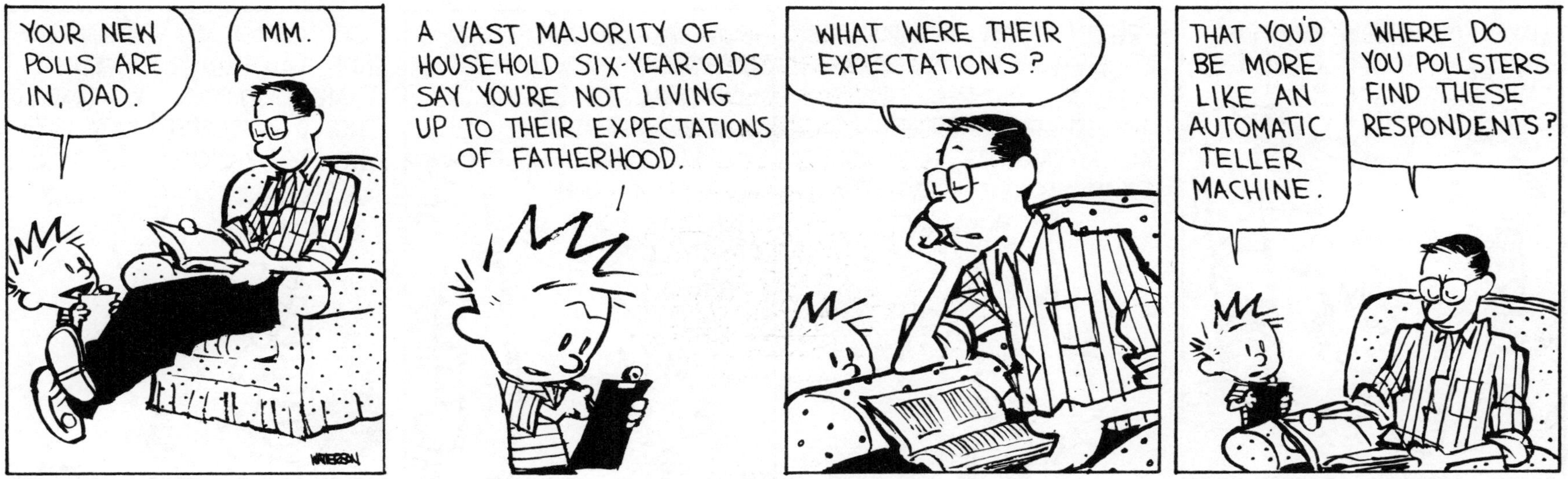
YOUR NEW POLLS ARE IN, DAD.
MM.
A VAST MAJORITY OF HOUSEHOLD SIX-YEAR-OLDS SAY YOU'RE NOT LIVING UP TO THEIR EXPECTATIONS OF FATHERHOOD.
WHAT WERE THEIR EXPECTATIONS?
THAT YOU'D BE MORE LIKE AN AUTOMATIC TELLER MACHINE.
WHERE DO YOU POLLSTERS FIND THESE RESPONDENTS?

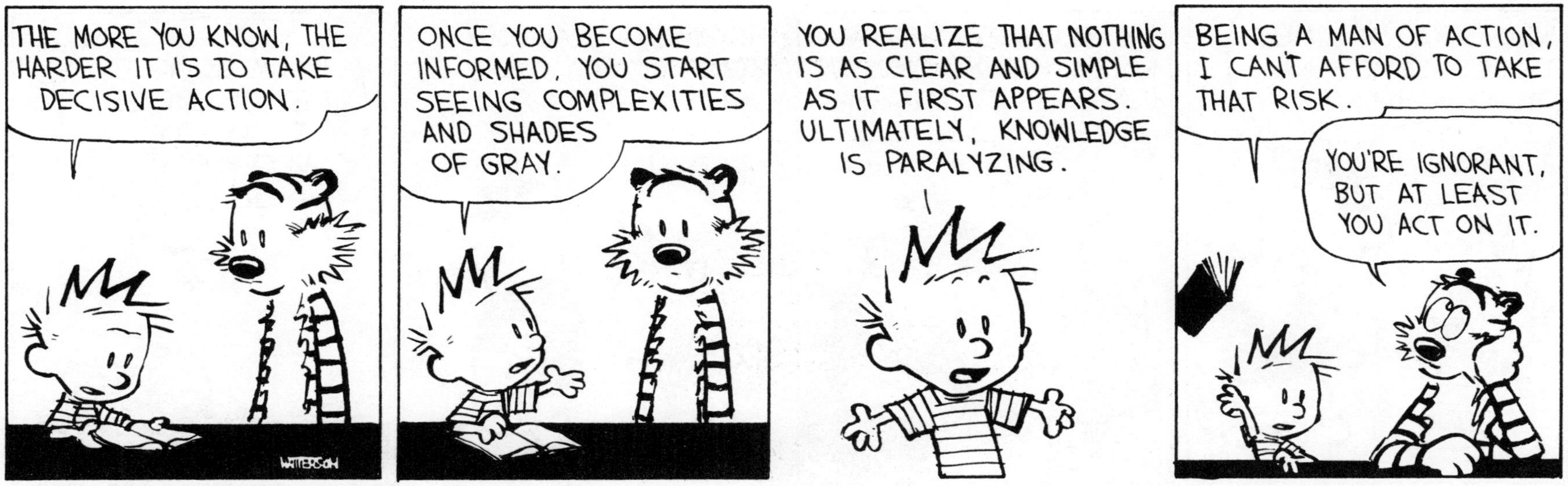
THE MORE YOU KNOW, THE HARDER IT IS TO TAKE DECISIVE ACTION.
ONCE YOU BECOME INFORMED, YOU START SEEING COMPLEXITIES AND SHADES OF GRAY.
YOU REALIZE THAT NOTHING IS AS CLEAR AND SIMPLE AS IT FIRST APPEARS. ULTIMATELY, KNOWLEDGE IS PARALYZING.
BEING A MAN OF ACTION, I CAN'T AFFORD TO TAKE THAT RISK.
YOU'RE IGNORANT, BUT AT LEAST YOU ACT ON IT.

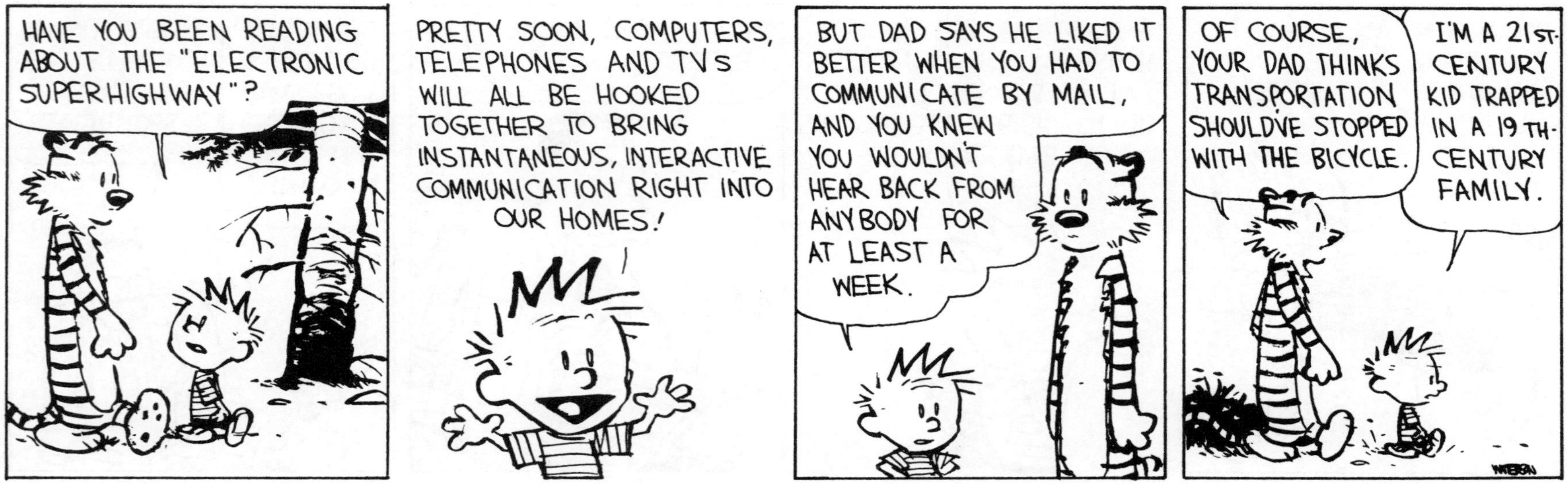
HAVE YOU BEEN READING ABOUT THE "ELECTRONIC SUPERHIGHWAY"?
PRETTY SOON, COMPUTERS, TELEPHONES AND TVs WILL ALL BE HOOKED TOGETHER TO BRING INSTANTANEOUS, INTERACTIVE COMMUNICATION RIGHT INTO OUR HOMES!
BUT DAD SAYS HE LIKED IT BETTER WHEN YOU HAD TO COMMUNICATE BY MAIL, AND YOU KNEW YOU WOULDN'T HEAR BACK FROM ANYBODY FOR AT LEAST A WEEK.
OF COURSE, YOUR DAD THINKS TRANSPORTATION SHOULD'VE STOPPED WITH THE BICYCLE.
I'M A 21ST-CENTURY KID TRAPPED IN A 19TH-CENTURY FAMILY.

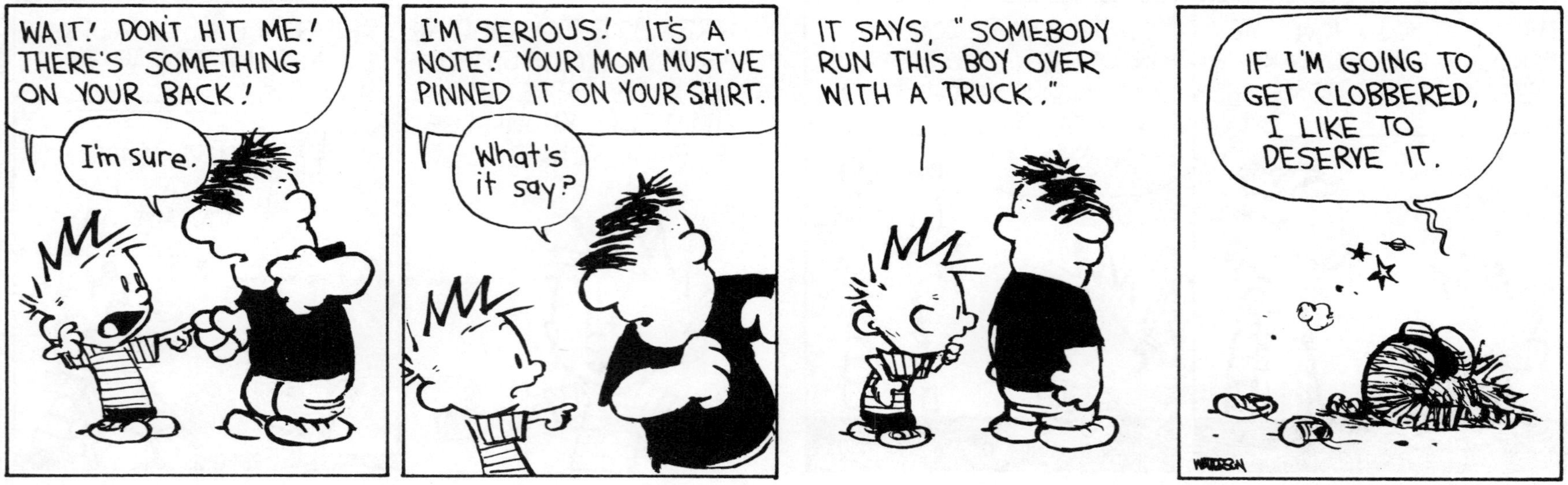
WAIT! DON'T HIT ME! THERE'S SOMETHING ON YOUR BACK!
I'm sure.
I'M SERIOUS! IT'S A NOTE! YOUR MOM MUST'VE PINNED IT ON YOUR SHIRT.
What's it say?
IT SAYS, "SOMEBODY RUN THIS BOY OVER WITH A TRUCK."
IF I'M GOING TO GET CLOBBERED, I LIKE TO DESERVE IT.

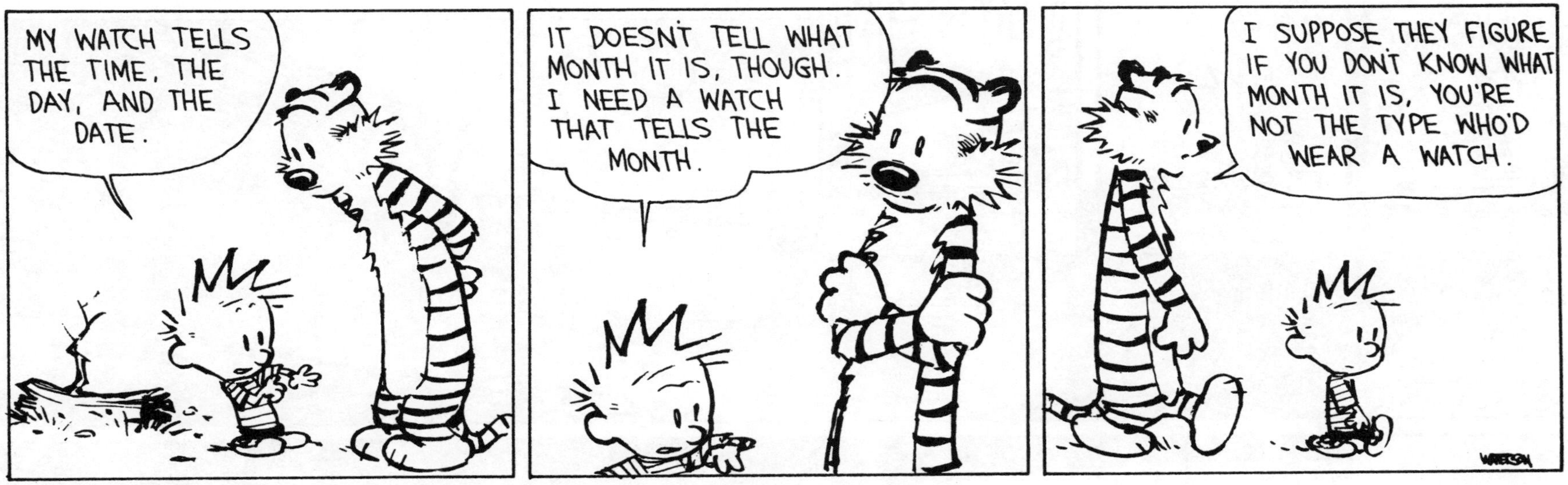
MY WATCH TELLS THE TIME, THE DAY, AND THE DATE.
IT DOESN'T TELL WHAT MONTH IT IS, THOUGH. I NEED A WATCH THAT TELLS THE MONTH.
I SUPPOSE THEY FIGURE IF YOU DON'T KNOW WHAT MONTH IT IS, YOU'RE NOT THE TYPE WHO'D WEAR A WATCH.
WATTERSON

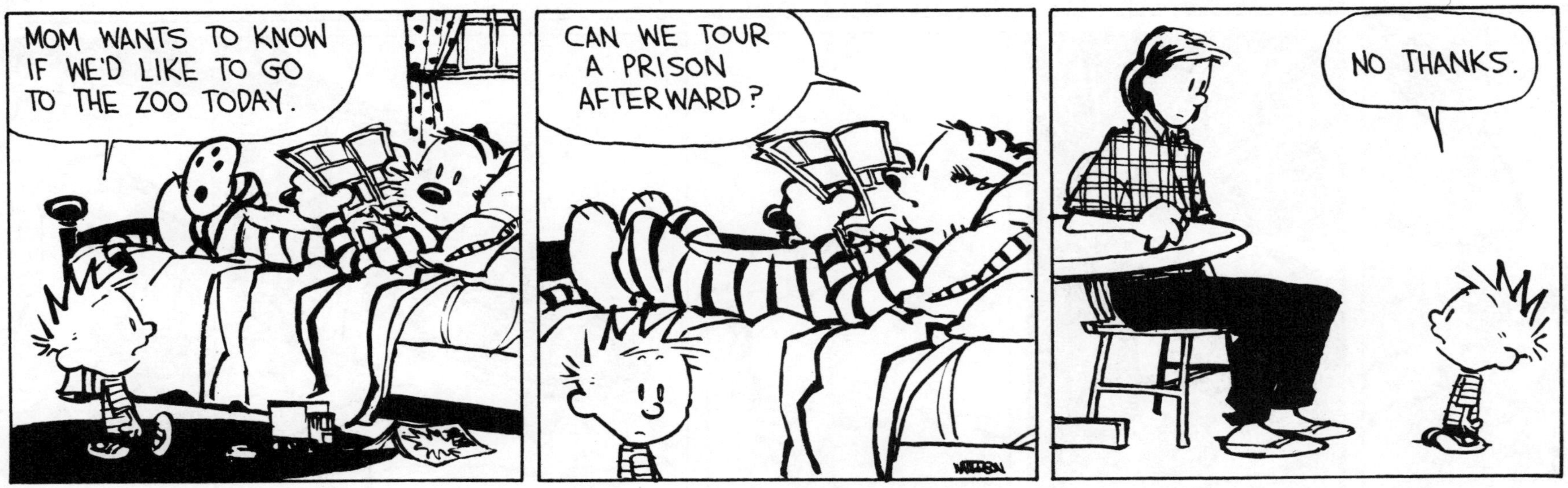
MOM WANTS TO KNOW IF WE'D LIKE TO GO TO THE ZOO TODAY.
CAN WE TOUR A PRISON AFTERWARD?
NO THANKS.
WATTERSON

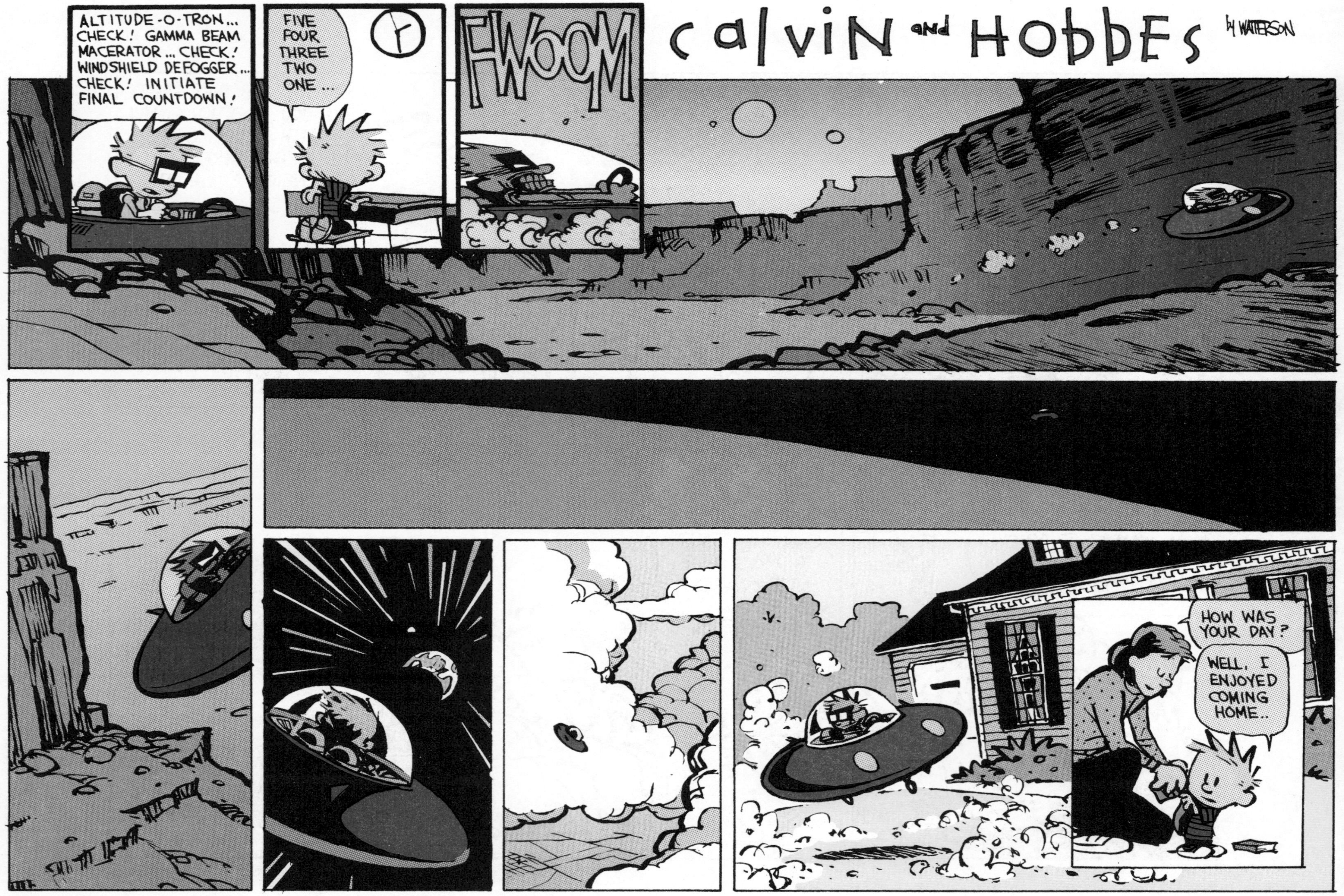
ALTITUDE-O-TRON... CHECK! GAMMA BEAM MACERATOR ... CHECK! WINDSHIELD DEFOGGER... CHECK! INITIATE FINAL COUNTDOWN!
FIVE FOUR THREE TWO ONE...
FWOOM
calvin and HOBBES
by WATTERSON
HOW WAS YOUR DAY?
WELL, I ENJOYED COMING HOME..

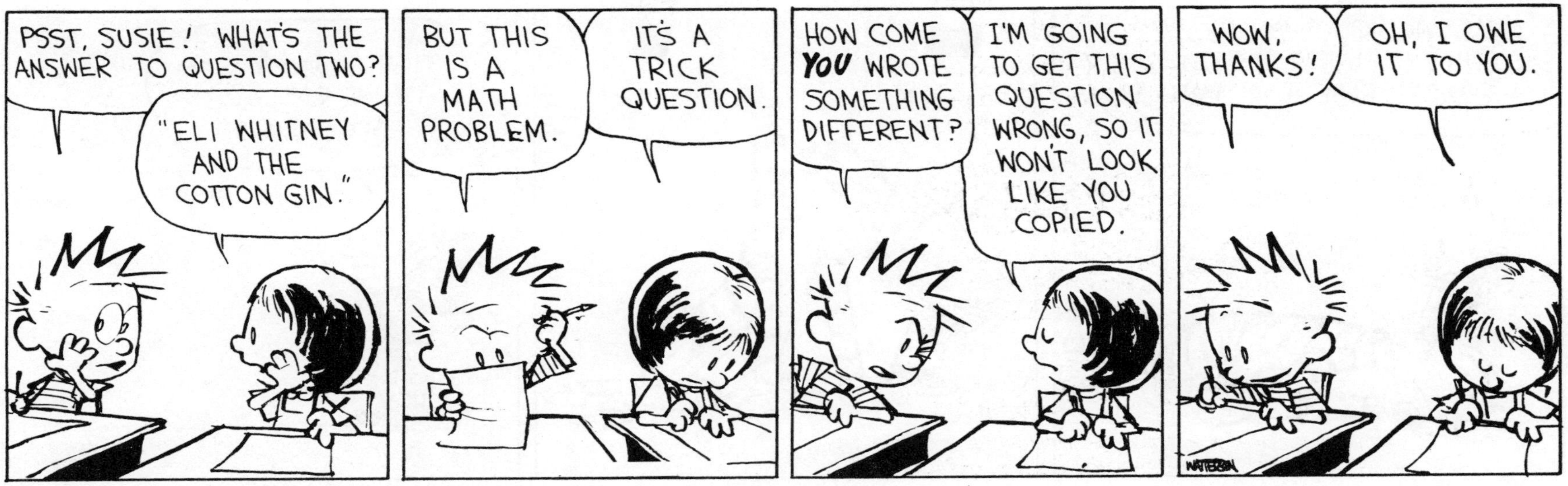
PSST, SUSIE! WHAT'S THE ANSWER TO QUESTION TWO?
"ELI WHITNEY AND THE COTTON GIN."
BUT THIS IS A MATH PROBLEM.
IT'S A TRICK QUESTION.
HOW COME YOU WROTE SOMETHING DIFFERENT?
I'M GOING TO GET THIS QUESTION WRONG, SO IT WON'T LOOK LIKE YOU COPIED.
WOW, THANKS!
OH, I OWE IT TO YOU.

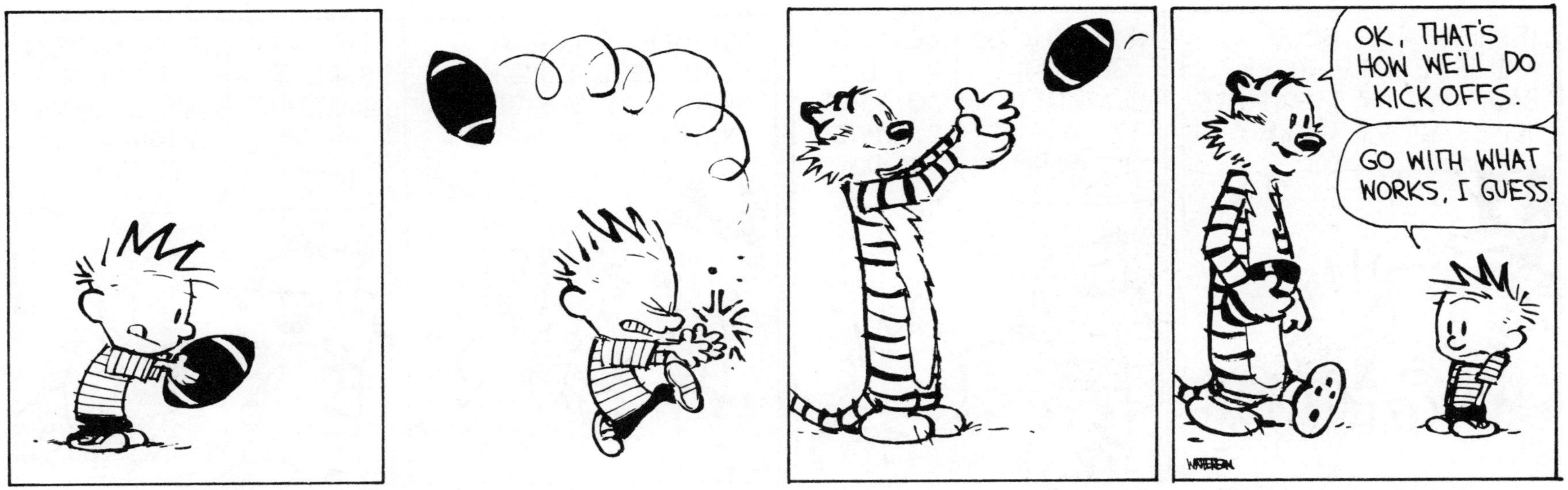
OK, THAT'S HOW WE'LL DO KICK OFFS.
GO WITH WHAT WORKS, I GUESS.

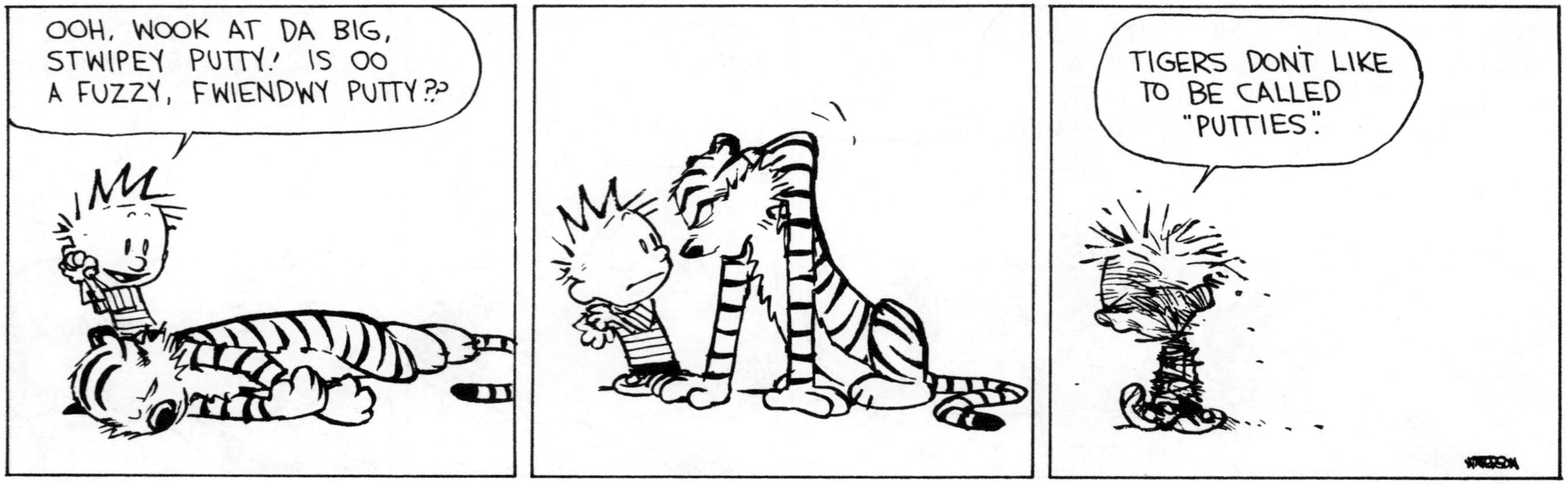
OOH, WOOK AT DA BIG, STWIPEY PUTTY! IS OO A FUZZY, FWIENDWY PUTTY?>
TIGERS DON'T LIKE TO BE CALLED "PUTTIES".

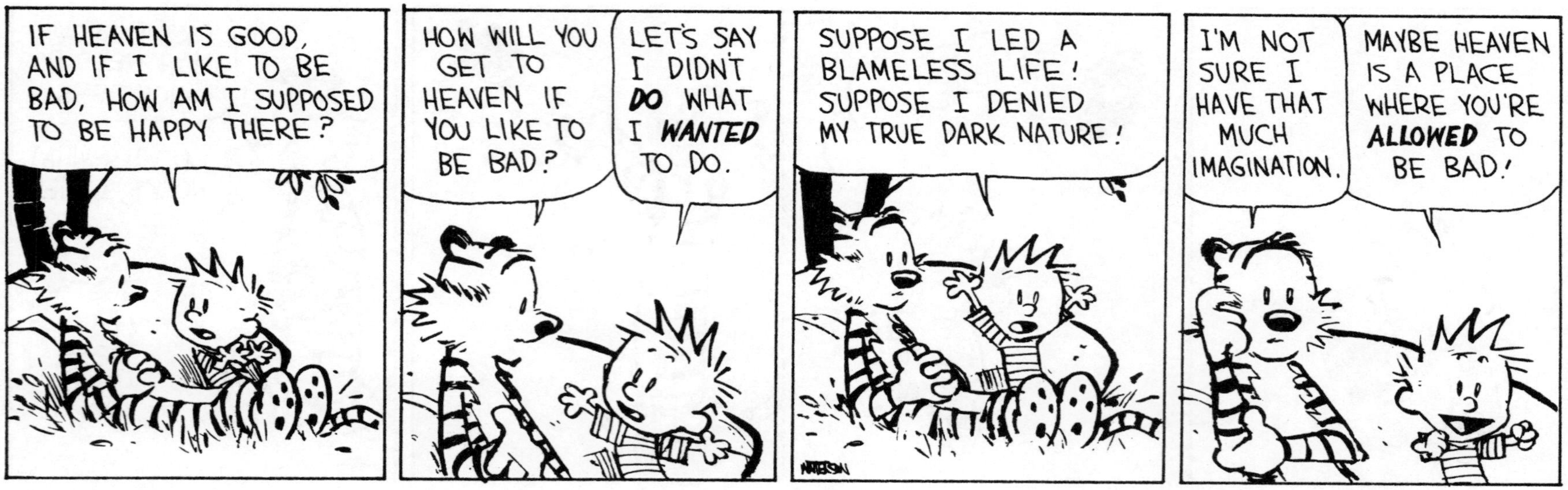
IF HEAVEN IS GOOD, AND IF I LIKE TO BE BAD, HOW AM I SUPPOSED TO BE HAPPY THERE?
HOW WILL YOU GET TO HEAVEN IF YOU LIKE TO BE BAD?
LET'S SAY I DIDN'T DO WHAT I WANTED TO DO.
SUPPOSE I LED A BLAMELESS LIFE! SUPPOSE I DENIED MY TRUE DARK NATURE!
I'M NOT SURE I HAVE THAT MUCH IMAGINATION.
MAYBE HEAVEN IS A PLACE WHERE YOU'RE ALLOWED TO BE BAD!

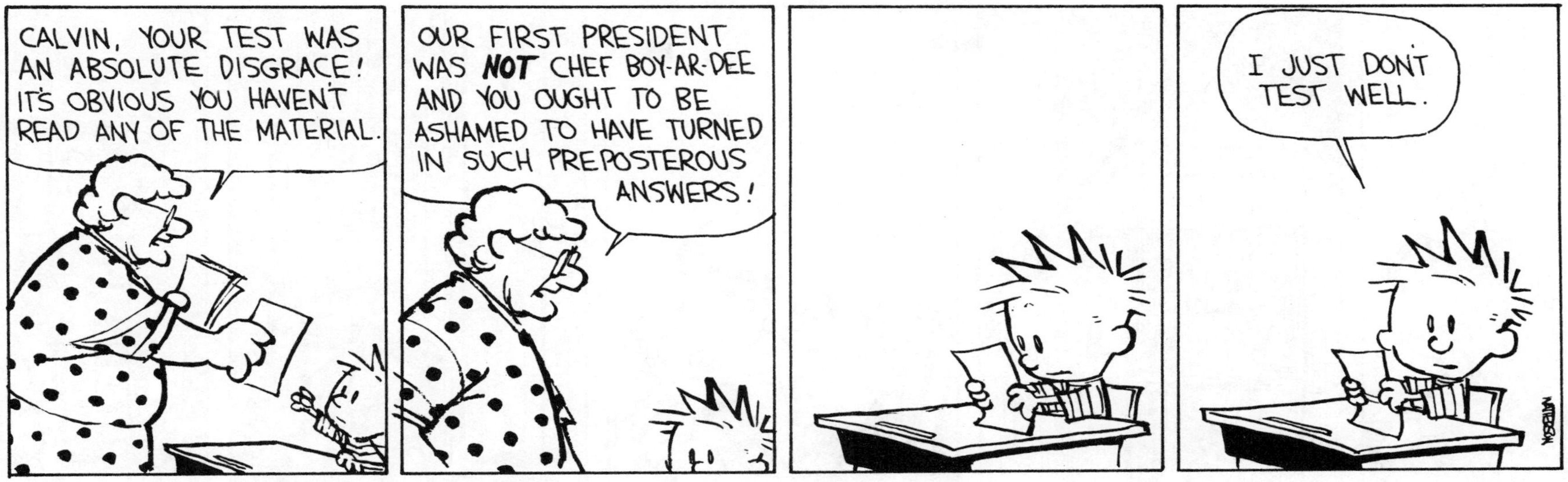
CALVIN, YOUR TEST WAS AN ABSOLUTE DISGRACE! IT'S OBVIOUS YOU HAVEN'T READ ANY OF THE MATERIAL.
OUR FIRST PRESIDENT WAS **NOT** CHEF BOY-AR-DEE AND YOU OUGHT TO BE ASHAMED TO HAVE TURNED IN SUCH PREPOSTEROUS ANSWERS!
I JUST DON'T TEST WELL.
WATTERSON

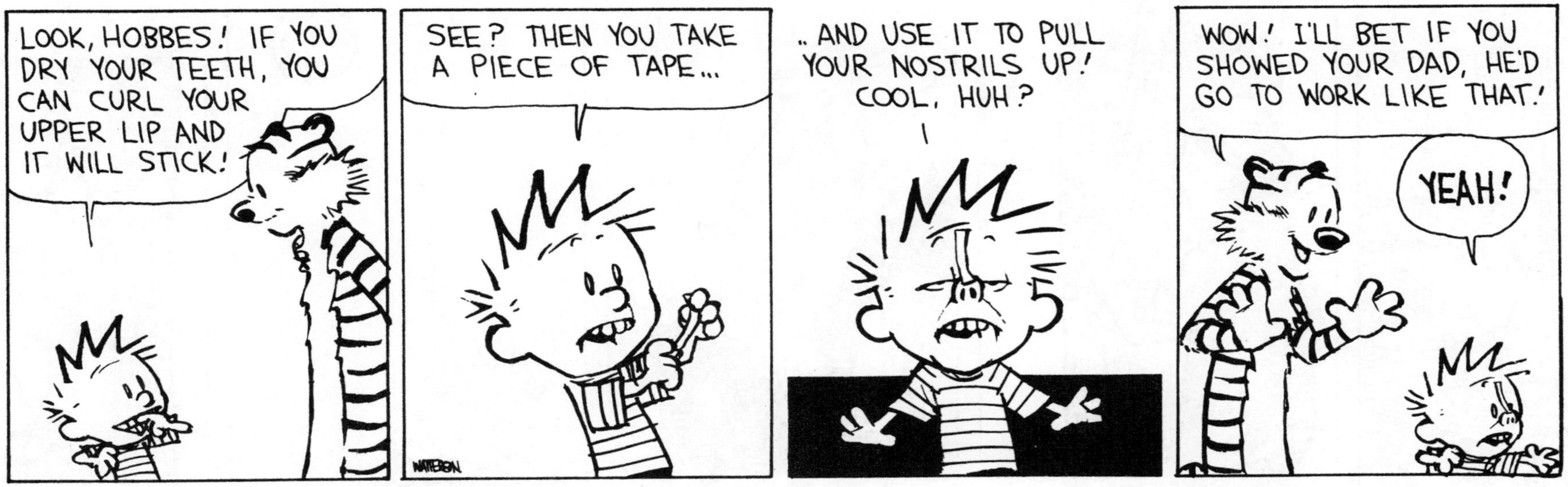
LOOK, HOBBES! IF YOU DRY YOUR TEETH, YOU CAN CURL YOUR UPPER LIP AND IT WILL STICK!
SEE? THEN YOU TAKE A PIECE OF TAPE...
WATTERSON
.. AND USE IT TO PULL YOUR NOSTRILS UP! COOL, HUH?
WOW! I'LL BET IF YOU SHOWED YOUR DAD, HE'D GO TO WORK LIKE THAT!
YEAH!

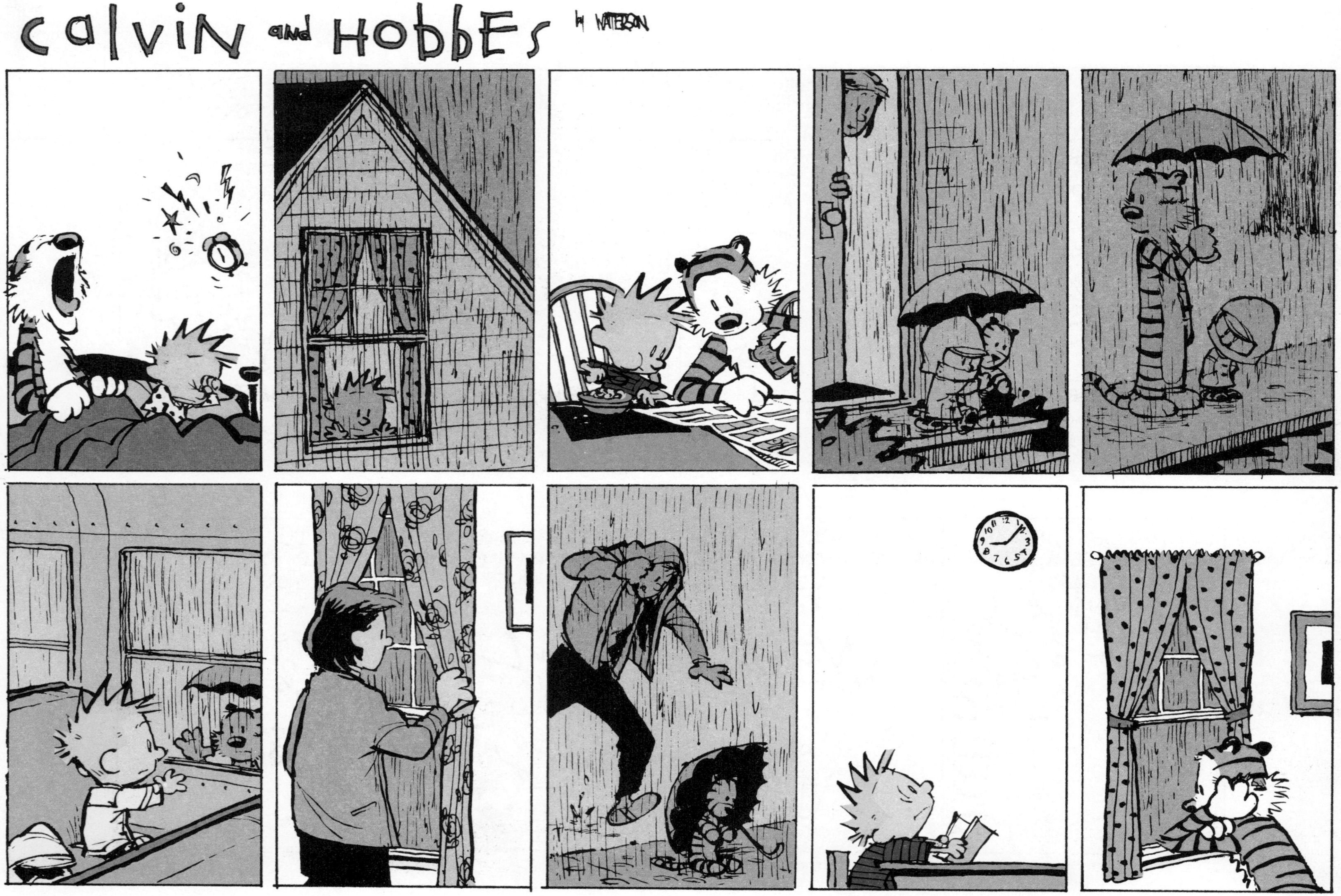
calvin and HOBBES

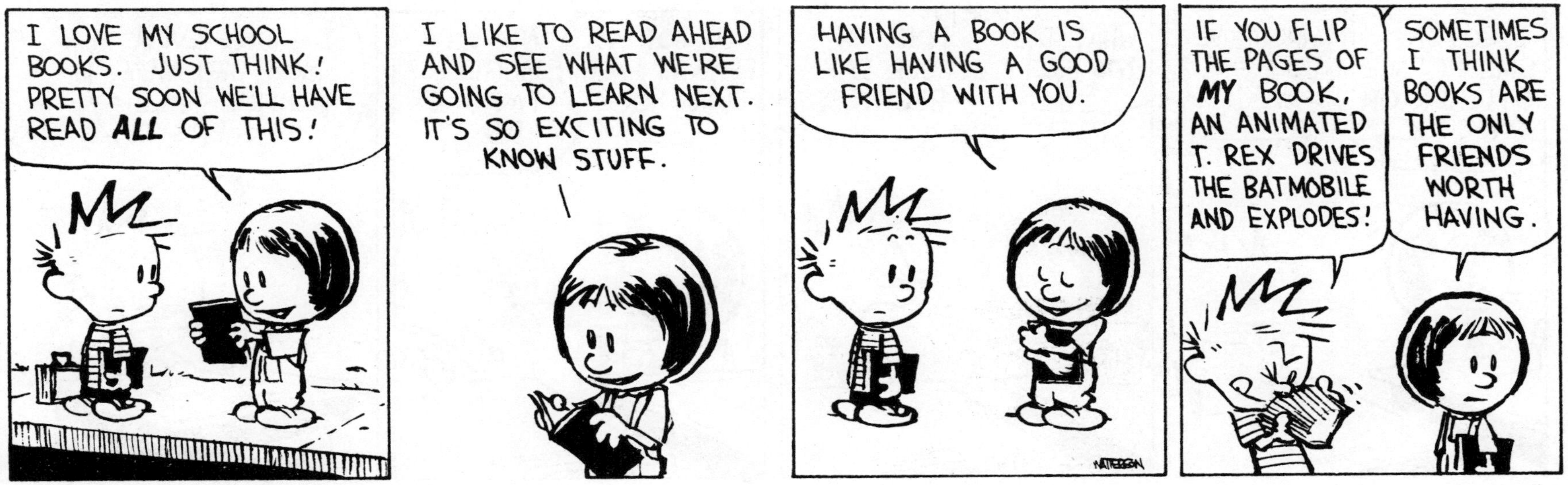
I LOVE MY SCHOOL BOOKS. JUST THINK! PRETTY SOON WE'LL HAVE READ **ALL** OF THIS!
I LIKE TO READ AHEAD AND SEE WHAT WE'RE GOING TO LEARN NEXT. IT'S SO EXCITING TO KNOW STUFF.
HAVING A BOOK IS LIKE HAVING A GOOD FRIEND WITH YOU.
IF YOU FLIP THE PAGES OF **MY** BOOK, AN ANIMATED T. REX DRIVES THE BATMOBILE AND EXPLODES!
SOMETIMES I THINK BOOKS ARE THE ONLY FRIENDS WORTH HAVING.

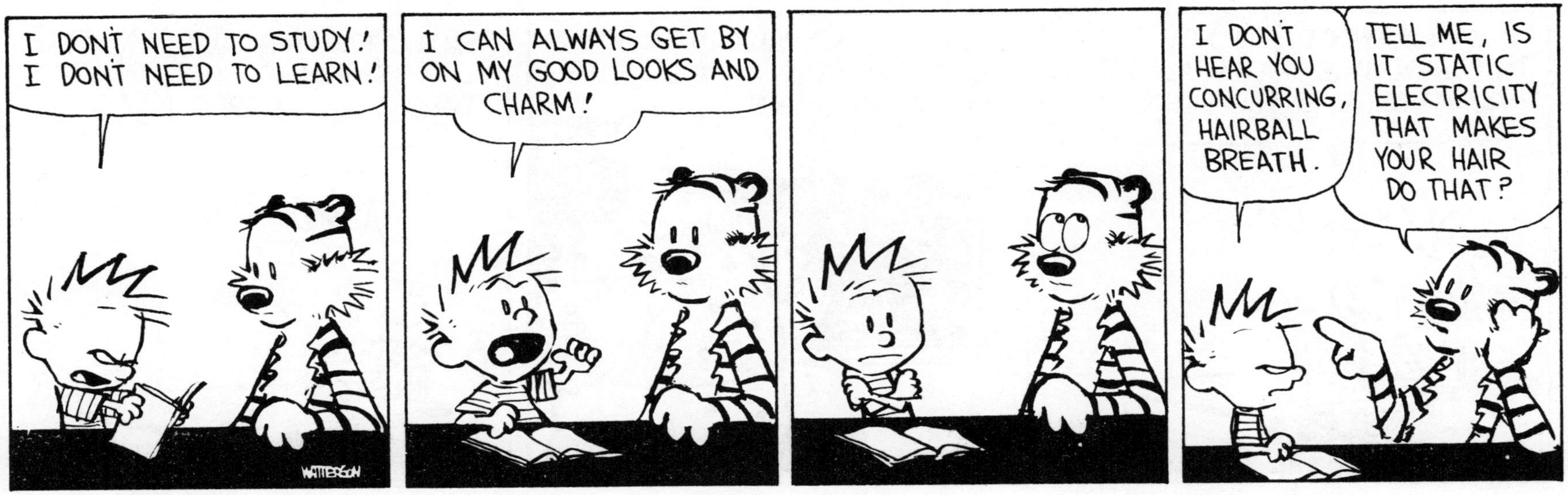
I DON'T NEED TO STUDY! I DON'T NEED TO LEARN!
I CAN ALWAYS GET BY ON MY GOOD LOOKS AND CHARM!
I DON'T HEAR YOU CONCURRING, HAIRBALL BREATH.
TELL ME, IS IT STATIC ELECTRICITY THAT MAKES YOUR HAIR DO THAT?

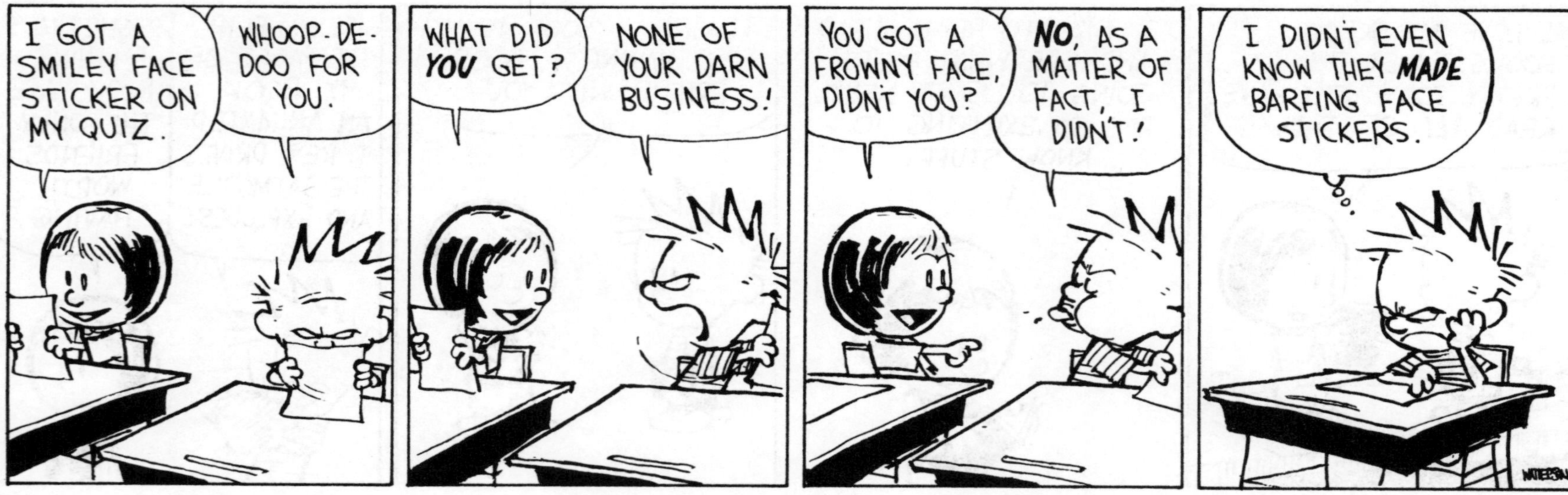
I GOT A SMILEY FACE STICKER ON MY QUIZ.
WHOOP-DE-DOO FOR YOU.
WHAT DID YOU GET?
NONE OF YOUR DARN BUSINESS!
YOU GOT A FROWNY FACE, DIDN'T YOU?
NO, AS A MATTER OF FACT, I DIDN'T!
I DIDN'T EVEN KNOW THEY MADE BARFING FACE STICKERS.
WATTERSON

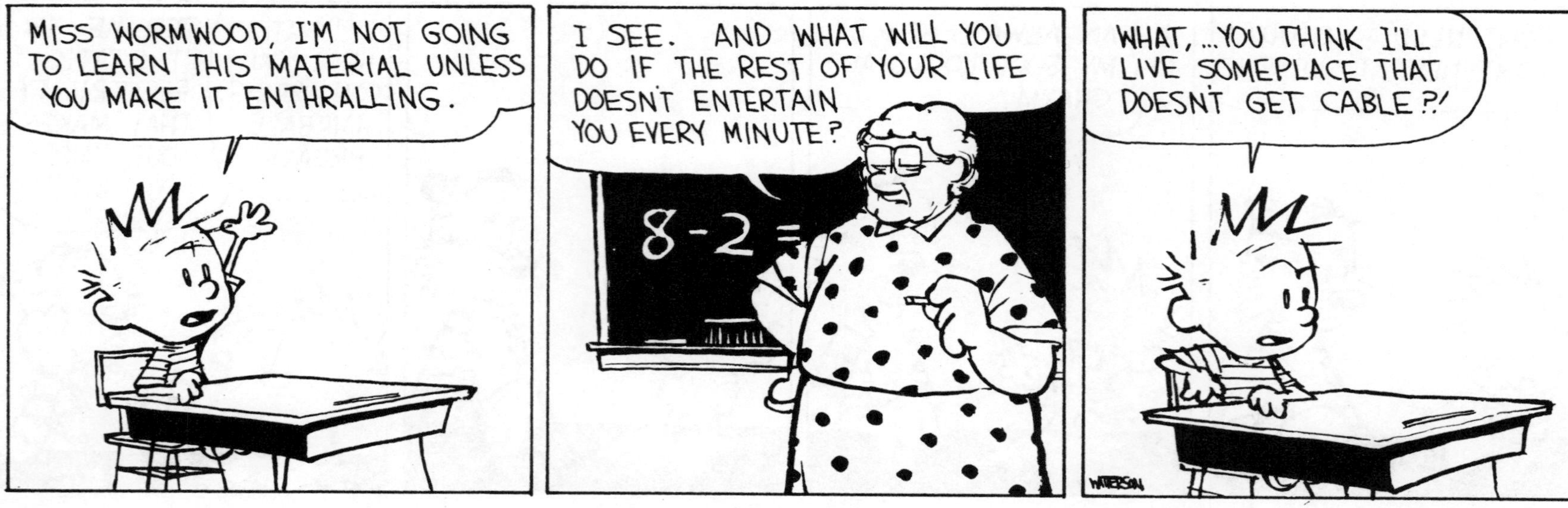
MISS WORMWOOD, I'M NOT GOING TO LEARN THIS MATERIAL UNLESS YOU MAKE IT ENTHRALLING.
I SEE. AND WHAT WILL YOU DO IF THE REST OF YOUR LIFE DOESN'T ENTERTAIN YOU EVERY MINUTE?
8-2=
WHAT, ...YOU THINK I'LL LIVE SOMEPLACE THAT DOESN'T GET CABLE?!
WATTERSON

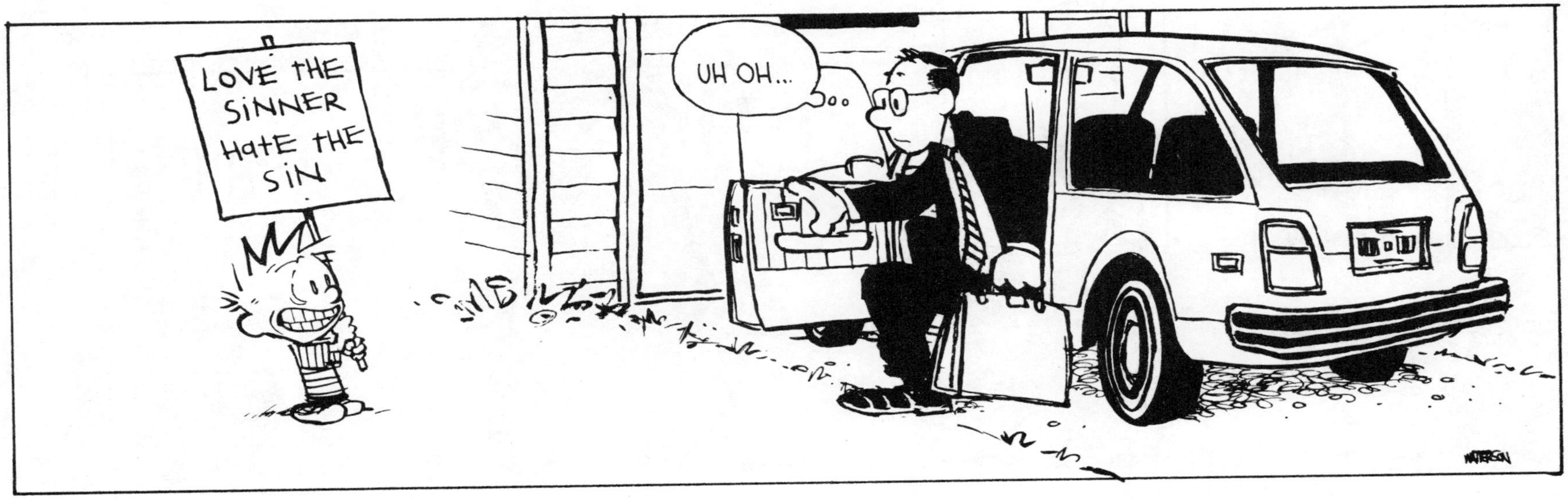
LOVE THE SINNER HATE THE SIN
UH OH...
WATTERSON

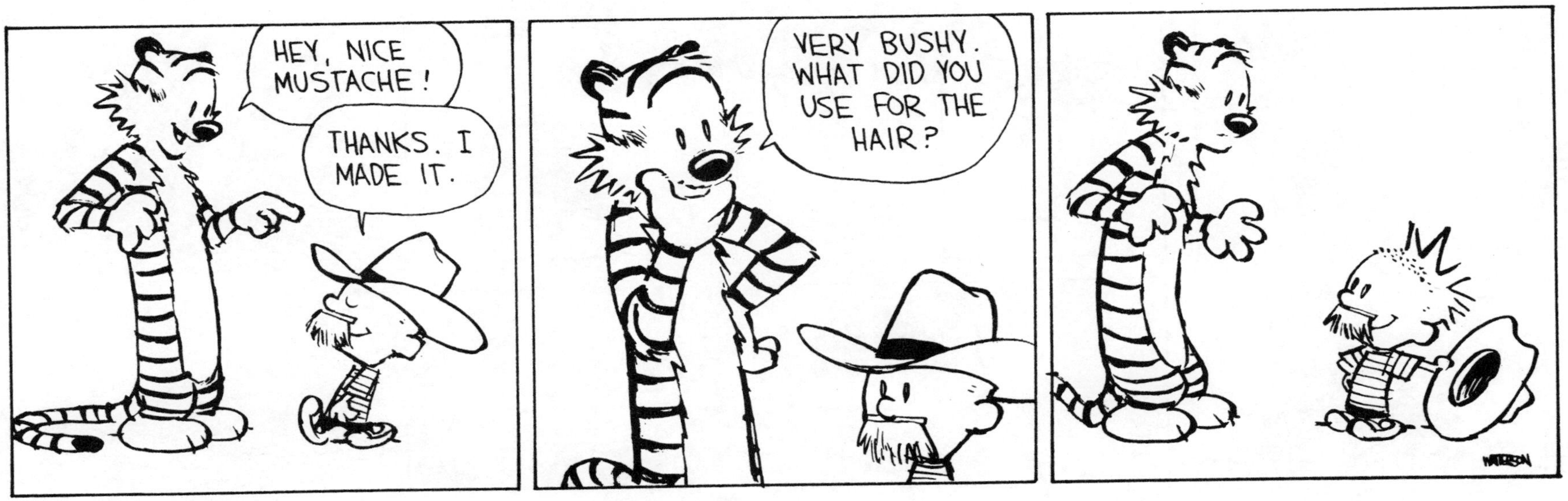
HEY, NICE MUSTACHE!
THANKS. I MADE IT.
VERY BUSHY. WHAT DID YOU USE FOR THE HAIR?
WATTERSON

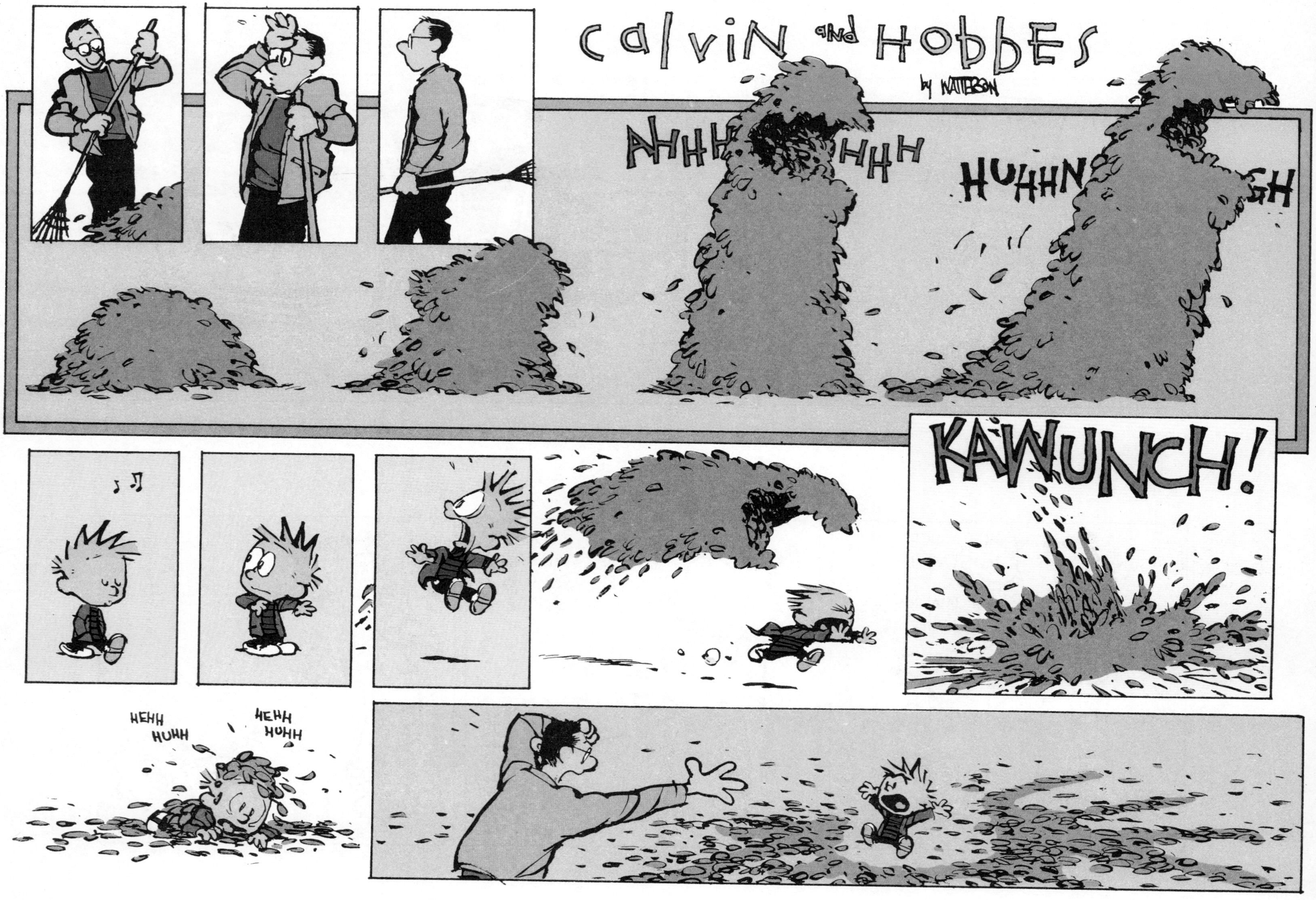

Calvin and HOBBES
by WATTERSON
AHHHHHHHH
HUHHN GH
KAWUNCH!
HEHH HUHH
HEHH HUHH

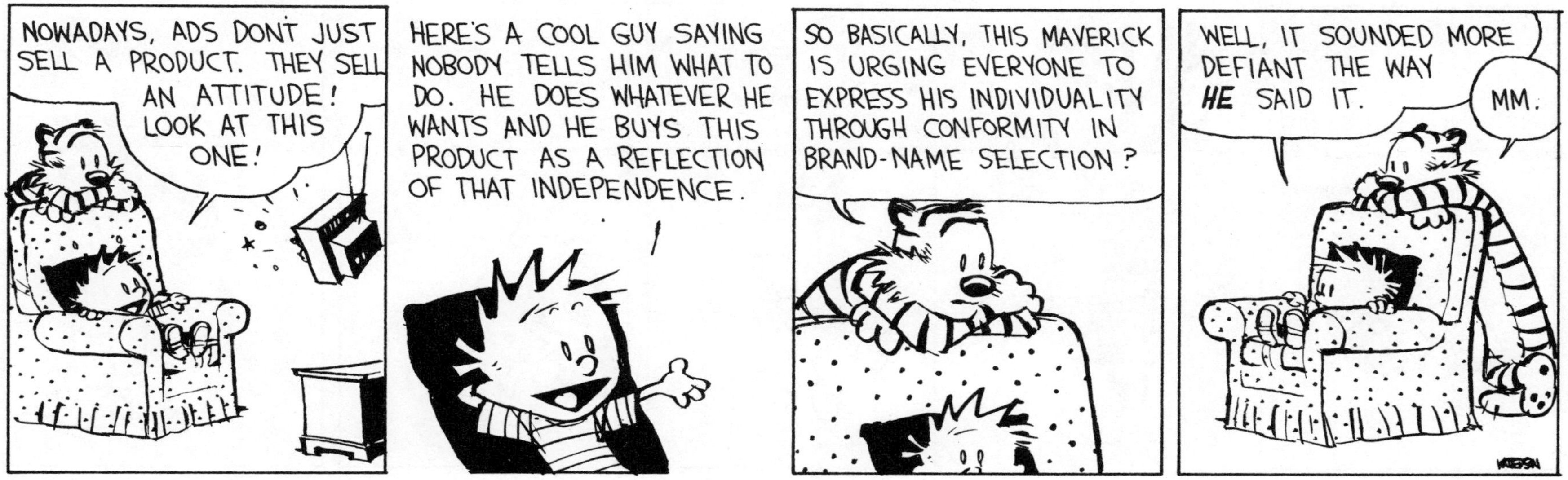
NOWADAYS, ADS DON'T JUST SELL A PRODUCT. THEY SELL AN ATTITUDE! LOOK AT THIS ONE!
HERE'S A COOL GUY SAYING NOBODY TELLS HIM WHAT TO DO. HE DOES WHATEVER HE WANTS AND HE BUYS THIS PRODUCT AS A REFLECTION OF THAT INDEPENDENCE.
SO BASICALLY, THIS MAVERICK IS URGING EVERYONE TO EXPRESS HIS INDIVIDUALITY THROUGH CONFORMITY IN BRAND-NAME SELECTION?
WELL, IT SOUNDED MORE DEFIANT THE WAY HE SAID IT.
MM.

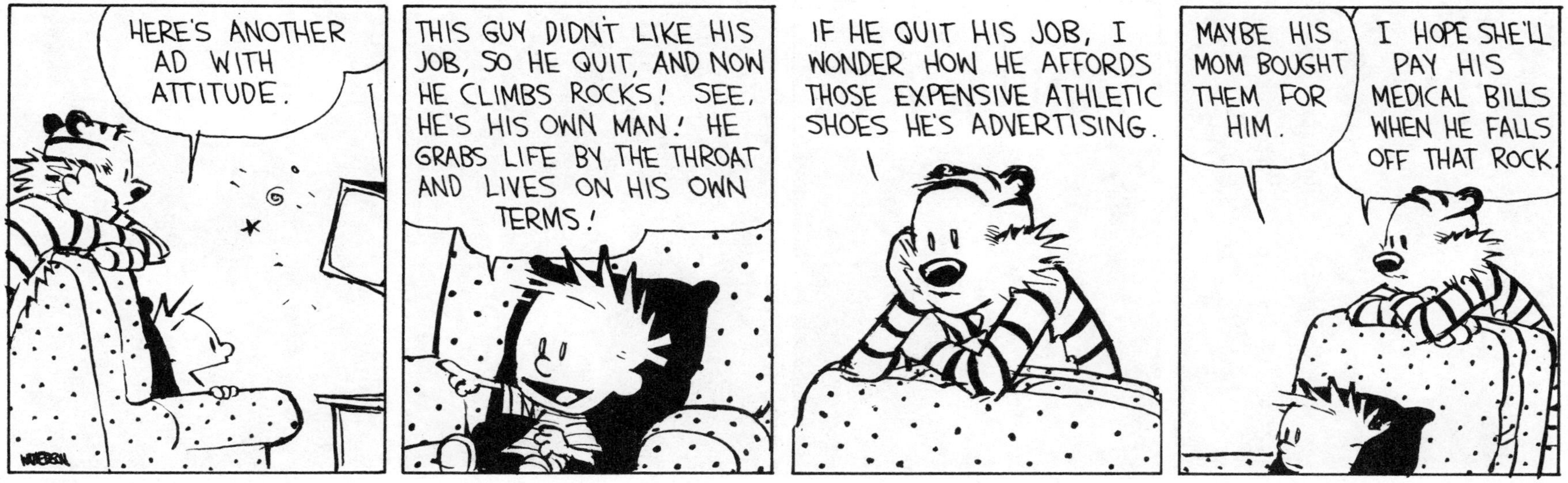
HERE'S ANOTHER AD WITH ATTITUDE.
THIS GUY DIDN'T LIKE HIS JOB, SO HE QUIT, AND NOW HE CLIMBS ROCKS! SEE, HE'S HIS OWN MAN! HE GRABS LIFE BY THE THROAT AND LIVES ON HIS OWN TERMS!
IF HE QUIT HIS JOB, I WONDER HOW HE AFFORDS THOSE EXPENSIVE ATHLETIC SHOES HE'S ADVERTISING.
MAYBE HIS MOM BOUGHT THEM FOR HIM.
I HOPE SHE'LL PAY HIS MEDICAL BILLS WHEN HE FALLS OFF THAT ROCK.

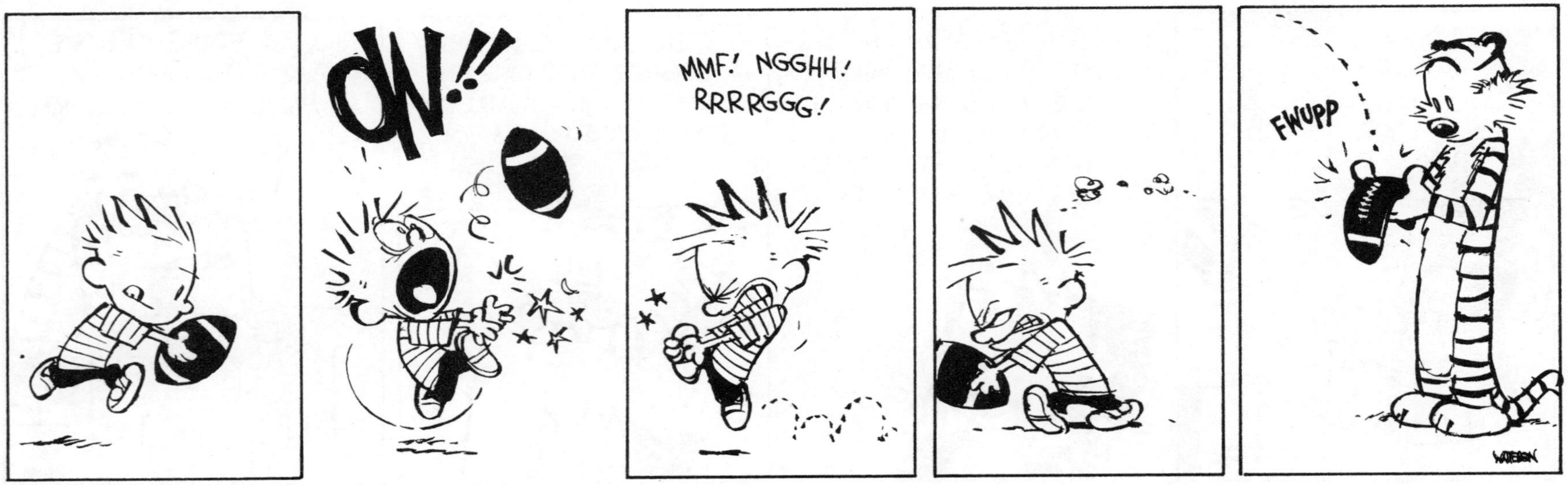
OW!!
MMF! NGGHH! RRRRGGG!
FWUPP
WATTERSON

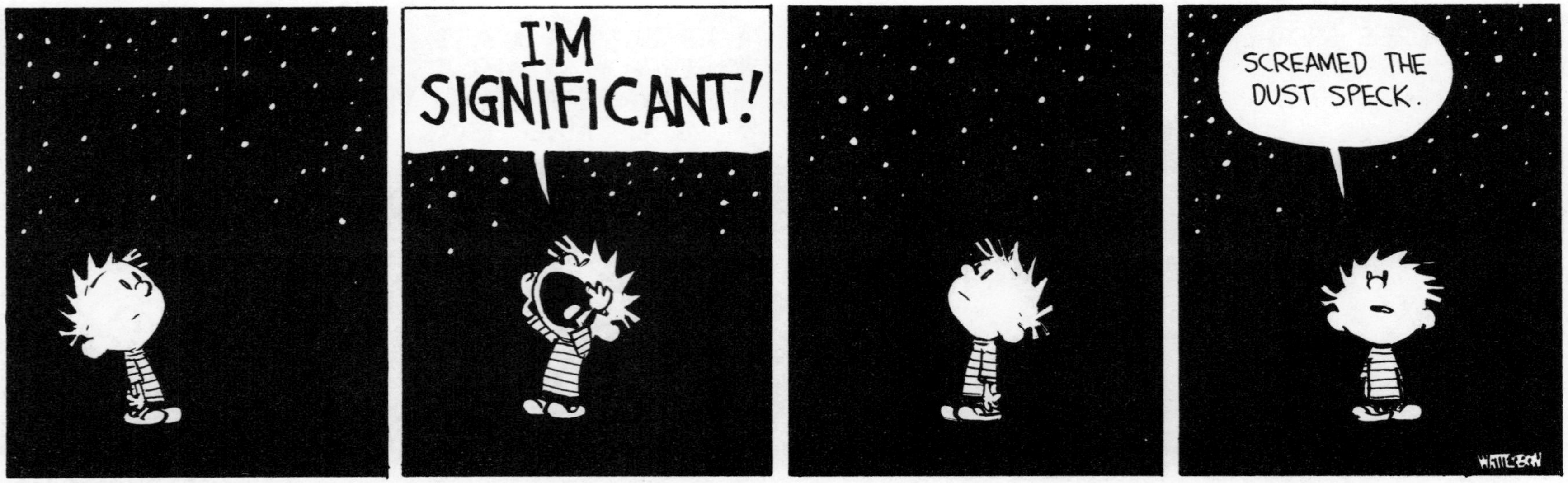
I'M SIGNIFICANT!
SCREAMED THE DUST SPECK.
WATTERSON

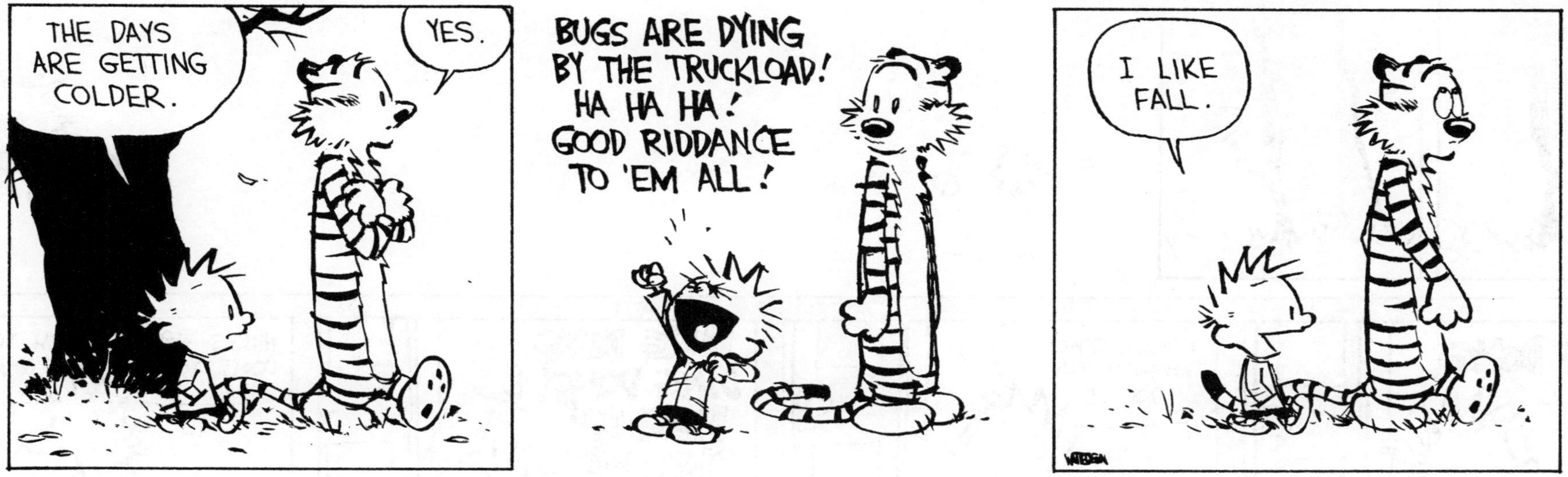
THE DAYS ARE GETTING COLDER.
YES.
BUGS ARE DYING BY THE TRUCKLOAD! HA HA HA! GOOD RIDDANCE TO 'EM ALL!
I LIKE FALL.

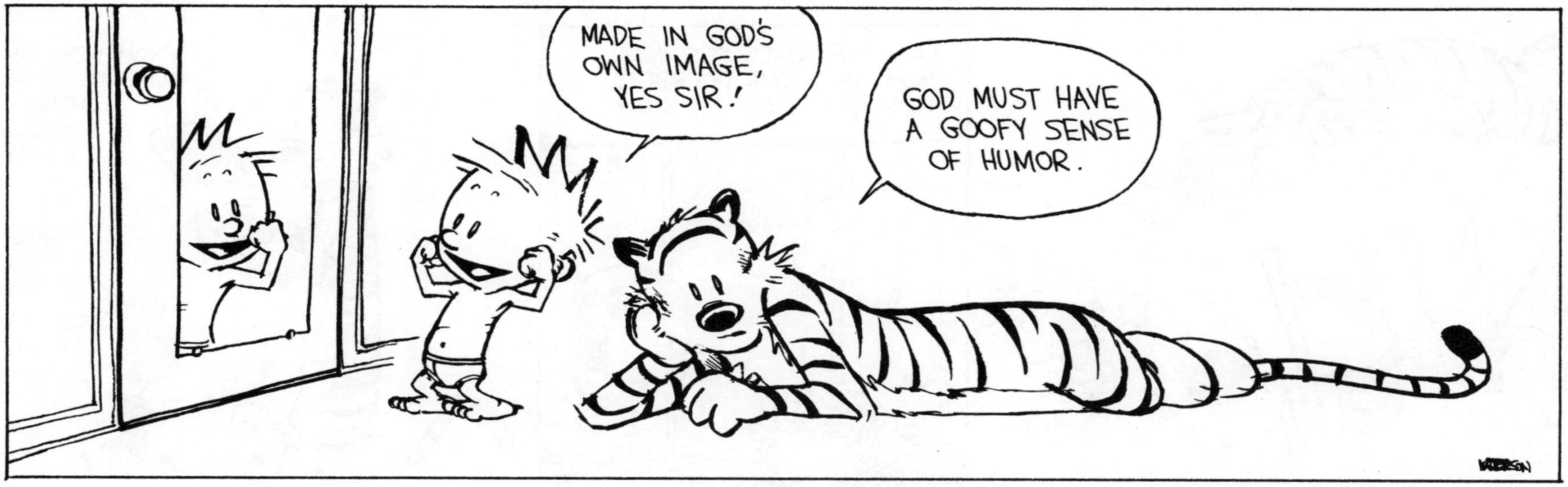
MADE IN GOD'S OWN IMAGE, YES SIR!
GOD MUST HAVE A GOOFY SENSE OF HUMOR.

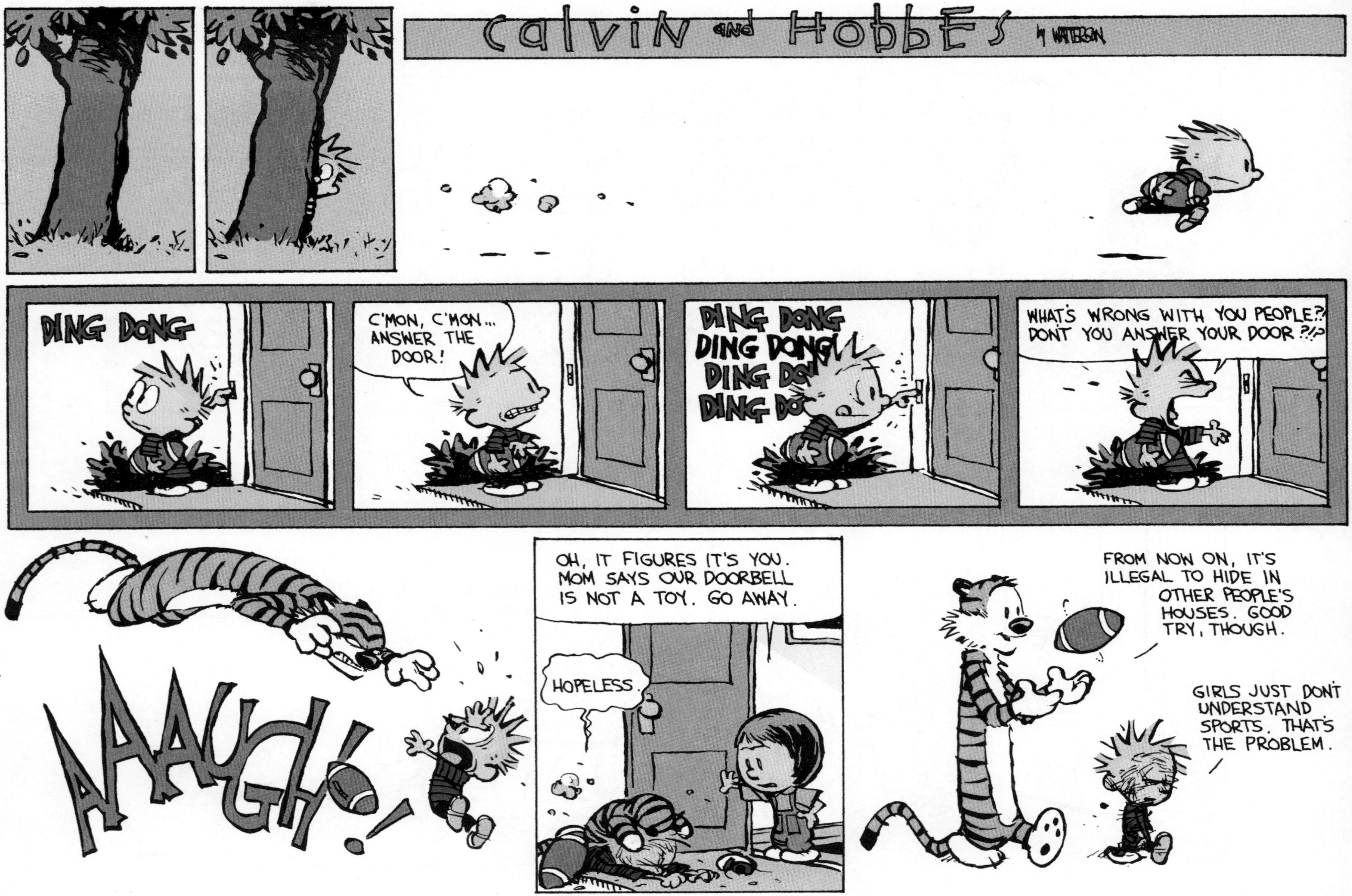
Calvin and Hobbes
by WATTERSON
DING DONG
C'MON, C'MON... ANSWER THE DOOR!
DING DONG
DING DONG
DING DO
DING DO
WHAT'S WRONG WITH YOU PEOPLE?! DON'T YOU ANSWER YOUR DOOR?!?
AAAUGH!!
OH, IT FIGURES IT'S YOU. MOM SAYS OUR DOORBELL IS NOT A TOY. GO AWAY.
HOPELESS.
FROM NOW ON, IT'S ILLEGAL TO HIDE IN OTHER PEOPLE'S HOUSES. GOOD TRY, THOUGH.
GIRLS JUST DON'T UNDERSTAND SPORTS. THAT'S THE PROBLEM.

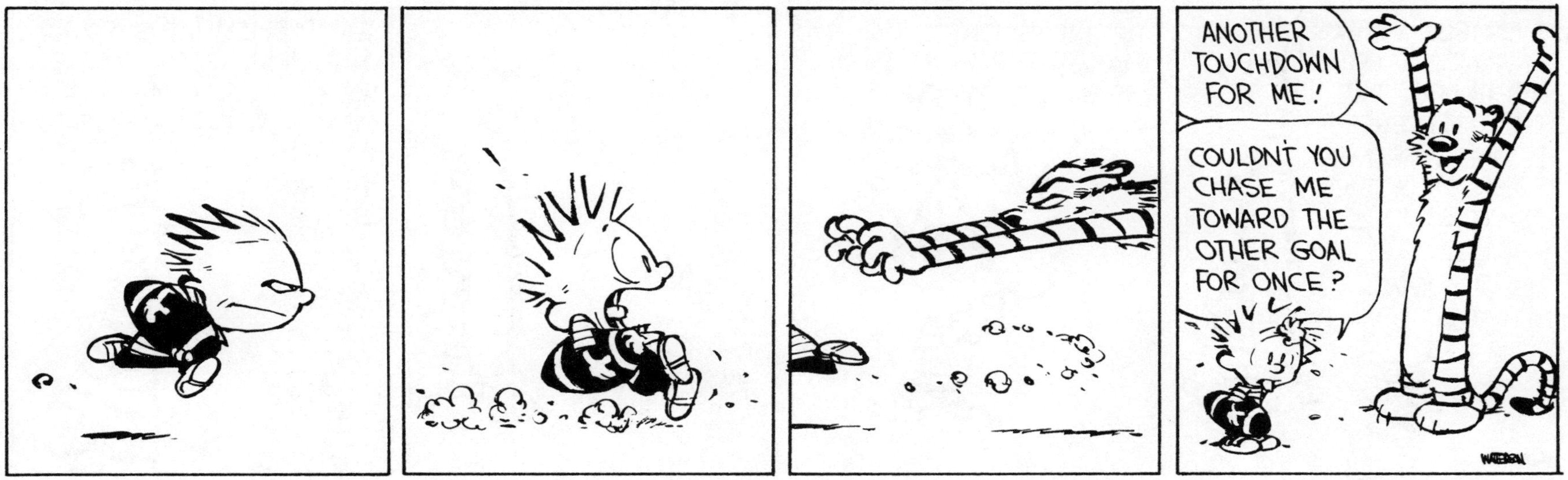
ANOTHER TOUCHDOWN FOR ME!
COULDN'T YOU CHASE ME TOWARD THE OTHER GOAL FOR ONCE?
WATTERSON

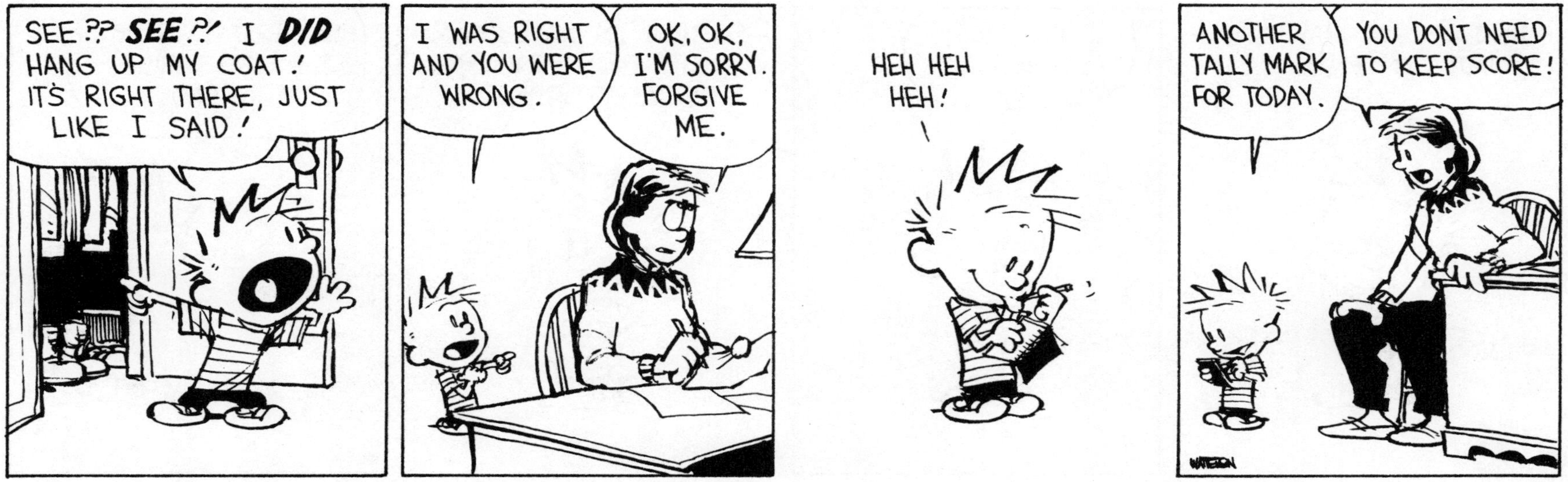
SEE?? SEE?! I DID HANG UP MY COAT! IT'S RIGHT THERE, JUST LIKE I SAID!
I WAS RIGHT AND YOU WERE WRONG.
OK, OK, I'M SORRY. FORGIVE ME.
HEH HEH HEH!
ANOTHER TALLY MARK FOR TODAY.
YOU DON'T NEED TO KEEP SCORE!
WATTERSON

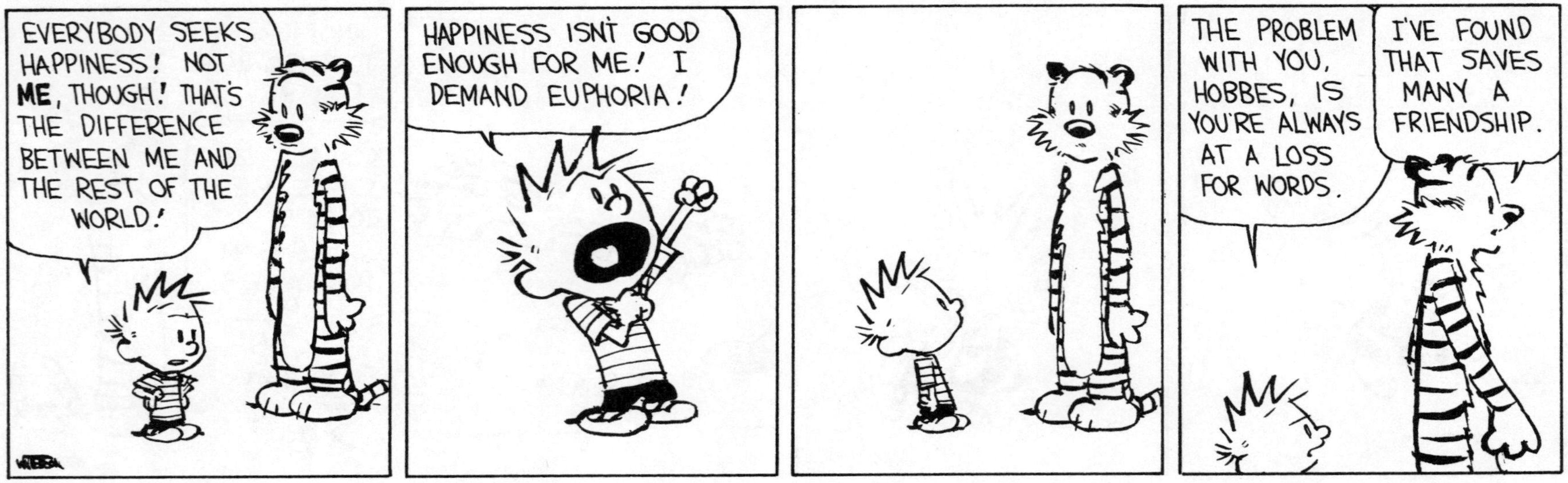
EVERYBODY SEEKS HAPPINESS! NOT ME, THOUGH! THAT'S THE DIFFERENCE BETWEEN ME AND THE REST OF THE WORLD!
HAPPINESS ISN'T GOOD ENOUGH FOR ME! I DEMAND EUPHORIA!
THE PROBLEM WITH YOU, HOBBES, IS YOU'RE ALWAYS AT A LOSS FOR WORDS.
I'VE FOUND THAT SAVES MANY A FRIENDSHIP.

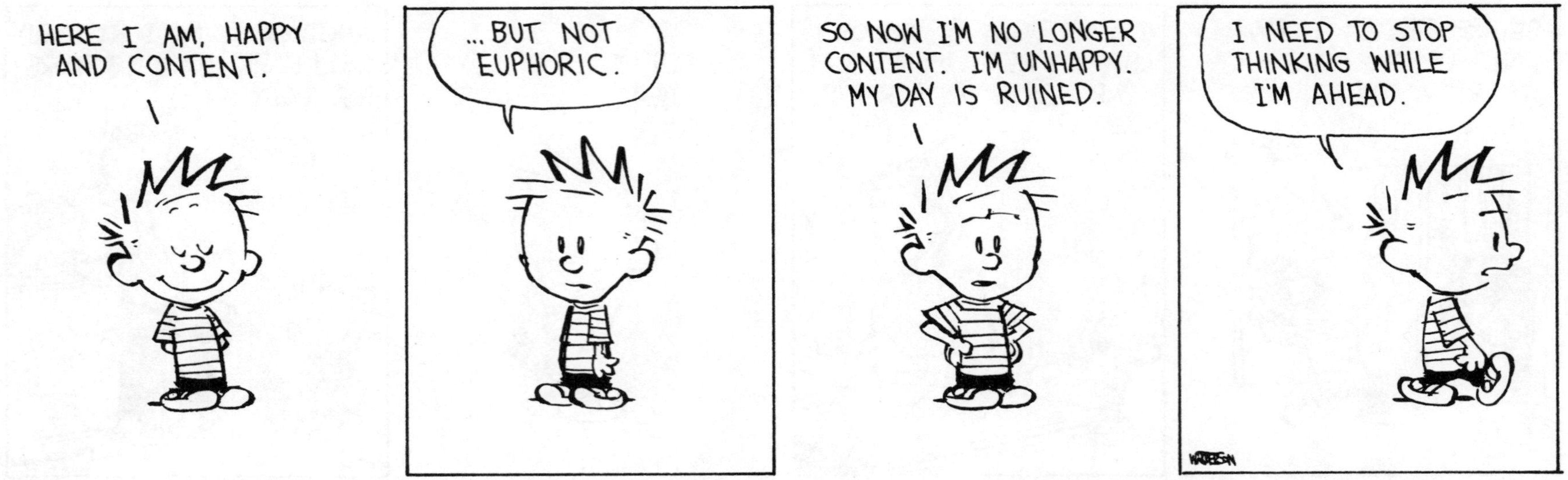
HERE I AM, HAPPY AND CONTENT.
...BUT NOT EUPHORIC.
SO NOW I'M NO LONGER CONTENT. I'M UNHAPPY. MY DAY IS RUINED.
I NEED TO STOP THINKING WHILE I'M AHEAD.

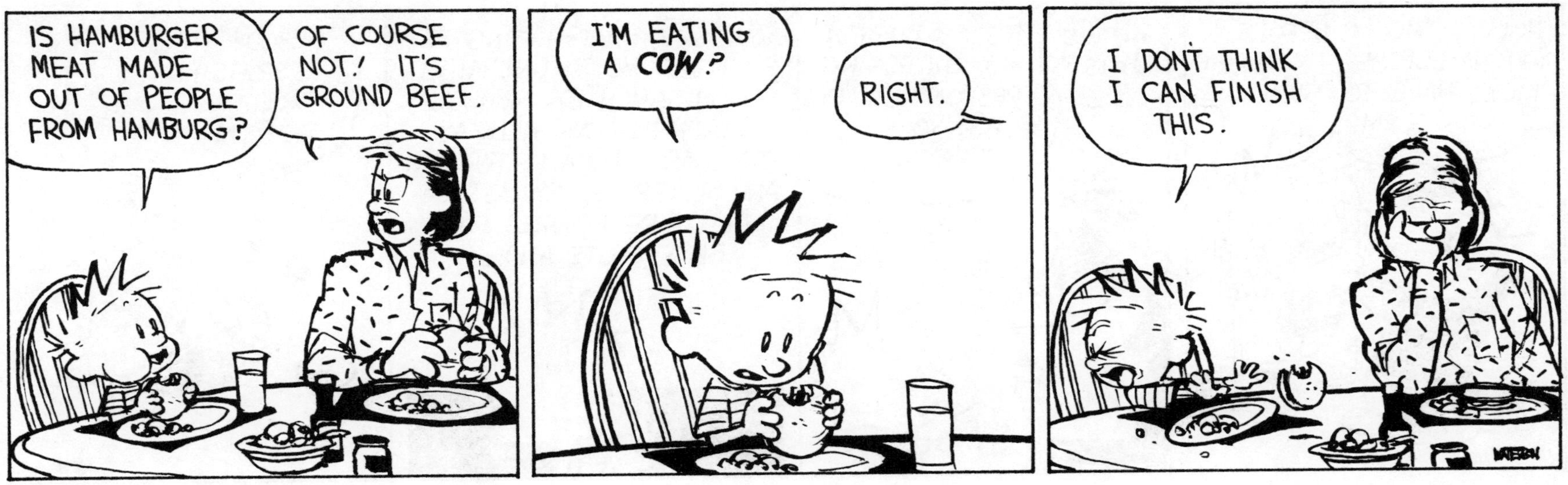
IS HAMBURGER MEAT MADE OUT OF PEOPLE FROM HAMBURG?
OF COURSE NOT! IT'S GROUND BEEF.
I'M EATING A COW?
RIGHT.
I DON'T THINK I CAN FINISH THIS.

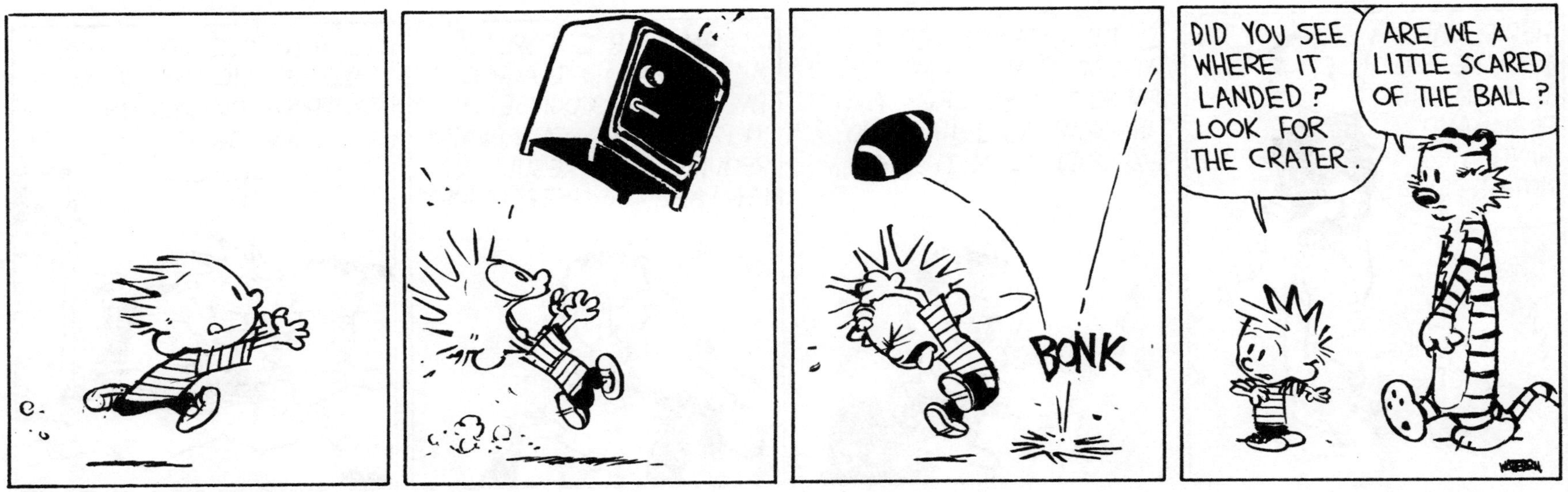
BONK
DID YOU SEE WHERE IT LANDED? LOOK FOR THE CRATER.
ARE WE A LITTLE SCARED OF THE BALL?

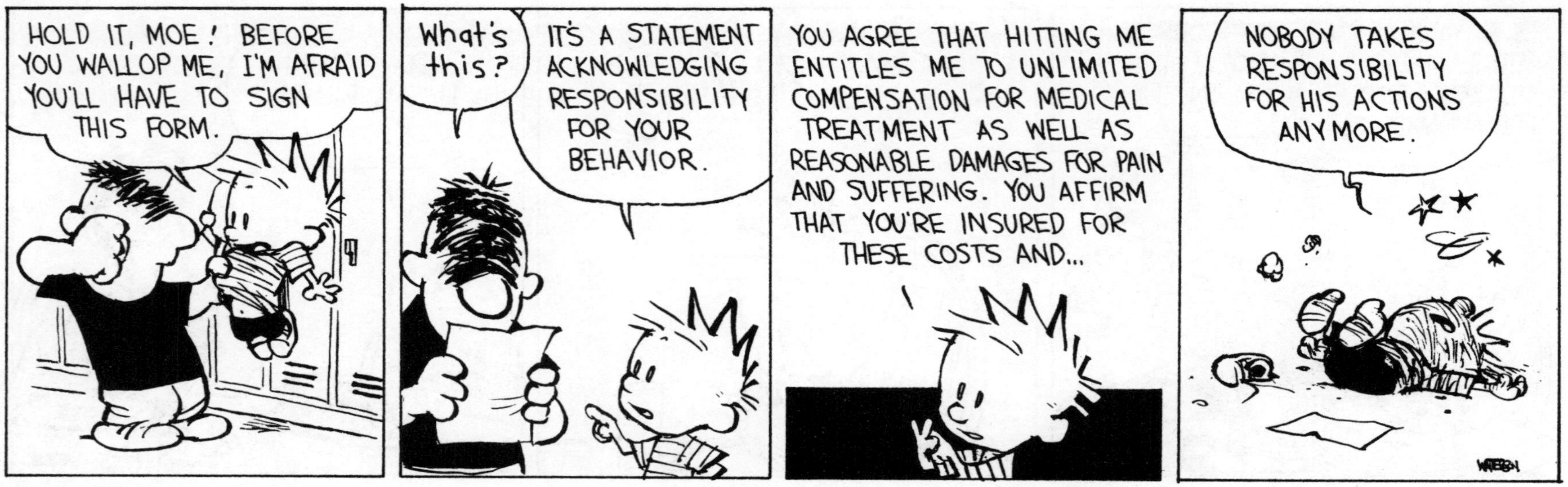
HOLD IT, MOE! BEFORE YOU WALLOP ME, I'M AFRAID YOU'LL HAVE TO SIGN THIS FORM.
What's this?
IT'S A STATEMENT ACKNOWLEDGING RESPONSIBILITY FOR YOUR BEHAVIOR.
YOU AGREE THAT HITTING ME ENTITLES ME TO UNLIMITED COMPENSATION FOR MEDICAL TREATMENT AS WELL AS REASONABLE DAMAGES FOR PAIN AND SUFFERING. YOU AFFIRM THAT YOU'RE INSURED FOR THESE COSTS AND...
NOBODY TAKES RESPONSIBILITY FOR HIS ACTIONS ANYMORE.
WATTERSON

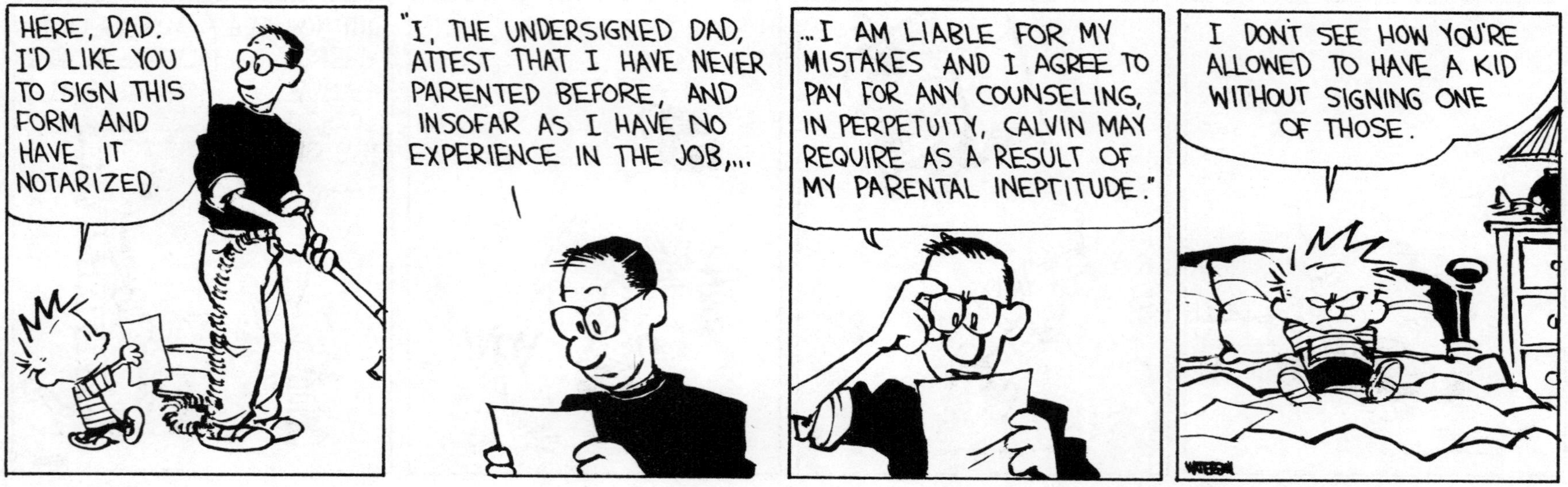
HERE, DAD. I'D LIKE YOU TO SIGN THIS FORM AND HAVE IT NOTARIZED.
"I, THE UNDERSIGNED DAD, ATTEST THAT I HAVE NEVER PARENTED BEFORE, AND INSOFAR AS I HAVE NO EXPERIENCE IN THE JOB,...
...I AM LIABLE FOR MY MISTAKES AND I AGREE TO PAY FOR ANY COUNSELING, IN PERPETUITY, CALVIN MAY REQUIRE AS A RESULT OF MY PARENTAL INEPTITUDE."
I DON'T SEE HOW YOU'RE ALLOWED TO HAVE A KID WITHOUT SIGNING ONE OF THOSE.
WATTERSON

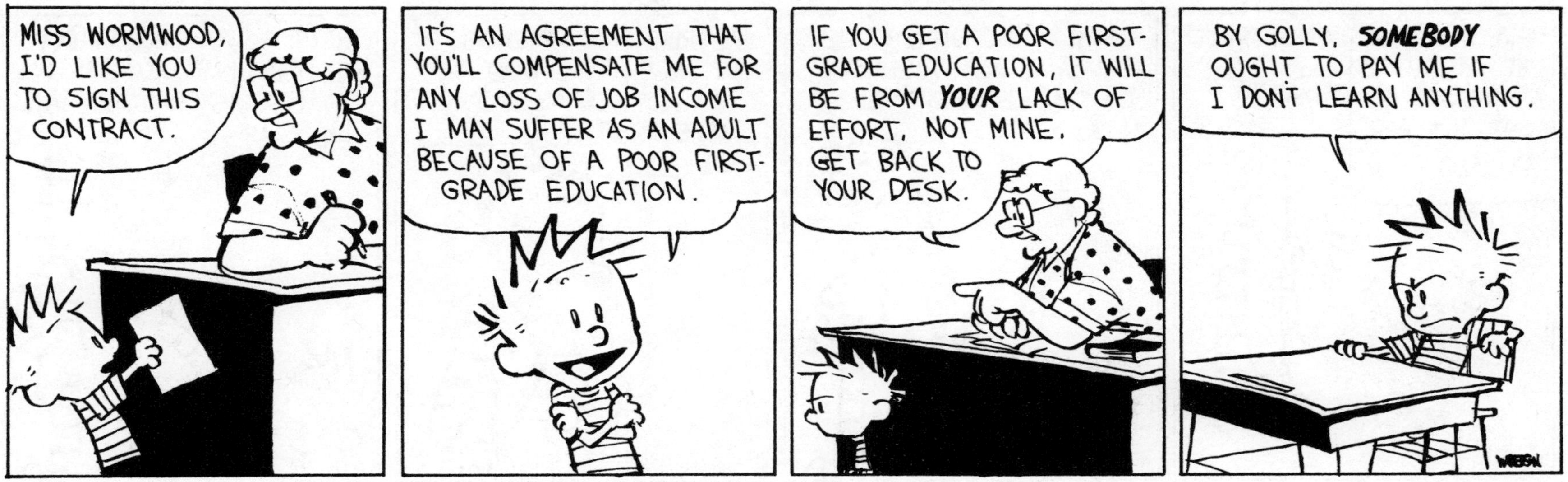
MISS WORMWOOD, I'D LIKE YOU TO SIGN THIS CONTRACT.
IT'S AN AGREEMENT THAT YOU'LL COMPENSATE ME FOR ANY LOSS OF JOB INCOME I MAY SUFFER AS AN ADULT BECAUSE OF A POOR FIRST-GRADE EDUCATION.
IF YOU GET A POOR FIRST-GRADE EDUCATION, IT WILL BE FROM ***YOUR*** LACK OF EFFORT, NOT MINE. GET BACK TO YOUR DESK.
BY GOLLY, ***SOMEBODY*** OUGHT TO PAY ME IF I DON'T LEARN ANYTHING.

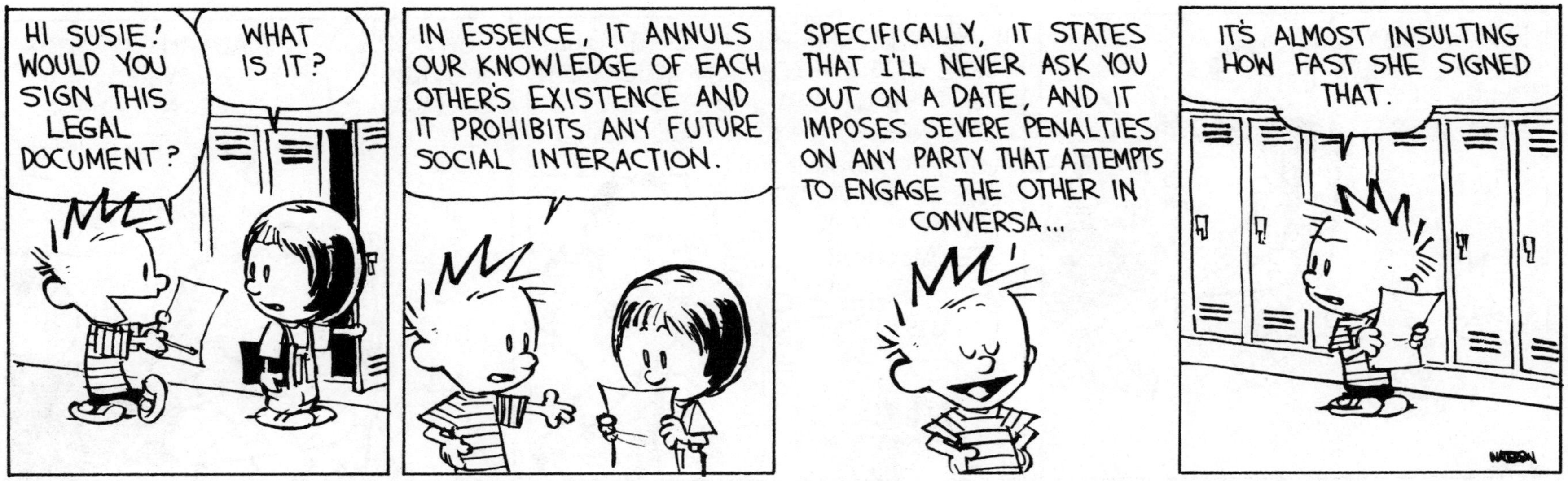
HI SUSIE! WOULD YOU SIGN THIS LEGAL DOCUMENT?
WHAT IS IT?
IN ESSENCE, IT ANNULS OUR KNOWLEDGE OF EACH OTHER'S EXISTENCE AND IT PROHIBITS ANY FUTURE SOCIAL INTERACTION.
SPECIFICALLY, IT STATES THAT I'LL NEVER ASK YOU OUT ON A DATE, AND IT IMPOSES SEVERE PENALTIES ON ANY PARTY THAT ATTEMPTS TO ENGAGE THE OTHER IN CONVERSA...
IT'S ALMOST INSULTING HOW FAST SHE SIGNED THAT.

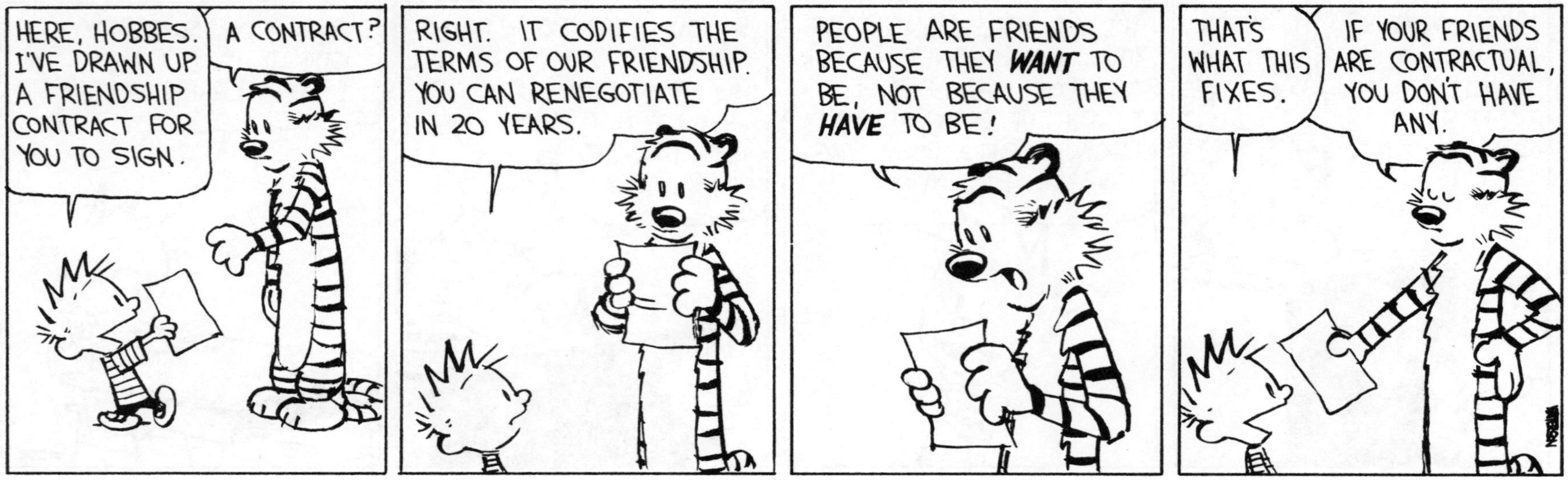
HERE, HOBBES. I'VE DRAWN UP A FRIENDSHIP CONTRACT FOR YOU TO SIGN.
A CONTRACT?
RIGHT. IT CODIFIES THE TERMS OF OUR FRIENDSHIP. YOU CAN RENEGOTIATE IN 20 YEARS.
PEOPLE ARE FRIENDS BECAUSE THEY **WANT** TO BE, NOT BECAUSE THEY **HAVE** TO BE!
THAT'S WHAT THIS FIXES.
IF YOUR FRIENDS ARE CONTRACTUAL, YOU DON'T HAVE ANY.

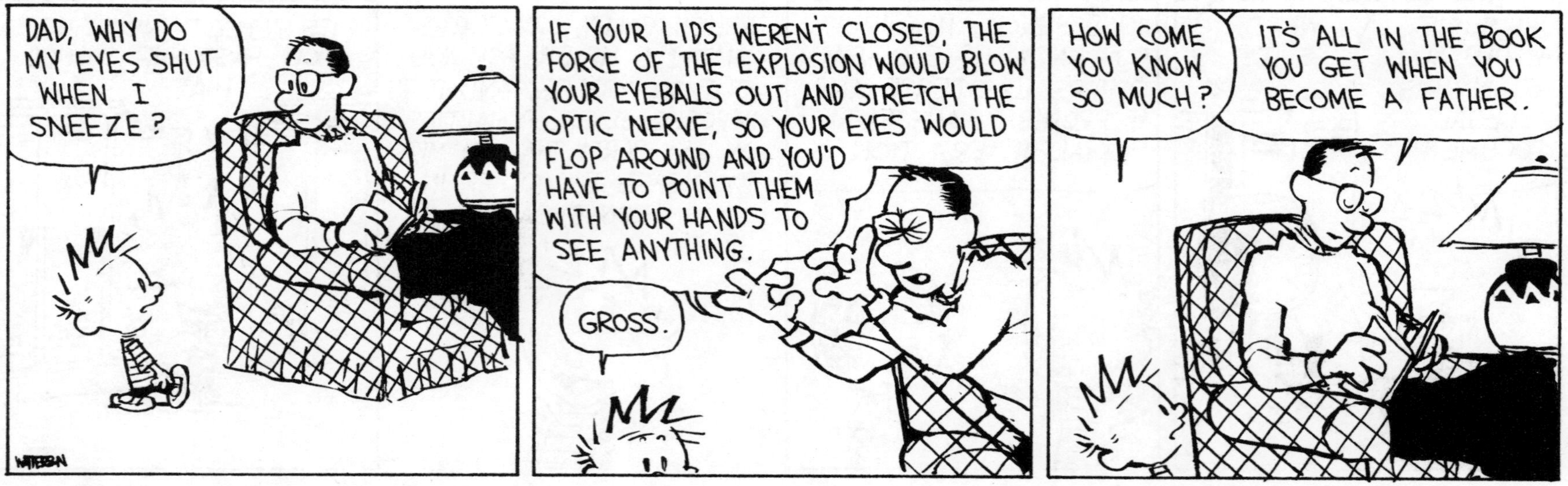
DAD, WHY DO MY EYES SHUT WHEN I SNEEZE?
IF YOUR LIDS WEREN'T CLOSED, THE FORCE OF THE EXPLOSION WOULD BLOW YOUR EYEBALLS OUT AND STRETCH THE OPTIC NERVE, SO YOUR EYES WOULD FLOP AROUND AND YOU'D HAVE TO POINT THEM WITH YOUR HANDS TO SEE ANYTHING.
GROSS.
HOW COME YOU KNOW SO MUCH?
IT'S ALL IN THE BOOK YOU GET WHEN YOU BECOME A FATHER.

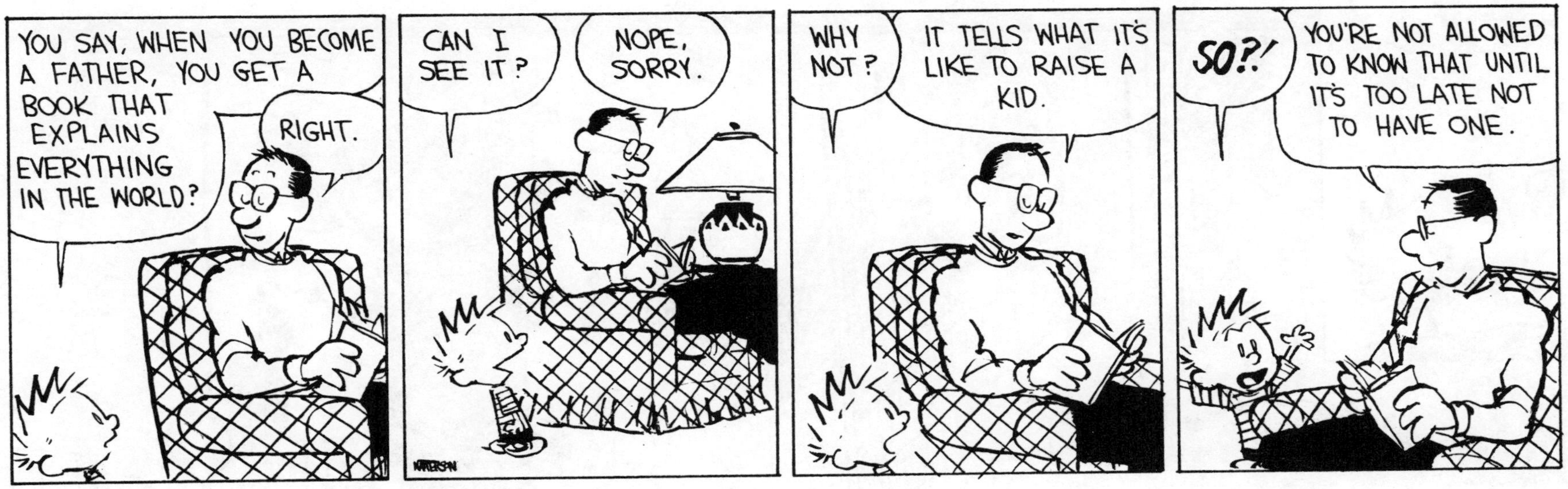
YOU SAY, WHEN YOU BECOME A FATHER, YOU GET A BOOK THAT EXPLAINS EVERYTHING IN THE WORLD?
RIGHT.
CAN I SEE IT?
NOPE, SORRY.
WHY NOT?
IT TELLS WHAT IT'S LIKE TO RAISE A KID.
SO?!
YOU'RE NOT ALLOWED TO KNOW THAT UNTIL IT'S TOO LATE NOT TO HAVE ONE.

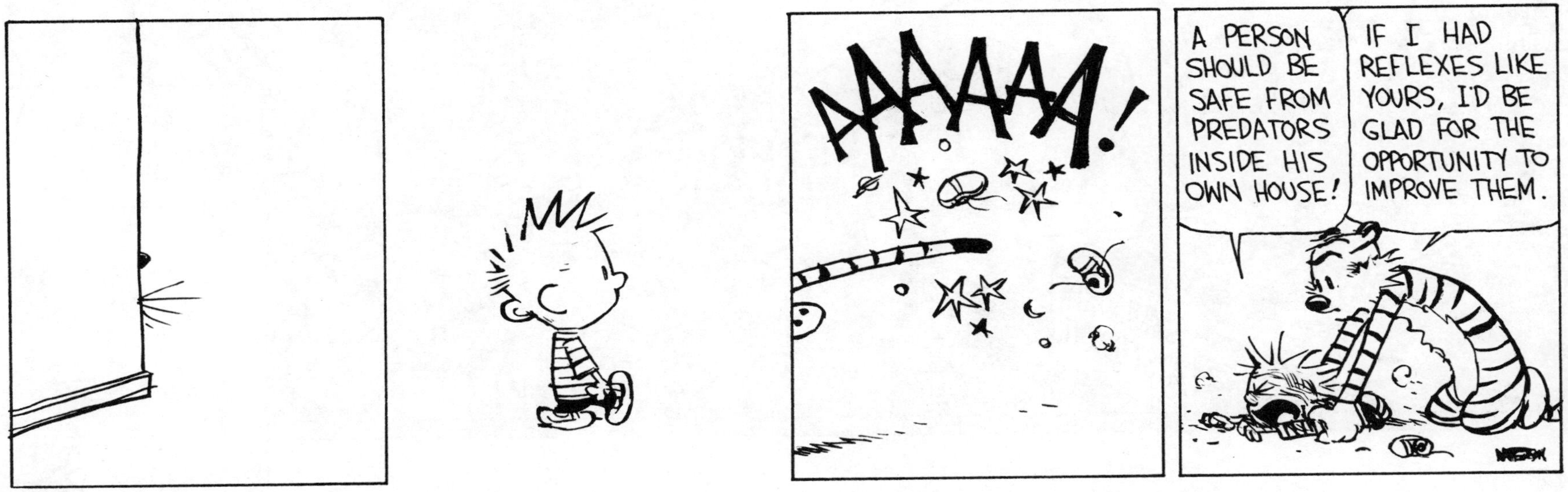
AAAAAA!
A PERSON SHOULD BE SAFE FROM PREDATORS INSIDE HIS OWN HOUSE!
IF I HAD REFLEXES LIKE YOURS, I'D BE GLAD FOR THE OPPORTUNITY TO IMPROVE THEM.

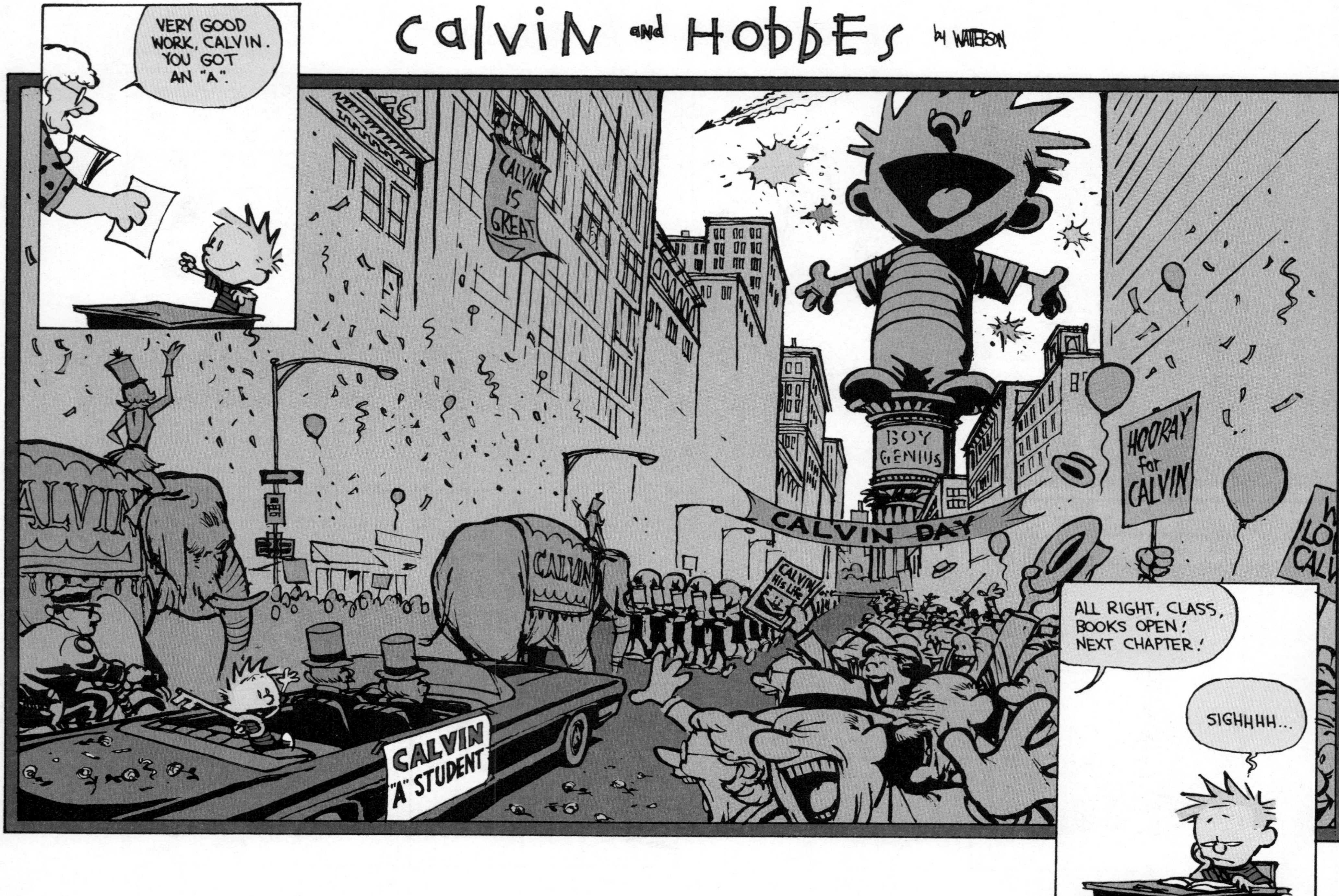

CALVIN and HOBBES by WATTERSON
VERY GOOD WORK, CALVIN. YOU GOT AN "A".
CALVIN IS GREAT
BOY GENIUS
HOORAY for CALVIN
CALVIN DAY
CALVIN His Life
CALVIN
"A" STUDENT
ALL RIGHT, CLASS, BOOKS OPEN! NEXT CHAPTER!
SIGHHHH...

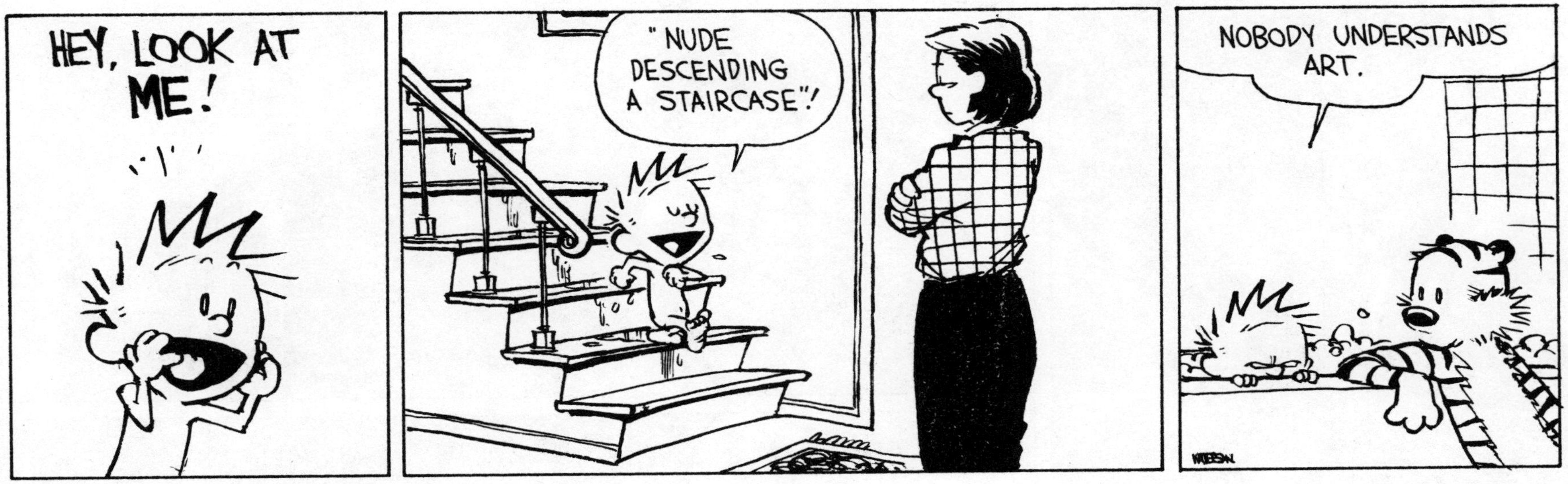
HEY, LOOK AT ME!
"NUDE DESCENDING A STAIRCASE"!
NOBODY UNDERSTANDS ART.

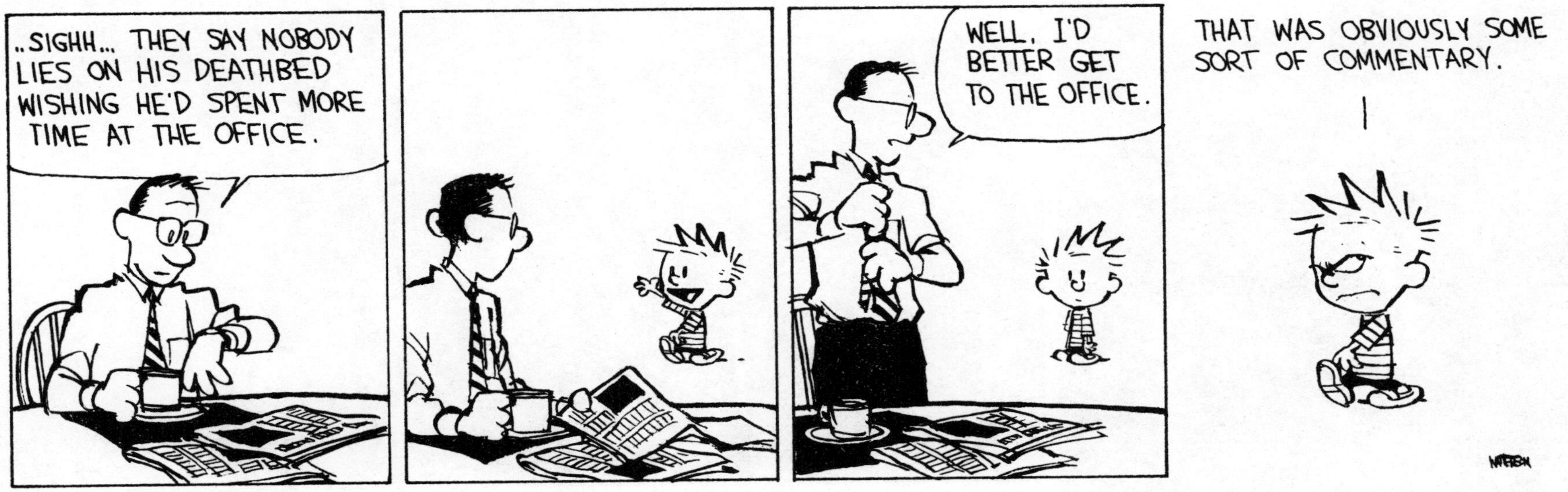
..SIGHH... THEY SAY NOBODY LIES ON HIS DEATHBED WISHING HE'D SPENT MORE TIME AT THE OFFICE.
WELL, I'D BETTER GET TO THE OFFICE.
THAT WAS OBVIOUSLY SOME SORT OF COMMENTARY.

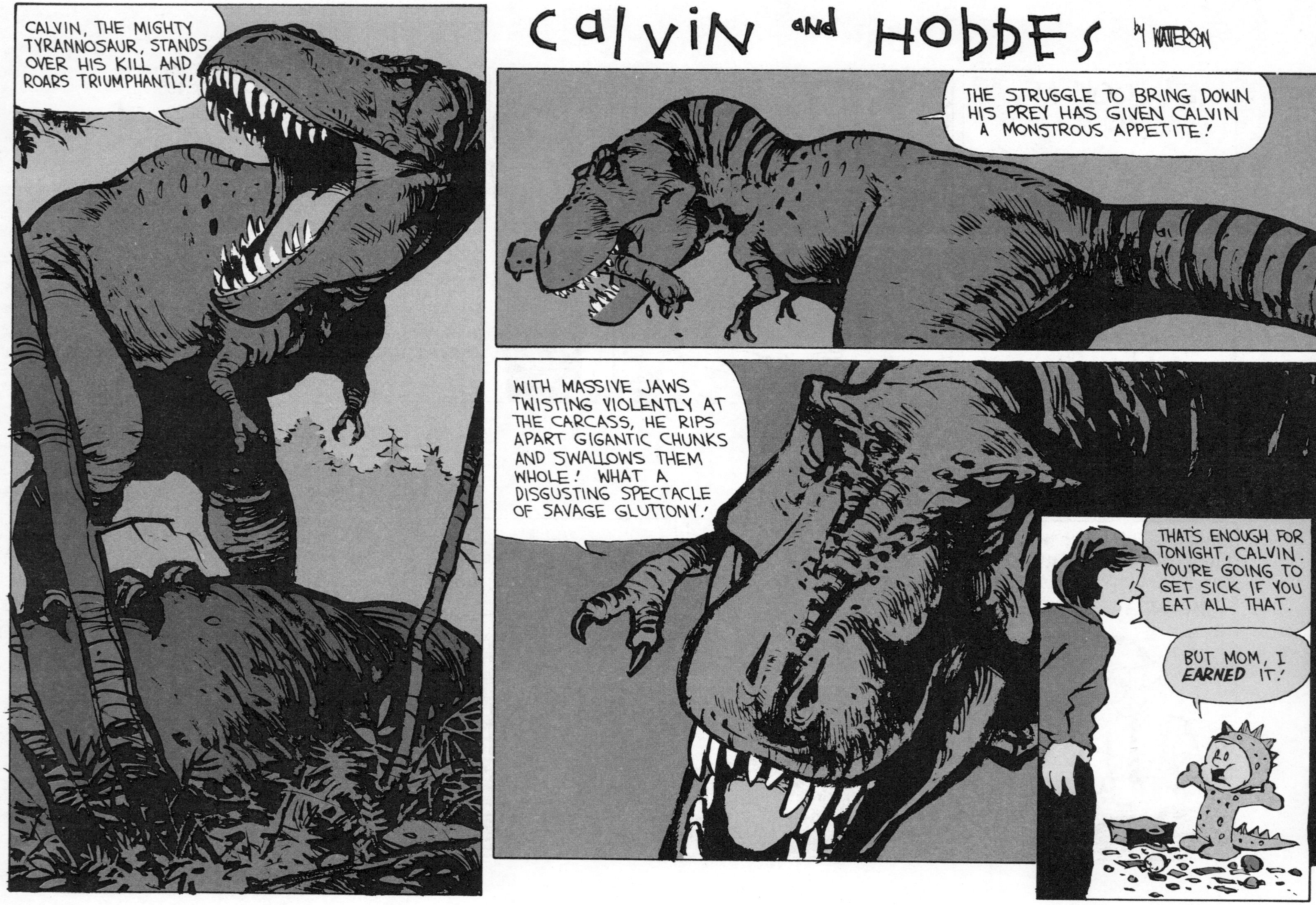
Calvin and Hobbes by WATTERSON
CALVIN, THE MIGHTY TYRANNOSAUR, STANDS OVER HIS KILL AND ROARS TRIUMPHANTLY!
THE STRUGGLE TO BRING DOWN HIS PREY HAS GIVEN CALVIN A MONSTROUS APPETITE!
WITH MASSIVE JAWS TWISTING VIOLENTLY AT THE CARCASS, HE RIPS APART GIGANTIC CHUNKS AND SWALLOWS THEM WHOLE! WHAT A DISGUSTING SPECTACLE OF SAVAGE GLUTTONY!
THAT'S ENOUGH FOR TONIGHT, CALVIN. YOU'RE GOING TO GET SICK IF YOU EAT ALL THAT.
BUT MOM, I EARNED IT!

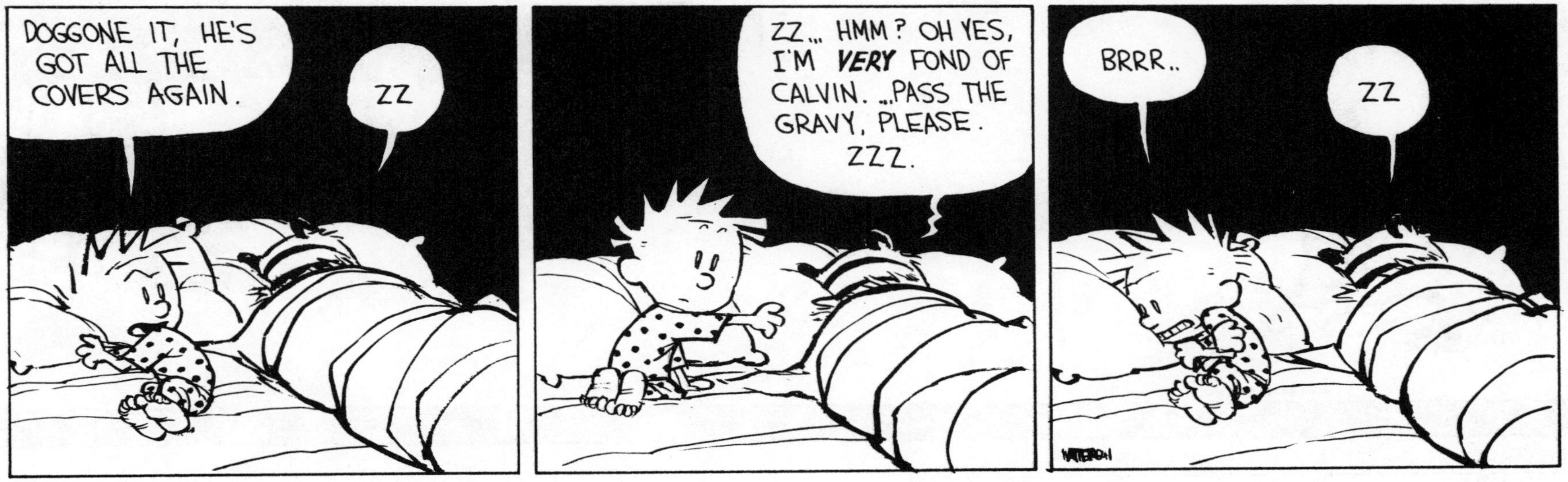
DOGGONE IT, HE'S GOT ALL THE COVERS AGAIN.
ZZ
ZZ... HMM? OH YES, I'M **VERY** FOND OF CALVIN. ...PASS THE GRAVY, PLEASE. ZZZ.
BRRR..
ZZ

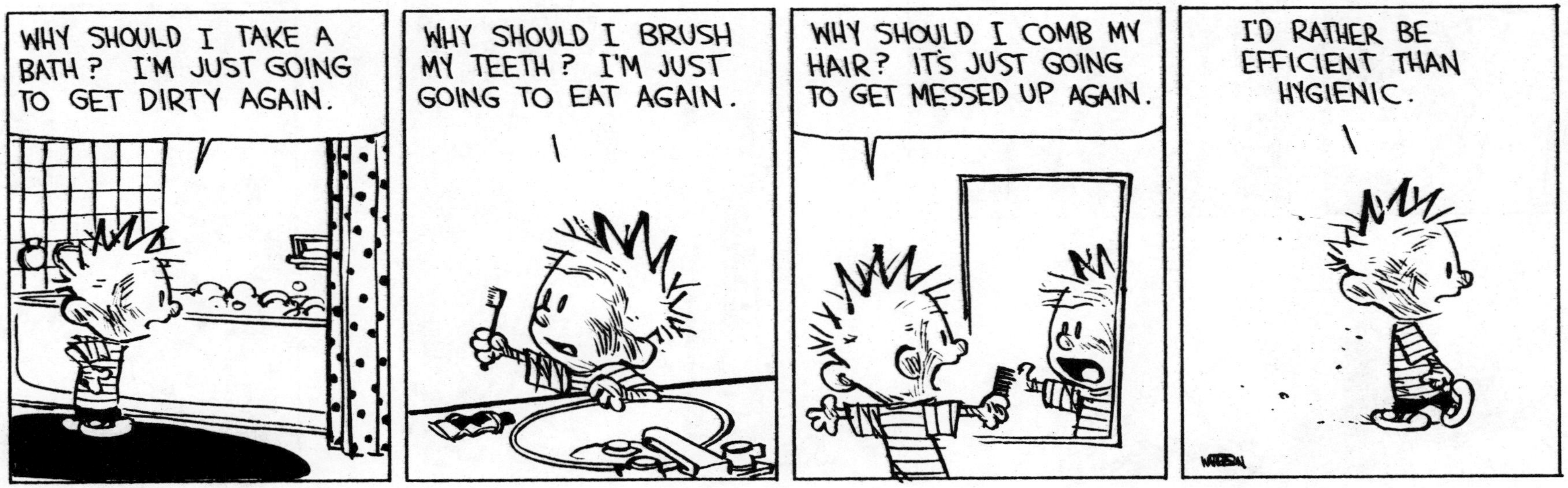
WHY SHOULD I TAKE A BATH? I'M JUST GOING TO GET DIRTY AGAIN.
WHY SHOULD I BRUSH MY TEETH? I'M JUST GOING TO EAT AGAIN.
WHY SHOULD I COMB MY HAIR? IT'S JUST GOING TO GET MESSED UP AGAIN.
I'D RATHER BE EFFICIENT THAN HYGIENIC.

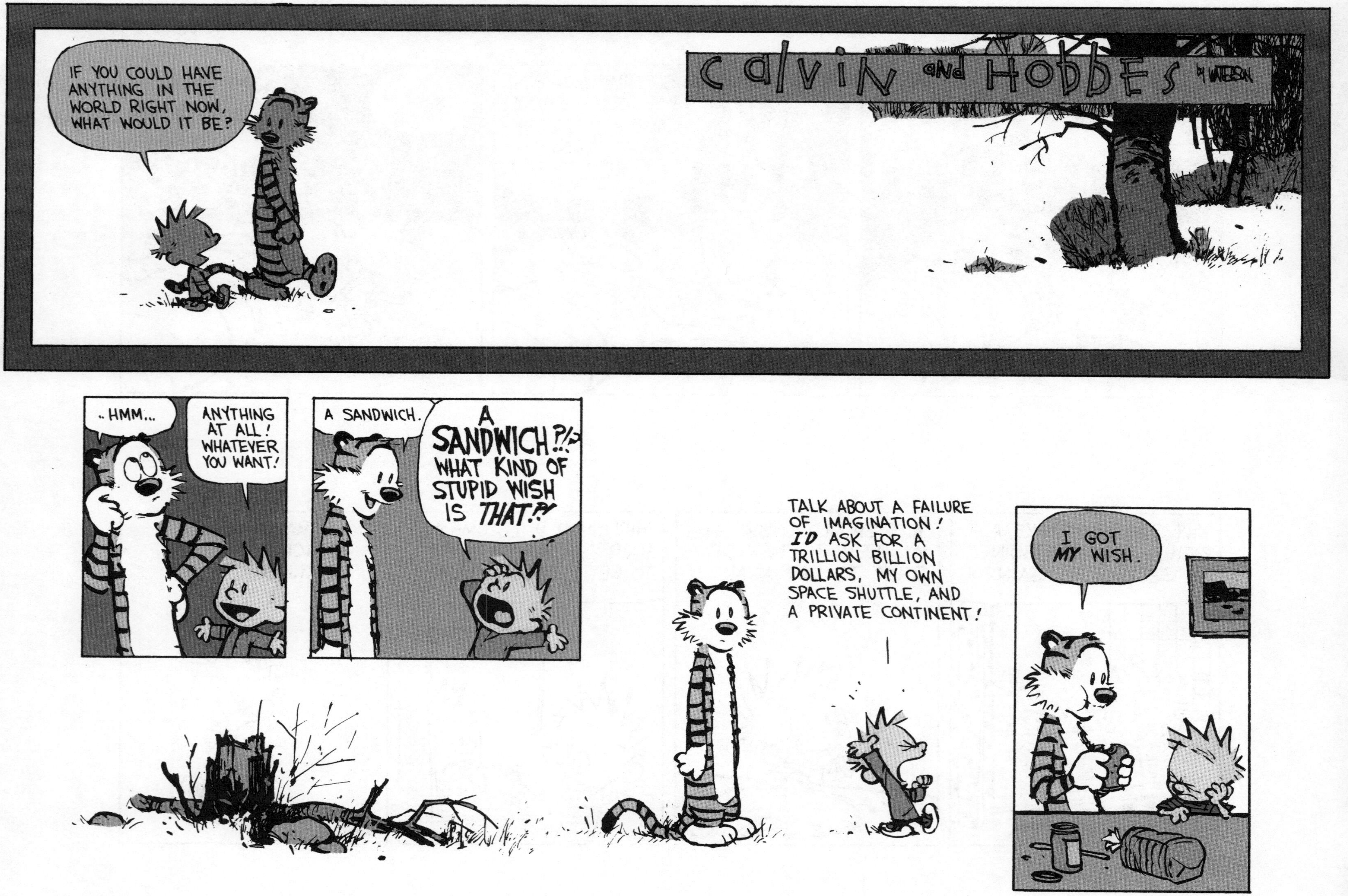
IF YOU COULD HAVE ANYTHING IN THE WORLD RIGHT NOW, WHAT WOULD IT BE?
Calvin and HOBBES by WATTERSON
..HMM...
ANYTHING AT ALL! WHATEVER YOU WANT!
A SANDWICH.
A SANDWICH?!? WHAT KIND OF STUPID WISH IS *THAT*?!
TALK ABOUT A FAILURE OF IMAGINATION! *I'D* ASK FOR A TRILLION BILLION DOLLARS, MY OWN SPACE SHUTTLE, AND A PRIVATE CONTINENT!
I GOT *MY* WISH.

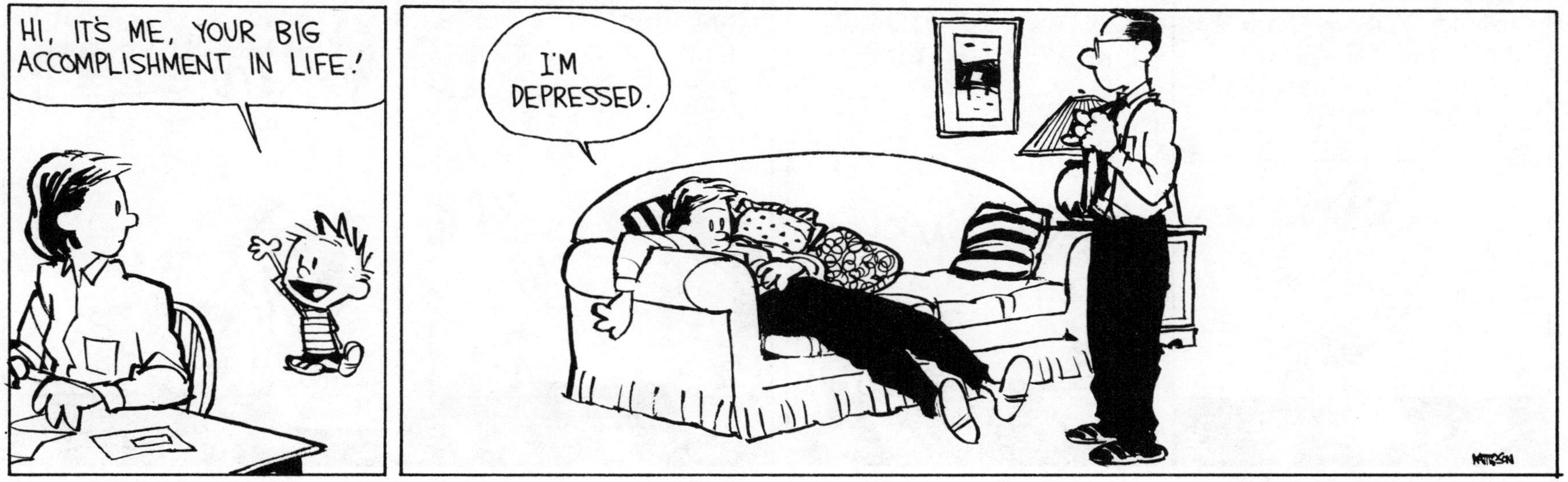

HI, IT'S ME, YOUR BIG ACCOMPLISHMENT IN LIFE!
I'M DEPRESSED.

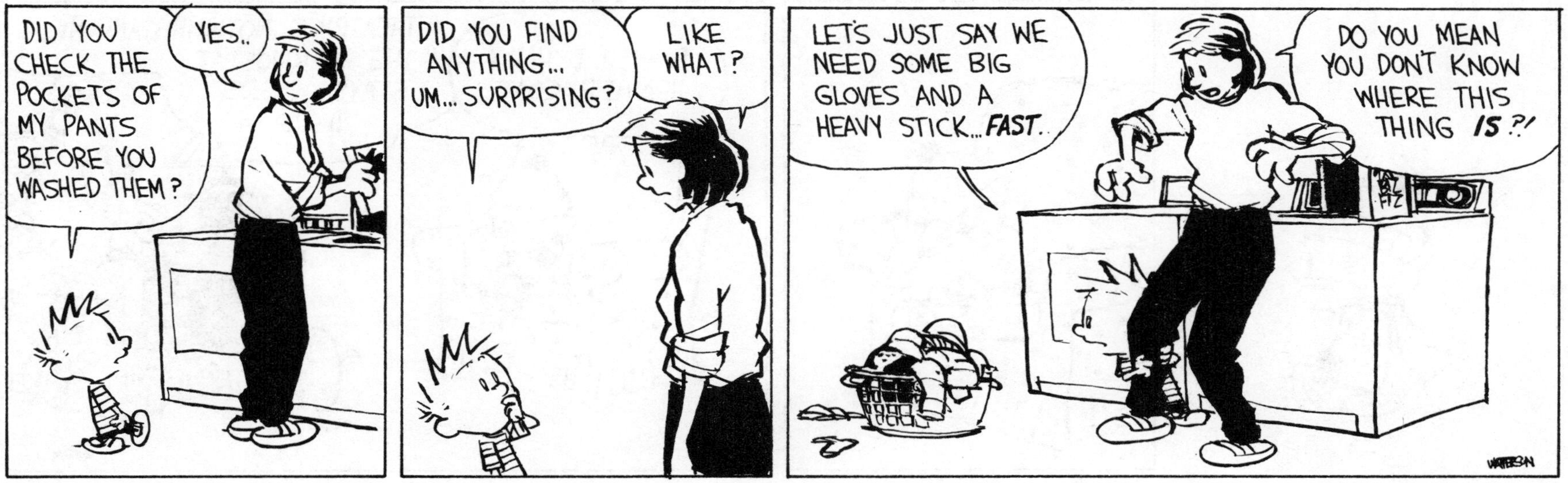

DID YOU CHECK THE POCKETS OF MY PANTS BEFORE YOU WASHED THEM?
YES..
DID YOU FIND ANYTHING... UM... SURPRISING?
LIKE WHAT?
LET'S JUST SAY WE NEED SOME BIG GLOVES AND A HEAVY STICK... FAST..
DO YOU MEAN YOU DON'T KNOW WHERE THIS THING IS?!

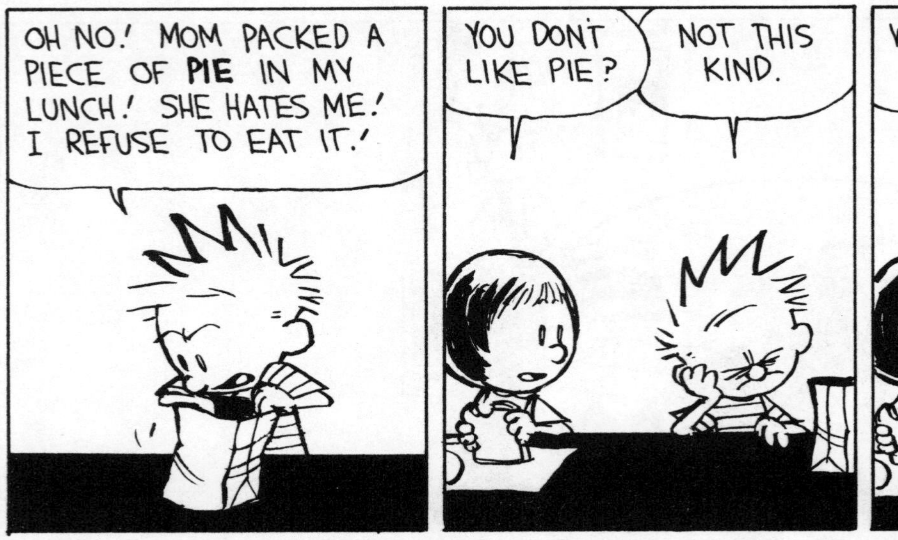
OH NO! MOM PACKED A PIECE OF **PIE** IN MY LUNCH! SHE HATES ME! I REFUSE TO EAT IT!
YOU DON'T LIKE PIE?
NOT THIS KIND.
WHAT KIND IS IT?
COW PIE.
MISS WORMWOOD!
WANT IT? IT'S FRESH.

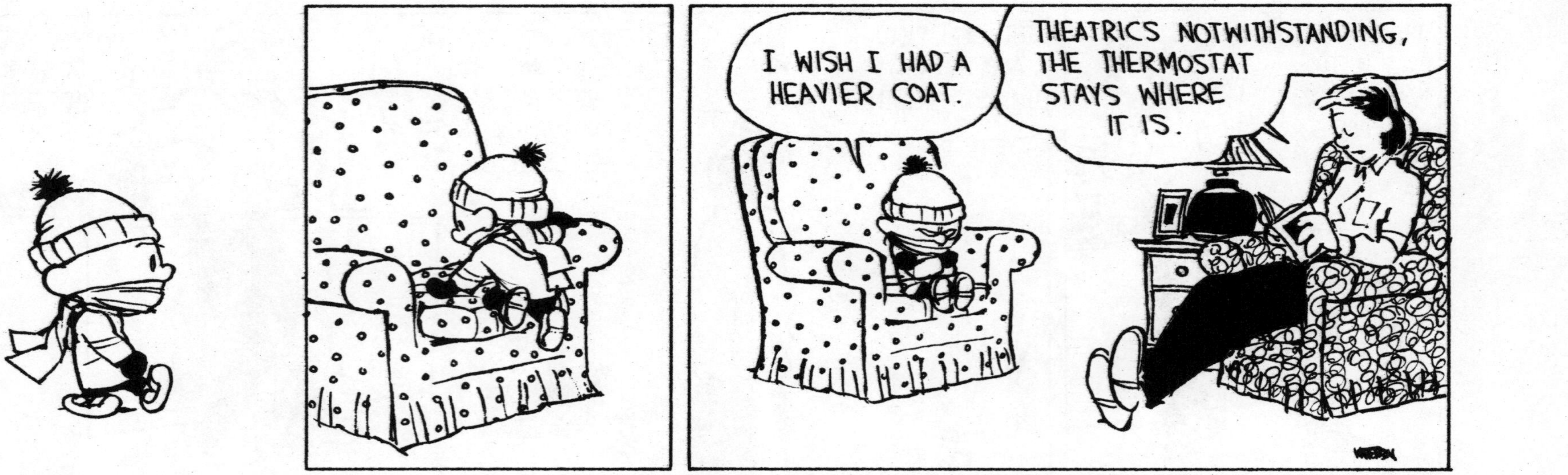
I WISH I HAD A HEAVIER COAT.
THEATRICS NOTWITHSTANDING, THE THERMOSTAT STAYS WHERE IT IS.

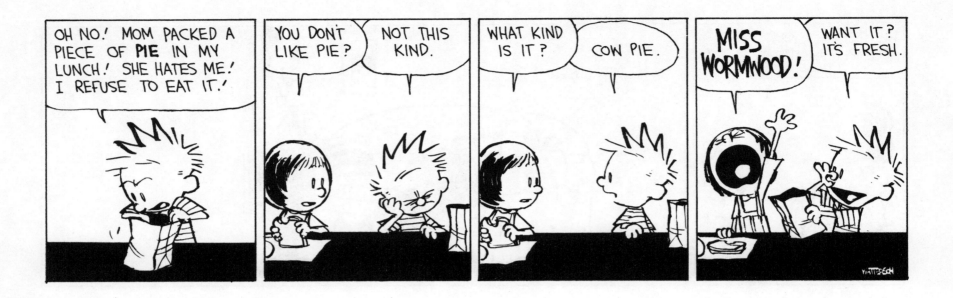

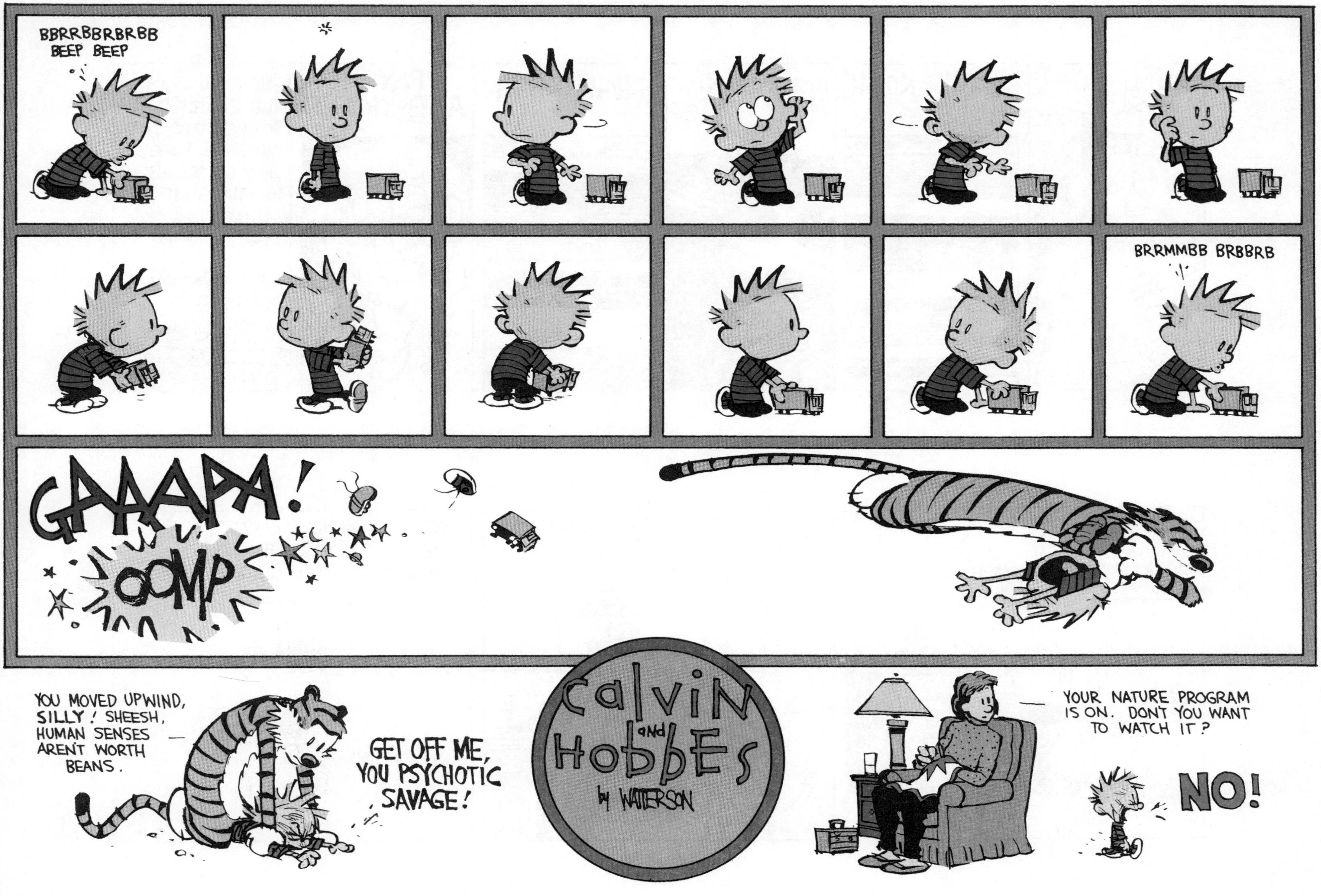
BBRRBBRBRBB
BEEP BEEP
BRRMMBB BRBBRB
GAAAPA!
OOMP
Calvin and Hobbes by WATTERSON
YOU MOVED UPWIND, SILLY! SHEESH, HUMAN SENSES AREN'T WORTH BEANS.
GET OFF ME, YOU PSYCHOTIC SAVAGE!
YOUR NATURE PROGRAM IS ON. DON'T YOU WANT TO WATCH IT?
NO!

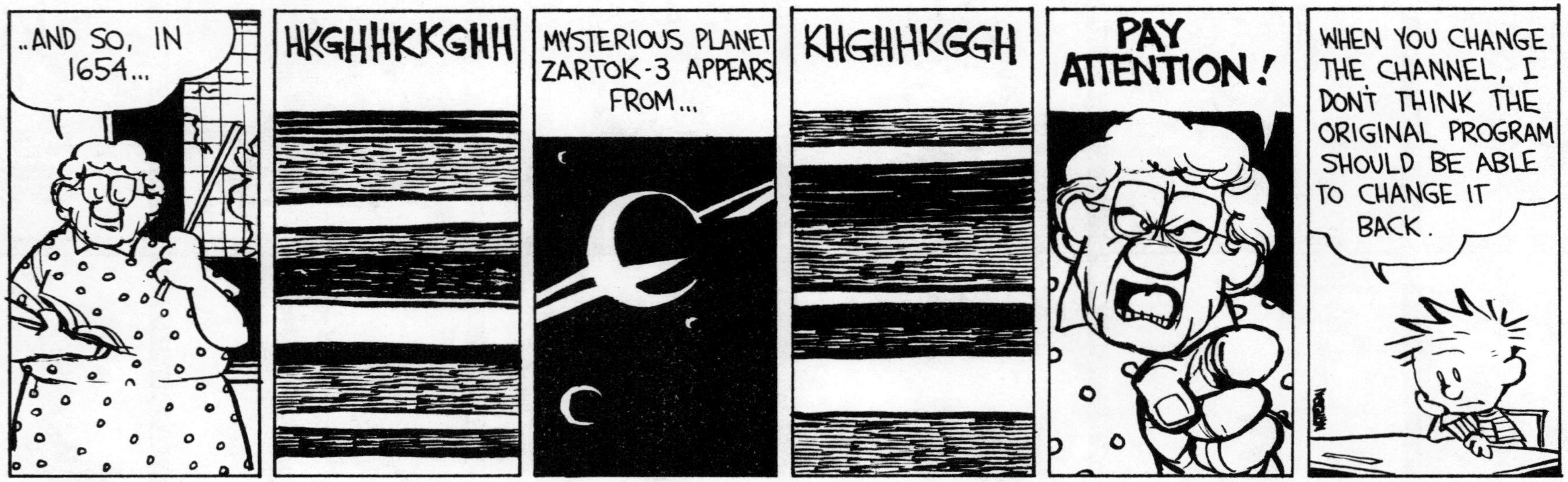
..AND SO, IN 1654...
HKGHHKKGHH
MYSTERIOUS PLANET ZARTOK-3 APPEARS FROM...
KHGHHKGGH
PAY ATTENTION!
WHEN YOU CHANGE THE CHANNEL, I DON'T THINK THE ORIGINAL PROGRAM SHOULD BE ABLE TO CHANGE IT BACK.

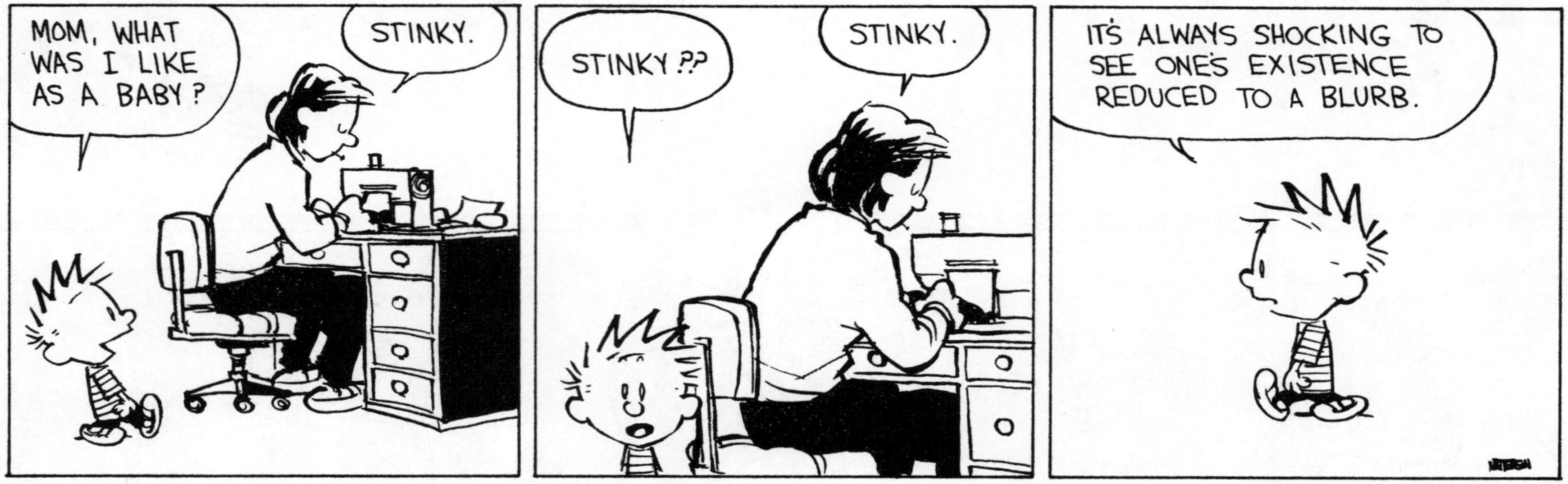
MOM, WHAT WAS I LIKE AS A BABY?
STINKY.
STINKY??
STINKY.
IT'S ALWAYS SHOCKING TO SEE ONE'S EXISTENCE REDUCED TO A BLURB.

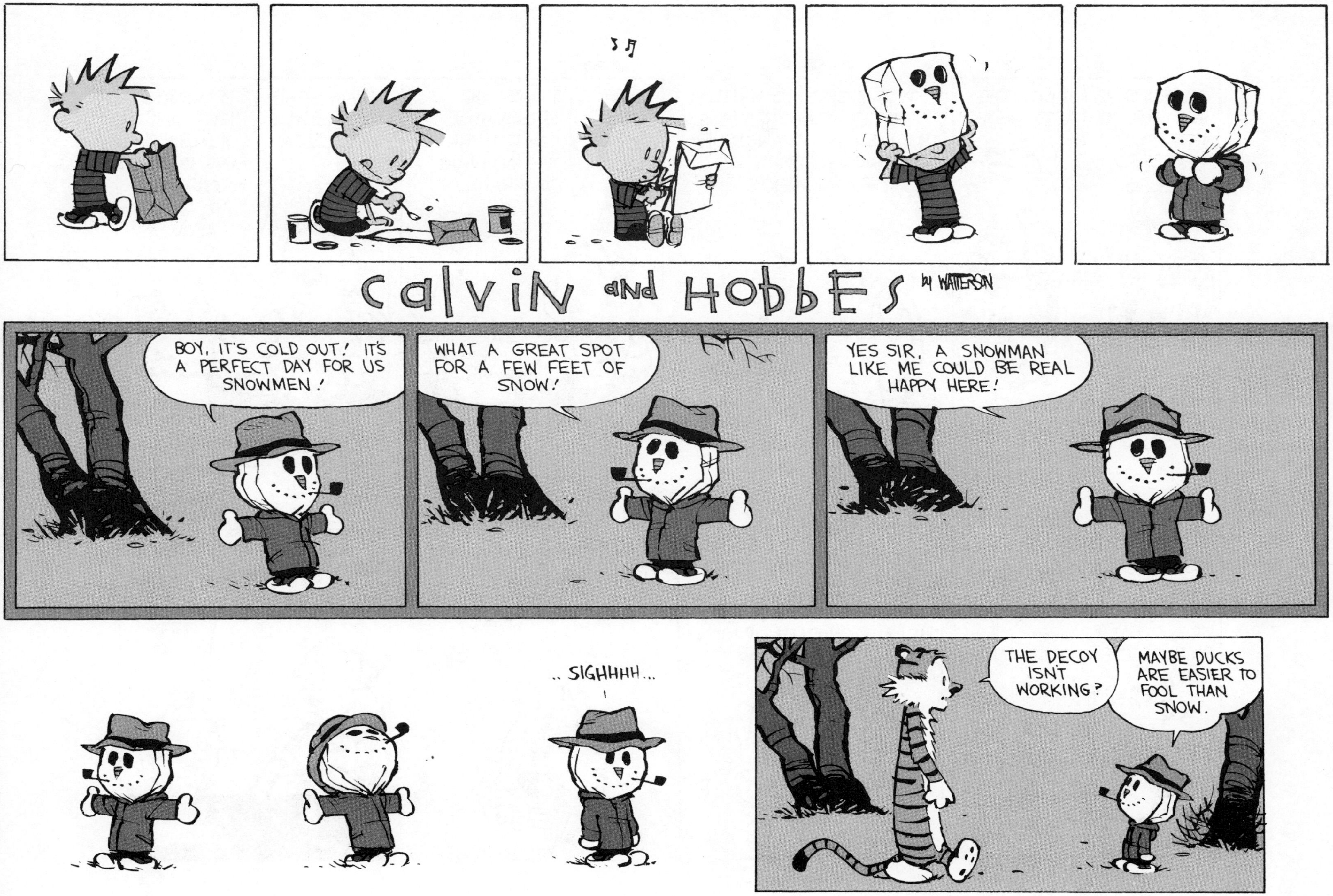
Calvin and HOBBES by WATTERSON
BOY, IT'S COLD OUT! IT'S A PERFECT DAY FOR US SNOWMEN!
WHAT A GREAT SPOT FOR A FEW FEET OF SNOW!
YES SIR, A SNOWMAN LIKE ME COULD BE REAL HAPPY HERE!
.. SIGHHHH...
THE DECOY ISN'T WORKING?
MAYBE DUCKS ARE EASIER TO FOOL THAN SNOW.

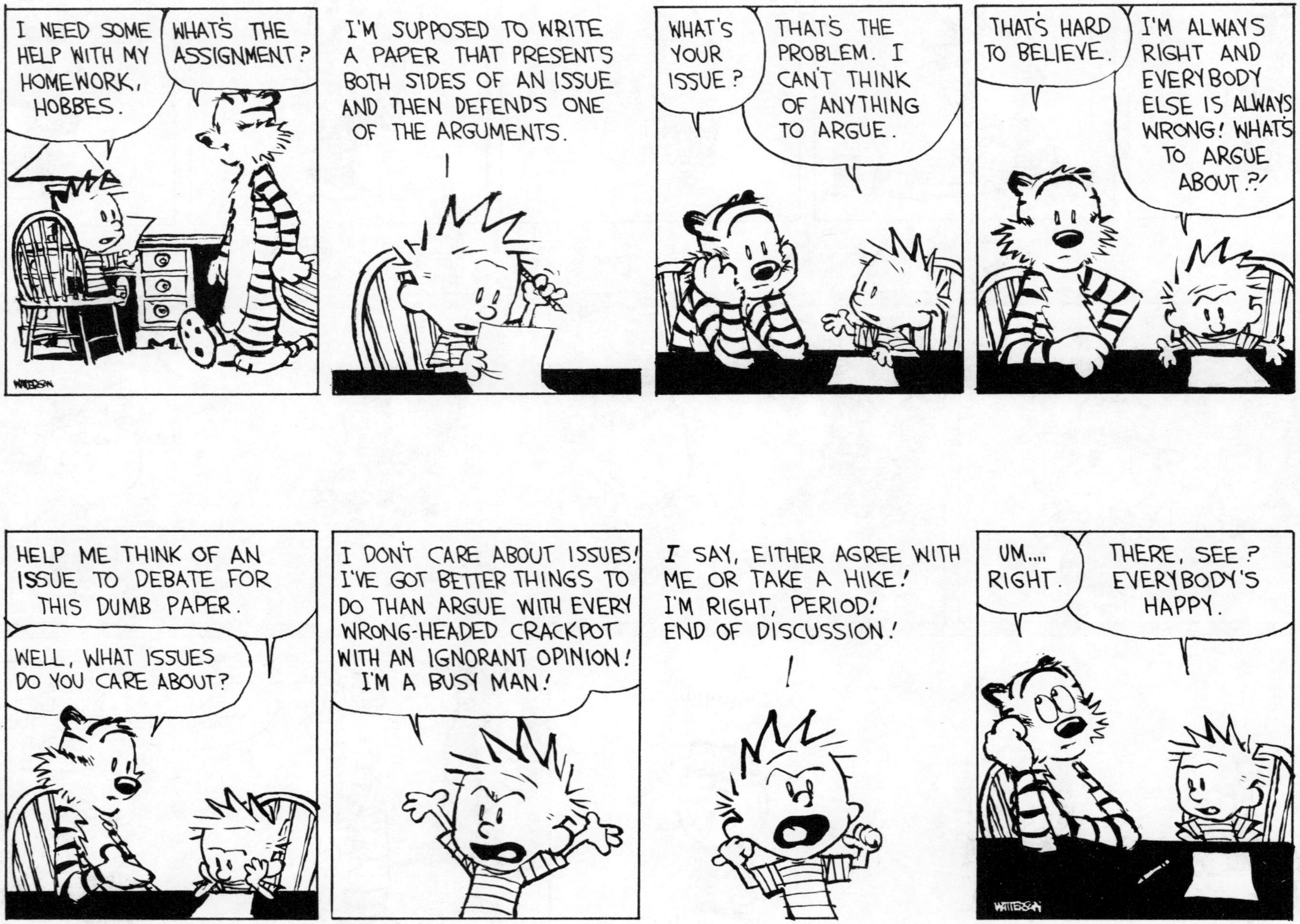
I NEED SOME HELP WITH MY HOMEWORK, HOBBES.
WHAT'S THE ASSIGNMENT?
I'M SUPPOSED TO WRITE A PAPER THAT PRESENTS BOTH SIDES OF AN ISSUE AND THEN DEFENDS ONE OF THE ARGUMENTS.
WHAT'S YOUR ISSUE?
THAT'S THE PROBLEM. I CAN'T THINK OF ANYTHING TO ARGUE.
THAT'S HARD TO BELIEVE.
I'M ALWAYS RIGHT AND EVERYBODY ELSE IS ALWAYS WRONG! WHAT'S TO ARGUE ABOUT?!
HELP ME THINK OF AN ISSUE TO DEBATE FOR THIS DUMB PAPER.
WELL, WHAT ISSUES DO YOU CARE ABOUT?
I DON'T CARE ABOUT ISSUES! I'VE GOT BETTER THINGS TO DO THAN ARGUE WITH EVERY WRONG-HEADED CRACKPOT WITH AN IGNORANT OPINION! I'M A BUSY MAN!
I SAY, EITHER AGREE WITH ME OR TAKE A HIKE! I'M RIGHT, PERIOD! END OF DISCUSSION!
UM.... RIGHT.
THERE, SEE? EVERYBODY'S HAPPY.

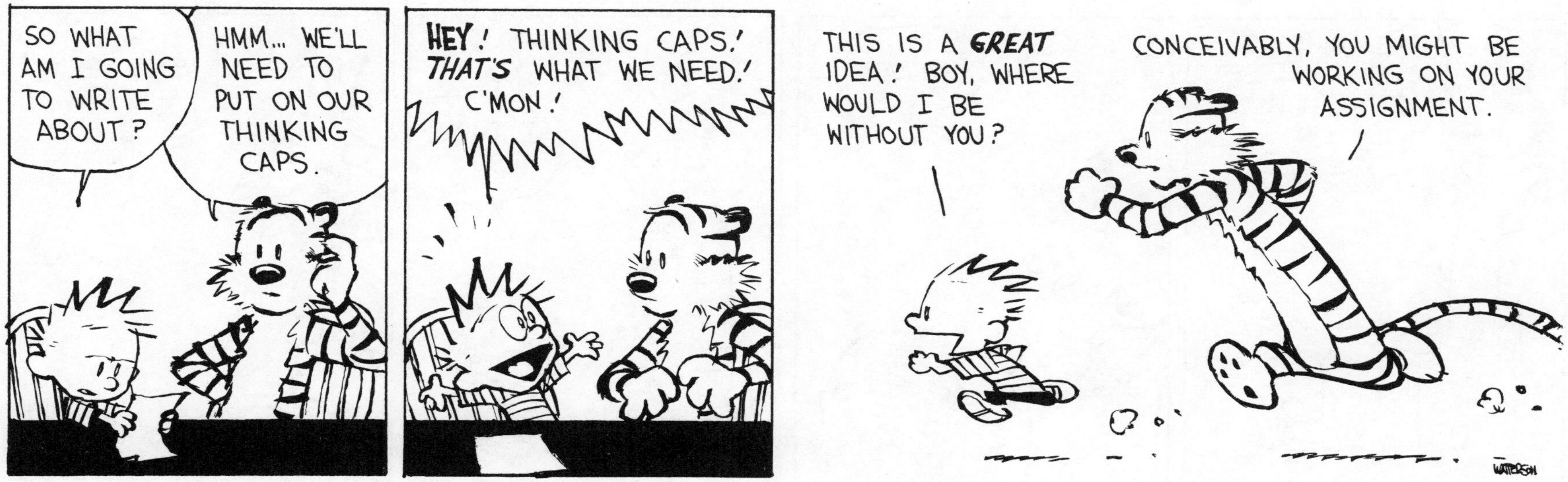
SO WHAT AM I GOING TO WRITE ABOUT?
HMM... WE'LL NEED TO PUT ON OUR THINKING CAPS.
HEY! THINKING CAPS! THAT'S WHAT WE NEED! C'MON!
THIS IS A GREAT IDEA! BOY, WHERE WOULD I BE WITHOUT YOU?
CONCEIVABLY, YOU MIGHT BE WORKING ON YOUR ASSIGNMENT.
WATTERSON

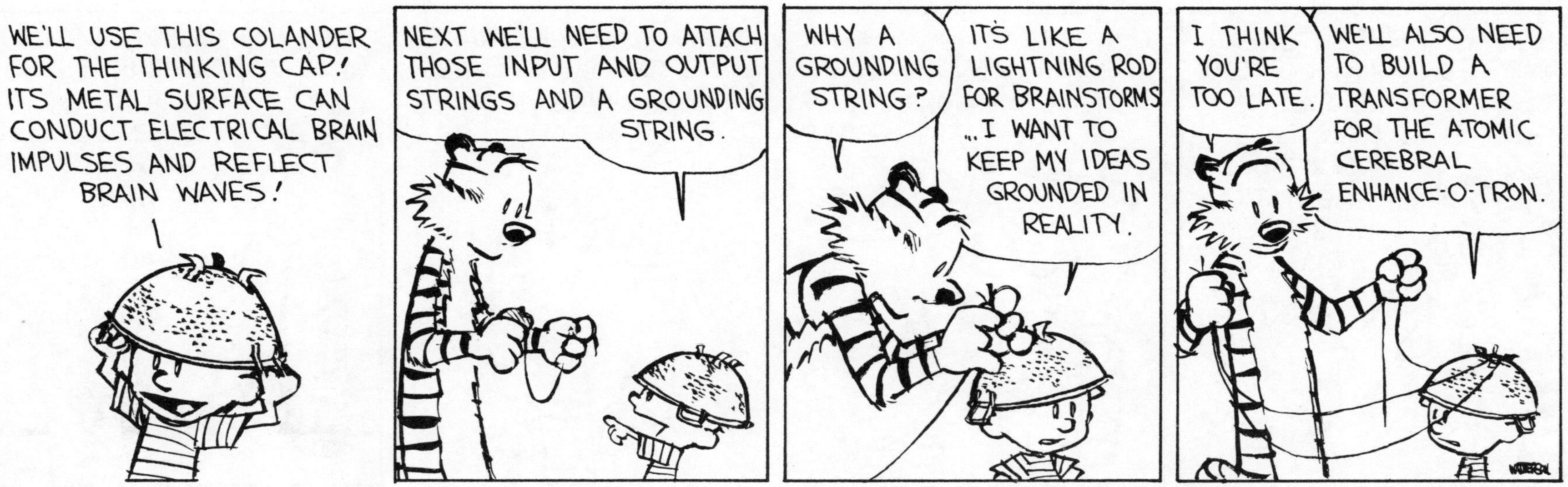
WE'LL USE THIS COLANDER FOR THE THINKING CAP! ITS METAL SURFACE CAN CONDUCT ELECTRICAL BRAIN IMPULSES AND REFLECT BRAIN WAVES!
NEXT WE'LL NEED TO ATTACH THOSE INPUT AND OUTPUT STRINGS AND A GROUNDING STRING.
WHY A GROUNDING STRING?
IT'S LIKE A LIGHTNING ROD FOR BRAINSTORMS ...I WANT TO KEEP MY IDEAS GROUNDED IN REALITY.
I THINK YOU'RE TOO LATE.
WE'LL ALSO NEED TO BUILD A TRANSFORMER FOR THE ATOMIC CEREBRAL ENHANCE-O-TRON.
WATTERSON

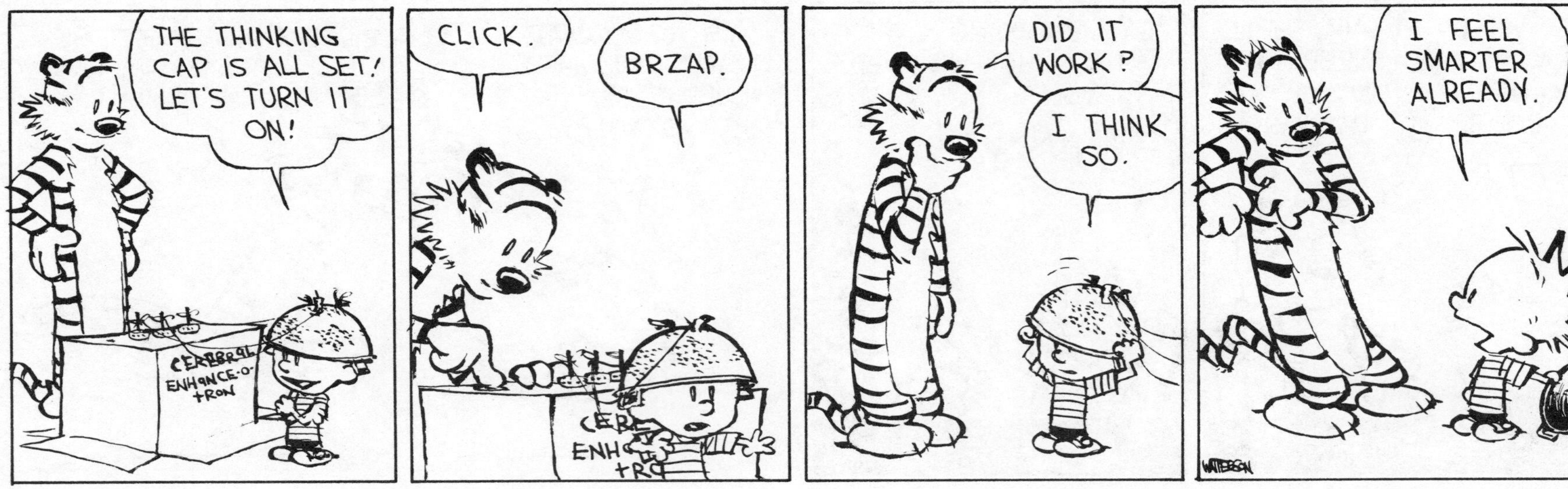
THE THINKING CAP IS ALL SET! LET'S TURN IT ON!
CEREBRAL ENHANCE-O-TRON
CLICK.
BRZAP.
DID IT WORK?
I THINK SO.
I FEEL SMARTER ALREADY.
WATTERSON

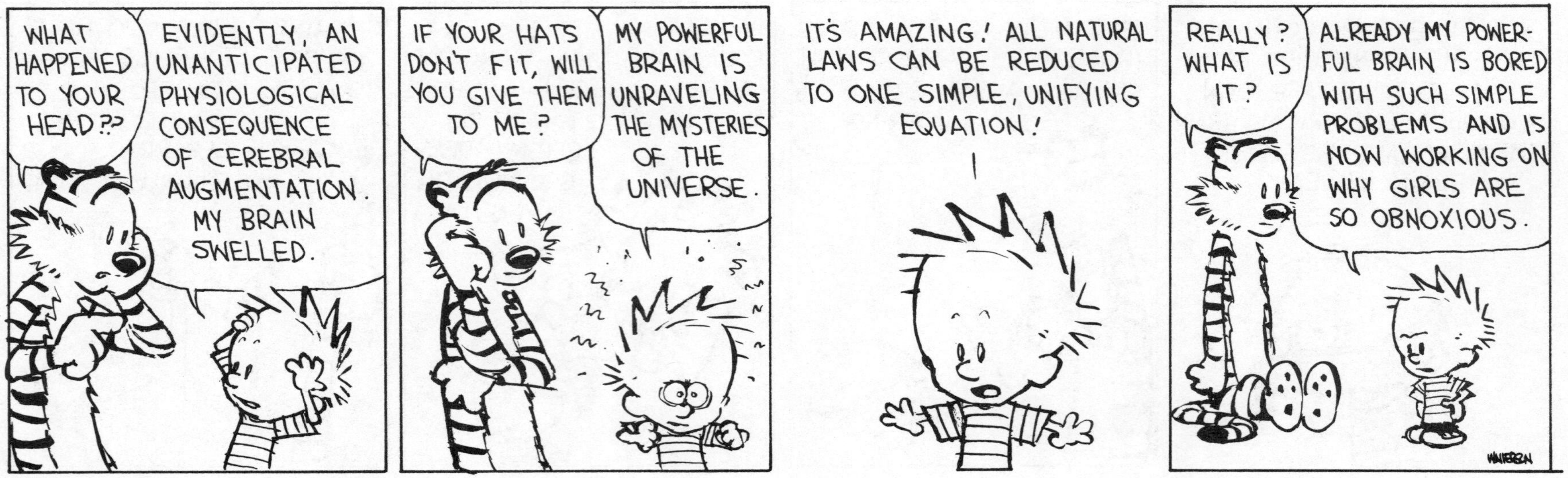
WHAT HAPPENED TO YOUR HEAD?!?
EVIDENTLY, AN UNANTICIPATED PHYSIOLOGICAL CONSEQUENCE OF CEREBRAL AUGMENTATION. MY BRAIN SWELLED.
IF YOUR HATS DON'T FIT, WILL YOU GIVE THEM TO ME?
MY POWERFUL BRAIN IS UNRAVELING THE MYSTERIES OF THE UNIVERSE.
IT'S AMAZING! ALL NATURAL LAWS CAN BE REDUCED TO ONE SIMPLE, UNIFYING EQUATION!
REALLY? WHAT IS IT?
ALREADY MY POWERFUL BRAIN IS BORED WITH SUCH SIMPLE PROBLEMS AND IS NOW WORKING ON WHY GIRLS ARE SO OBNOXIOUS.
WATTERSON

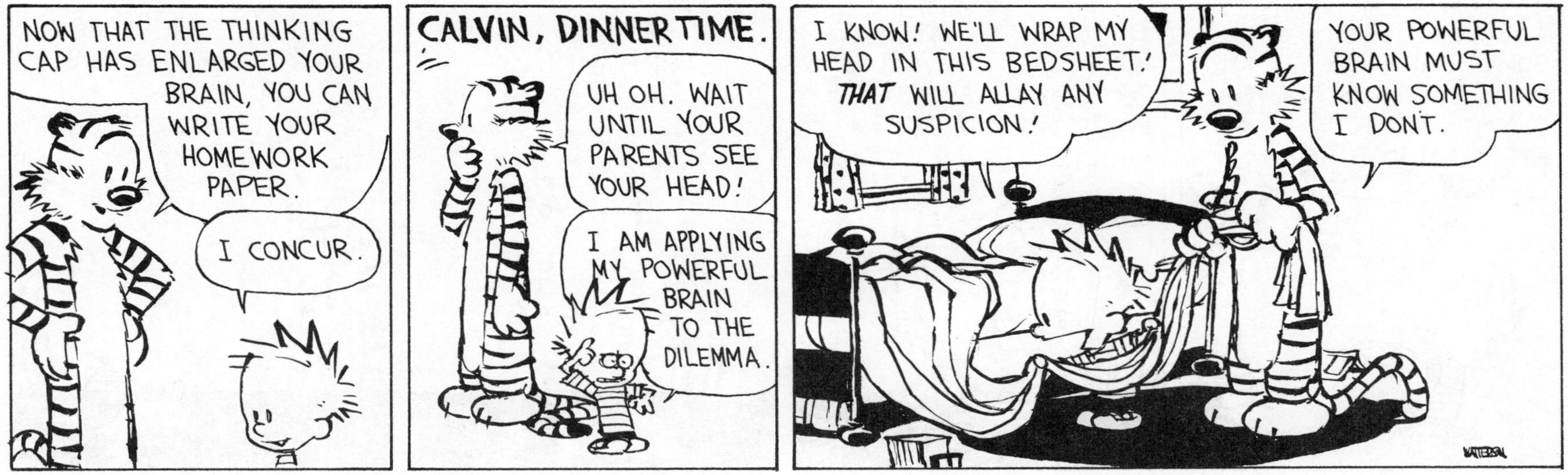

NOW THAT THE THINKING CAP HAS ENLARGED YOUR BRAIN, YOU CAN WRITE YOUR HOMEWORK PAPER.
I CONCUR.
CALVIN, DINNERTIME.
UH OH. WAIT UNTIL YOUR PARENTS SEE YOUR HEAD!
I AM APPLYING MY POWERFUL BRAIN TO THE DILEMMA.
I KNOW! WE'LL WRAP MY HEAD IN THIS BEDSHEET! THAT WILL ALLAY ANY SUSPICION!
YOUR POWERFUL BRAIN MUST KNOW SOMETHING I DON'T.

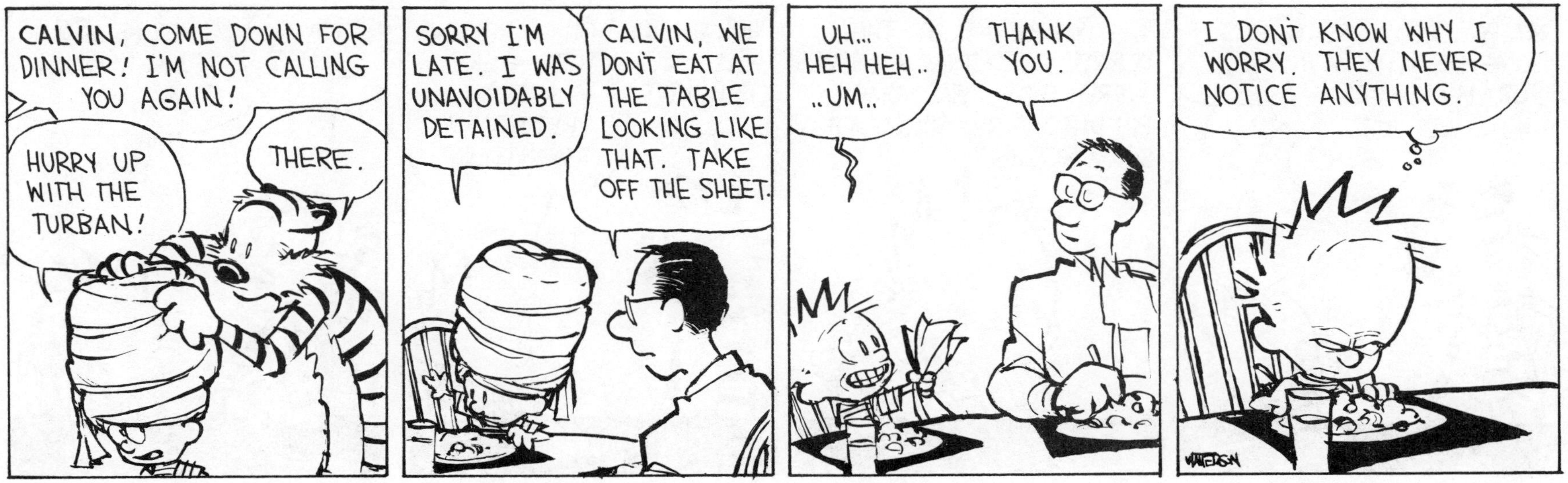

CALVIN, COME DOWN FOR DINNER! I'M NOT CALLING YOU AGAIN!
HURRY UP WITH THE TURBAN!
THERE.
SORRY I'M LATE. I WAS UNAVOIDABLY DETAINED.
CALVIN, WE DON'T EAT AT THE TABLE LOOKING LIKE THAT. TAKE OFF THE SHEET.
UH... HEH HEH.. ..UM..
THANK YOU.
I DON'T KNOW WHY I WORRY. THEY NEVER NOTICE ANYTHING.

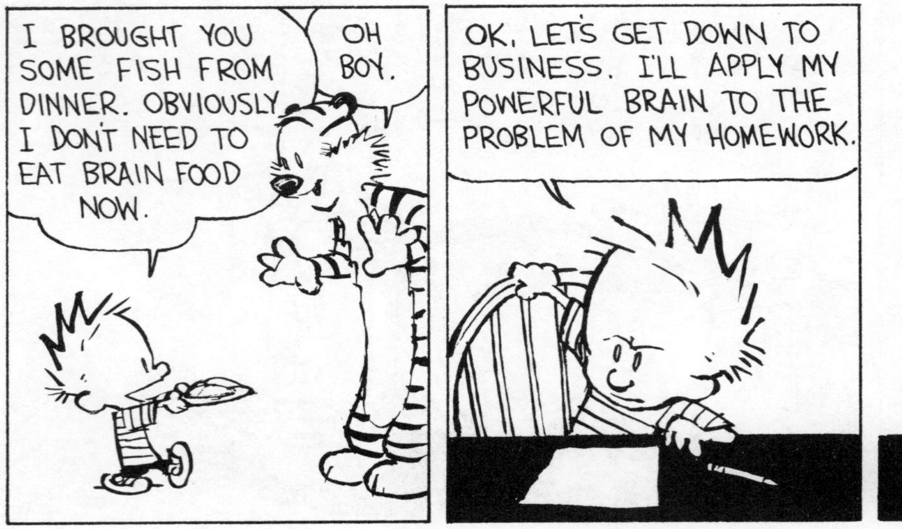
I BROUGHT YOU SOME FISH FROM DINNER. OBVIOUSLY I DON'T NEED TO EAT BRAIN FOOD NOW.
OH BOY.
OK, LET'S GET DOWN TO BUSINESS. I'LL APPLY MY POWERFUL BRAIN TO THE PROBLEM OF MY HOMEWORK.
... HMMMMMM ...
HOW'S IT GOING?
GOOD! I JUST REMEMBERED WHAT THE ASSIGNMENT WAS.
WATTERSON

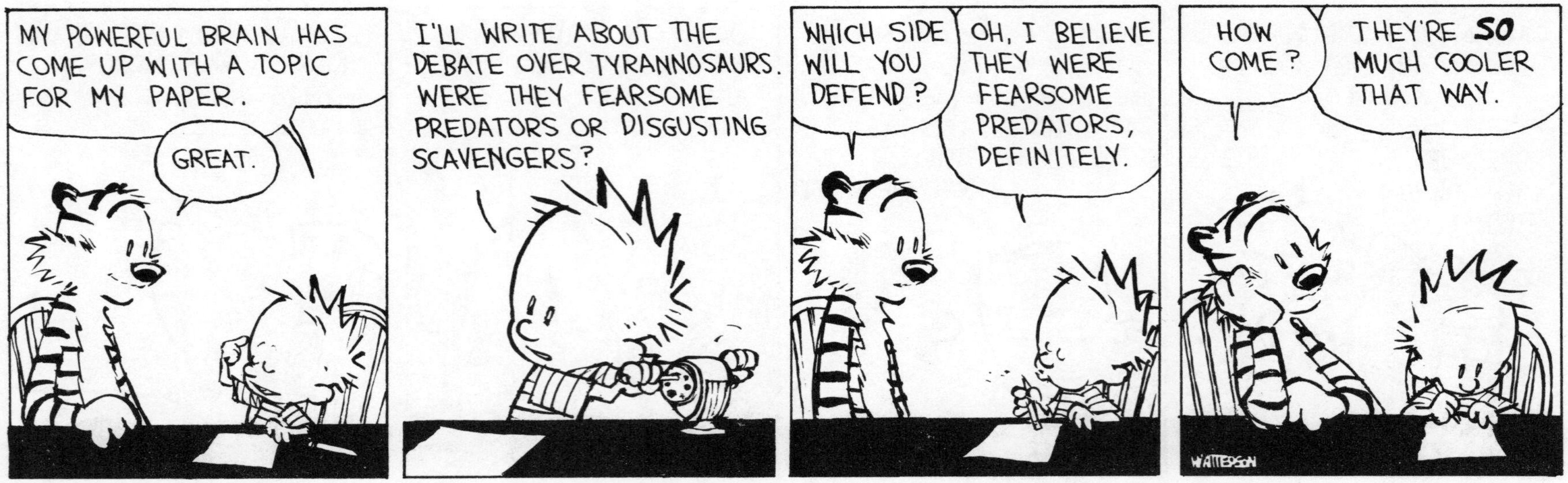
MY POWERFUL BRAIN HAS COME UP WITH A TOPIC FOR MY PAPER.
GREAT.
I'LL WRITE ABOUT THE DEBATE OVER TYRANNOSAURS. WERE THEY FEARSOME PREDATORS OR DISGUSTING SCAVENGERS?
WHICH SIDE WILL YOU DEFEND?
OH, I BELIEVE THEY WERE FEARSOME PREDATORS, DEFINITELY.
HOW COME?
THEY'RE **SO** MUCH COOLER THAT WAY.
WATTERSON

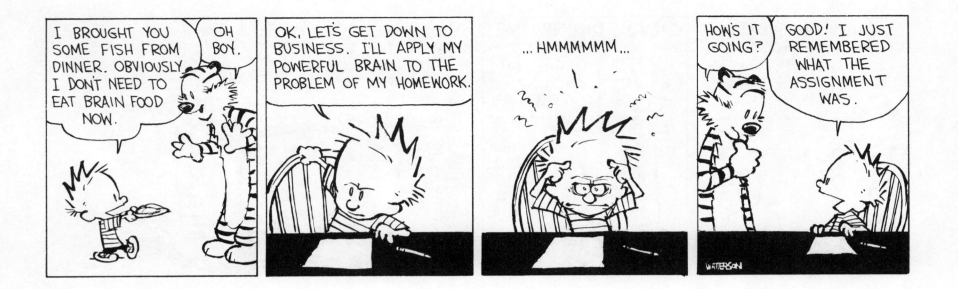

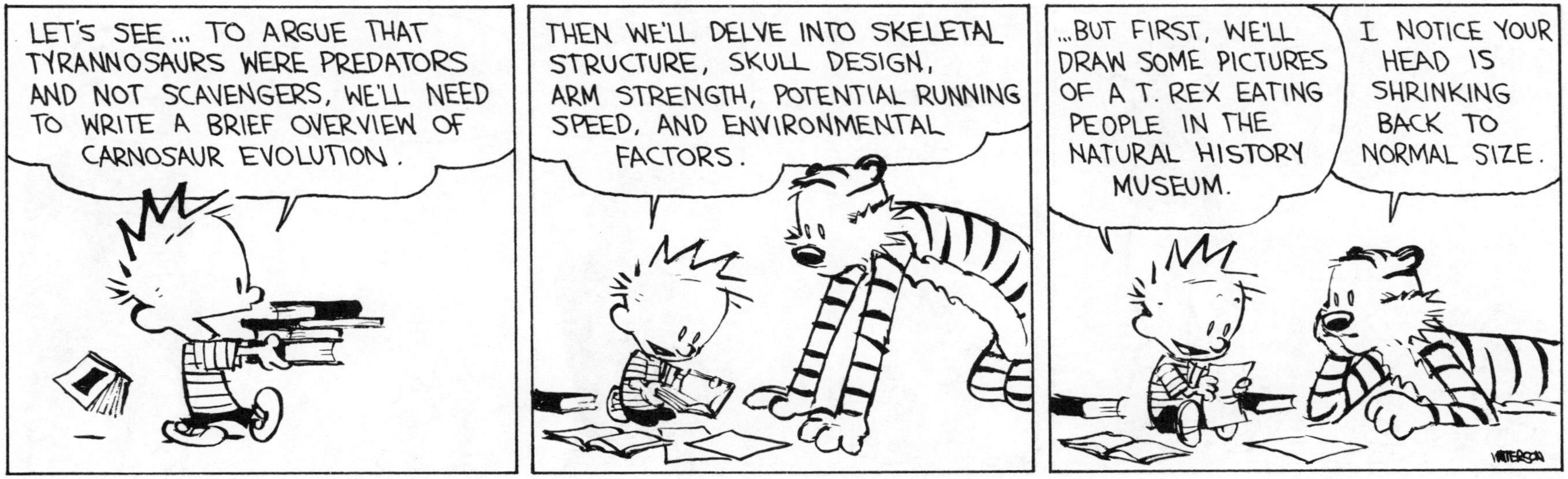
LET'S SEE... TO ARGUE THAT TYRANNOSAURS WERE PREDATORS AND NOT SCAVENGERS, WE'LL NEED TO WRITE A BRIEF OVERVIEW OF CARNOSAUR EVOLUTION.
THEN WE'LL DELVE INTO SKELETAL STRUCTURE, SKULL DESIGN, ARM STRENGTH, POTENTIAL RUNNING SPEED, AND ENVIRONMENTAL FACTORS.
...BUT FIRST, WE'LL DRAW SOME PICTURES OF A T. REX EATING PEOPLE IN THE NATURAL HISTORY MUSEUM.
I NOTICE YOUR HEAD IS SHRINKING BACK TO NORMAL SIZE.
WATTERSON

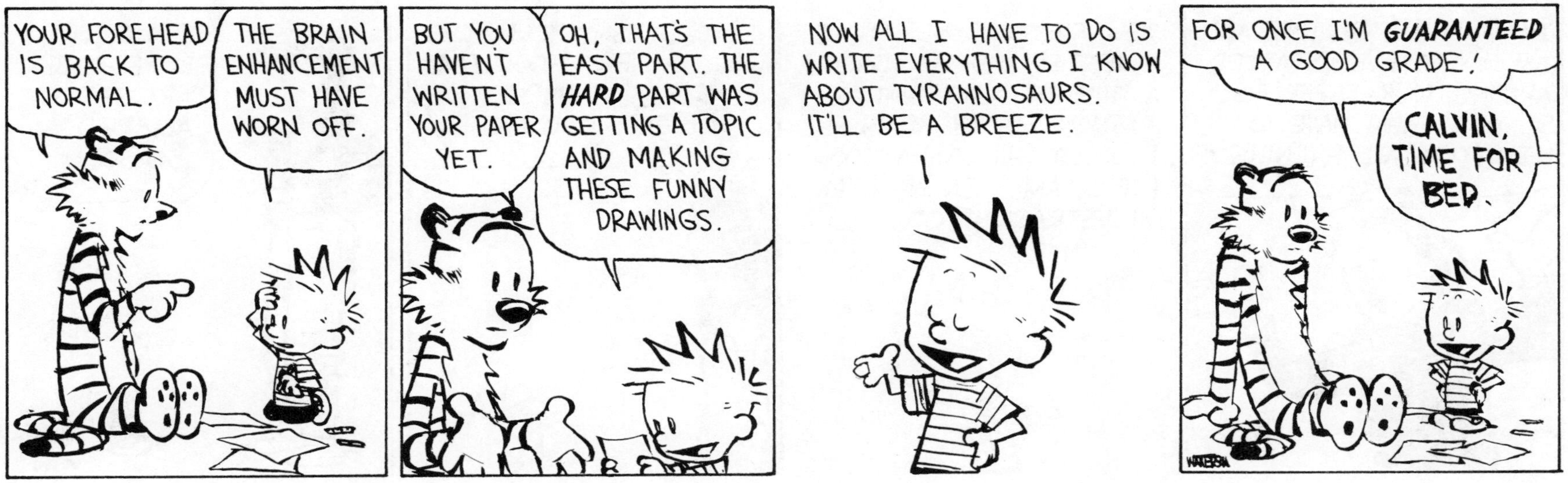
YOUR FOREHEAD IS BACK TO NORMAL.
THE BRAIN ENHANCEMENT MUST HAVE WORN OFF.
BUT YOU HAVEN'T WRITTEN YOUR PAPER YET.
OH, THAT'S THE EASY PART. THE HARD PART WAS GETTING A TOPIC AND MAKING THESE FUNNY DRAWINGS.
NOW ALL I HAVE TO DO IS WRITE EVERYTHING I KNOW ABOUT TYRANNOSAURS. IT'LL BE A BREEZE.
FOR ONCE I'M GUARANTEED A GOOD GRADE!
CALVIN, TIME FOR BED.
WATTERSON

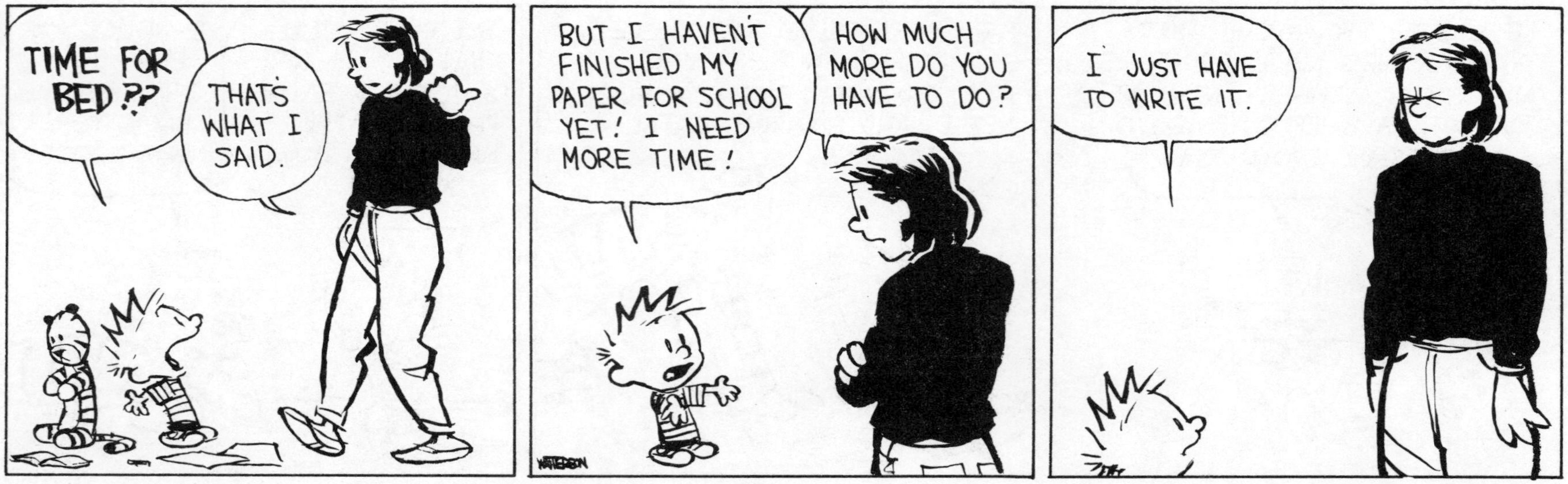
TIME FOR BED ??
THAT'S WHAT I SAID.
BUT I HAVEN'T FINISHED MY PAPER FOR SCHOOL YET! I NEED MORE TIME!
HOW MUCH MORE DO YOU HAVE TO DO?
I JUST HAVE TO WRITE IT.

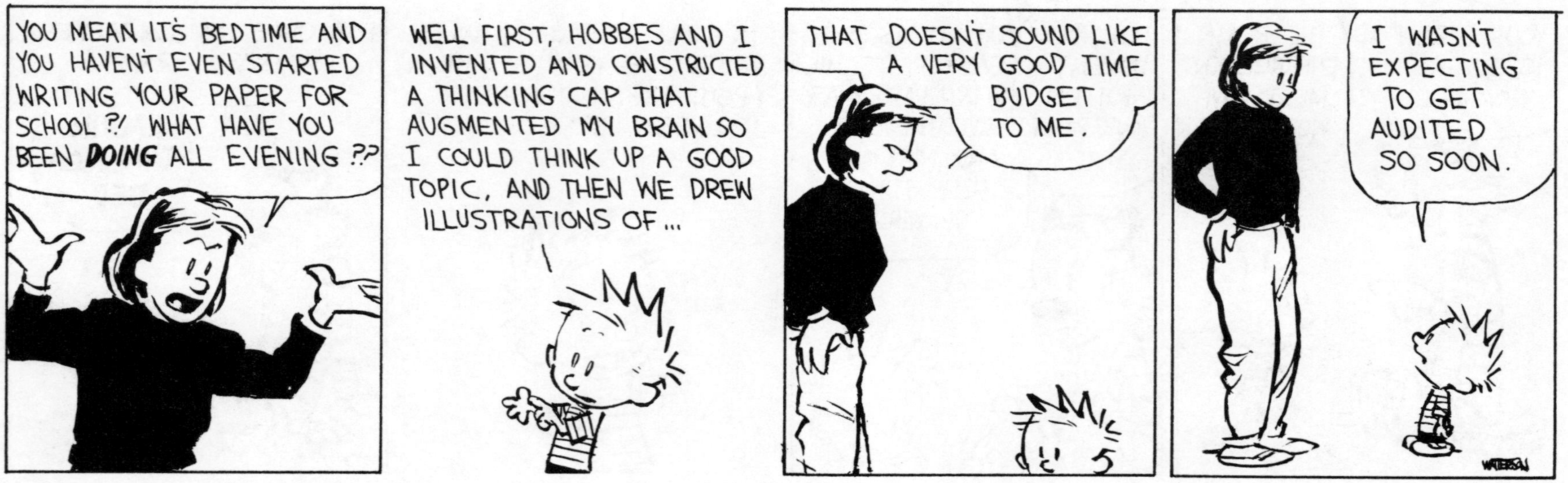
YOU MEAN IT'S BEDTIME AND YOU HAVEN'T EVEN STARTED WRITING YOUR PAPER FOR SCHOOL ?! WHAT HAVE YOU BEEN DOING ALL EVENING ??
WELL FIRST, HOBBES AND I INVENTED AND CONSTRUCTED A THINKING CAP THAT AUGMENTED MY BRAIN SO I COULD THINK UP A GOOD TOPIC, AND THEN WE DREW ILLUSTRATIONS OF...
THAT DOESN'T SOUND LIKE A VERY GOOD TIME BUDGET TO ME.
I WASN'T EXPECTING TO GET AUDITED SO SOON.

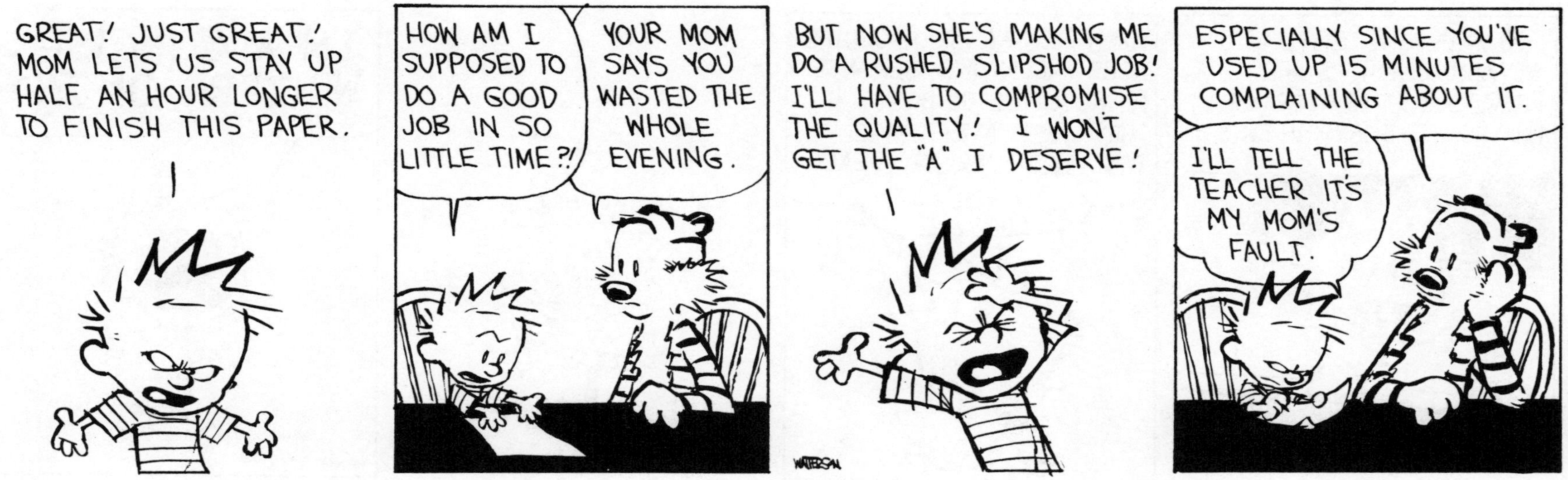
GREAT! JUST GREAT! MOM LETS US STAY UP HALF AN HOUR LONGER TO FINISH THIS PAPER.
HOW AM I SUPPOSED TO DO A GOOD JOB IN SO LITTLE TIME?!
YOUR MOM SAYS YOU WASTED THE WHOLE EVENING.
BUT NOW SHE'S MAKING ME DO A RUSHED, SLIPSHOD JOB! I'LL HAVE TO COMPROMISE THE QUALITY! I WON'T GET THE "A" I DESERVE!
ESPECIALLY SINCE YOU'VE USED UP 15 MINUTES COMPLAINING ABOUT IT.
I'LL TELL THE TEACHER IT'S MY MOM'S FAULT.

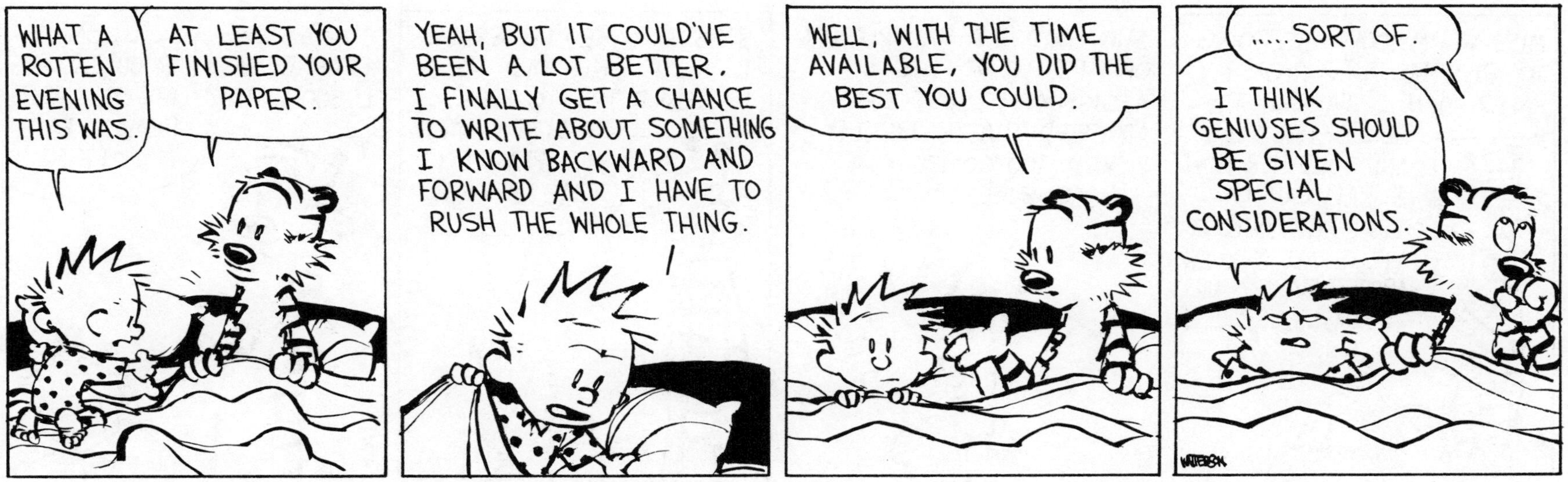
WHAT A ROTTEN EVENING THIS WAS.
AT LEAST YOU FINISHED YOUR PAPER.
YEAH, BUT IT COULD'VE BEEN A LOT BETTER. I FINALLY GET A CHANCE TO WRITE ABOUT SOMETHING I KNOW BACKWARD AND FORWARD AND I HAVE TO RUSH THE WHOLE THING.
WELL, WITH THE TIME AVAILABLE, YOU DID THE BEST YOU COULD.
.....SORT OF.
I THINK GENIUSES SHOULD BE GIVEN SPECIAL CONSIDERATIONS.

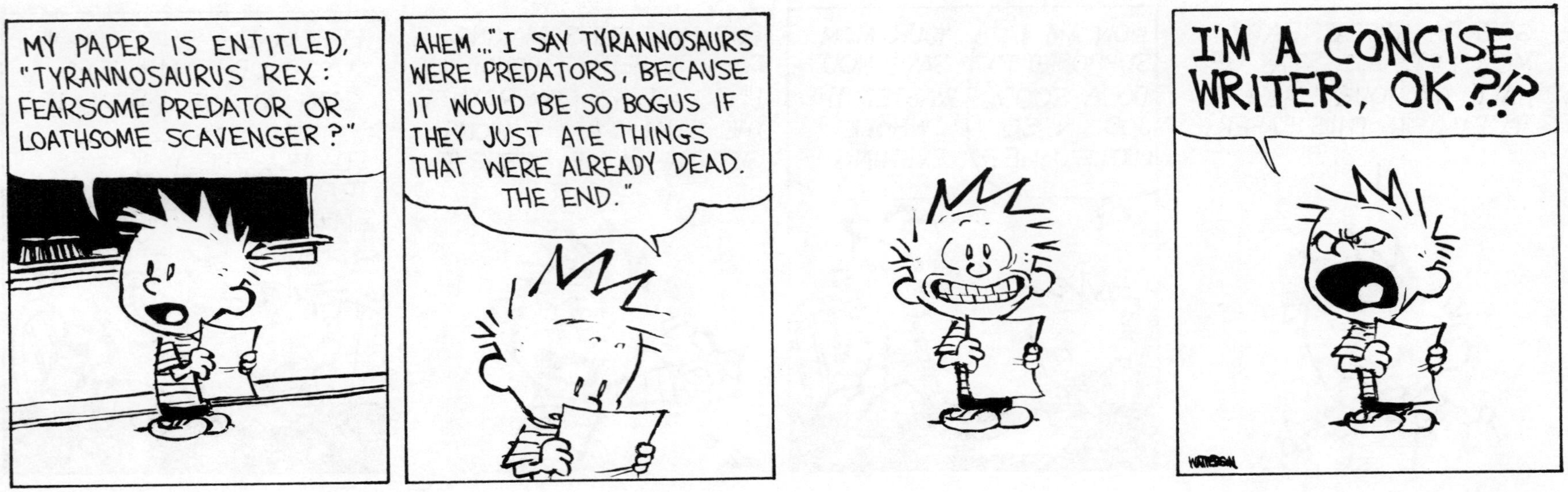
MY PAPER IS ENTITLED, "TYRANNOSAURUS REX: FEARSOME PREDATOR OR LOATHSOME SCAVENGER?"
AHEM..." I SAY TYRANNOSAURS WERE PREDATORS, BECAUSE IT WOULD BE SO BOGUS IF THEY JUST ATE THINGS THAT WERE ALREADY DEAD. THE END."
I'M A CONCISE WRITER, OK?!?

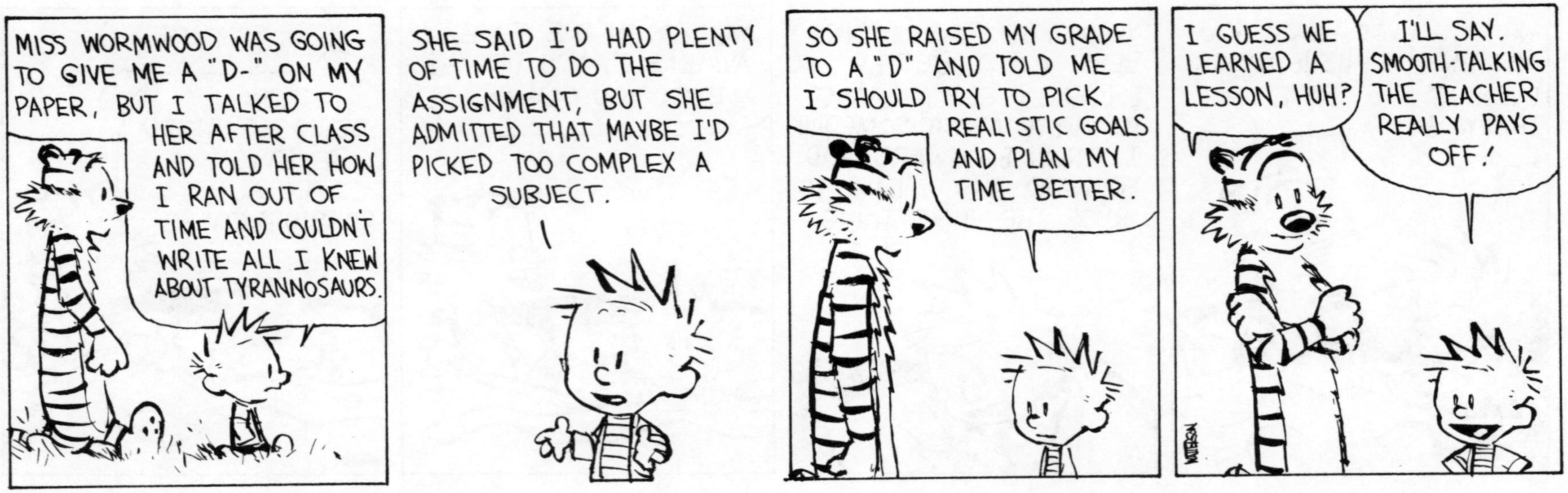
MISS WORMWOOD WAS GOING TO GIVE ME A "D-" ON MY PAPER, BUT I TALKED TO HER AFTER CLASS AND TOLD HER HOW I RAN OUT OF TIME AND COULDN'T WRITE ALL I KNEW ABOUT TYRANNOSAURS.
SHE SAID I'D HAD PLENTY OF TIME TO DO THE ASSIGNMENT, BUT SHE ADMITTED THAT MAYBE I'D PICKED TOO COMPLEX A SUBJECT.
SO SHE RAISED MY GRADE TO A "D" AND TOLD ME I SHOULD TRY TO PICK REALISTIC GOALS AND PLAN MY TIME BETTER.
I GUESS WE LEARNED A LESSON, HUH?
I'LL SAY. SMOOTH-TALKING THE TEACHER REALLY PAYS OFF!

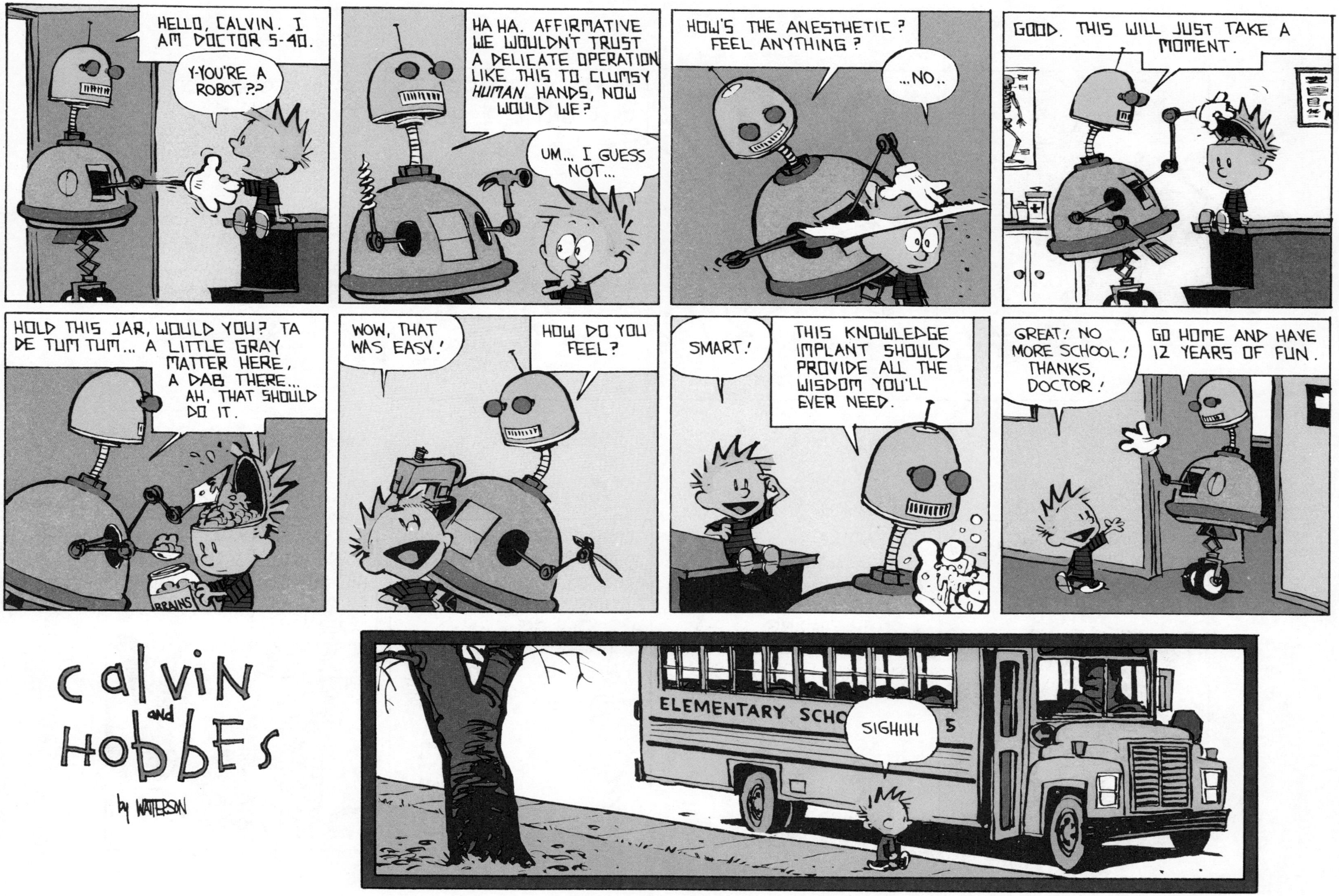
HELLO, CALVIN. I AM DOCTOR 5-40.
Y-YOU'RE A ROBOT ??
HA HA. AFFIRMATIVE WE WOULDN'T TRUST A DELICATE OPERATION LIKE THIS TO CLUMSY HUMAN HANDS, NOW WOULD WE?
UM... I GUESS NOT...
HOW'S THE ANESTHETIC? FEEL ANYTHING?
...NO..
GOOD. THIS WILL JUST TAKE A MOMENT.
HOLD THIS JAR, WOULD YOU? TA DE TUM TUM... A LITTLE GRAY MATTER HERE, A DAB THERE... AH, THAT SHOULD DO IT.
BRAINS
WOW, THAT WAS EASY!
HOW DO YOU FEEL?
SMART!
THIS KNOWLEDGE IMPLANT SHOULD PROVIDE ALL THE WISDOM YOU'LL EVER NEED.
GREAT! NO MORE SCHOOL! THANKS, DOCTOR!
GO HOME AND HAVE 12 YEARS OF FUN.
calvin and HobbEs
by WATTERSON
ELEMENTARY SCHO
5
SIGHHH

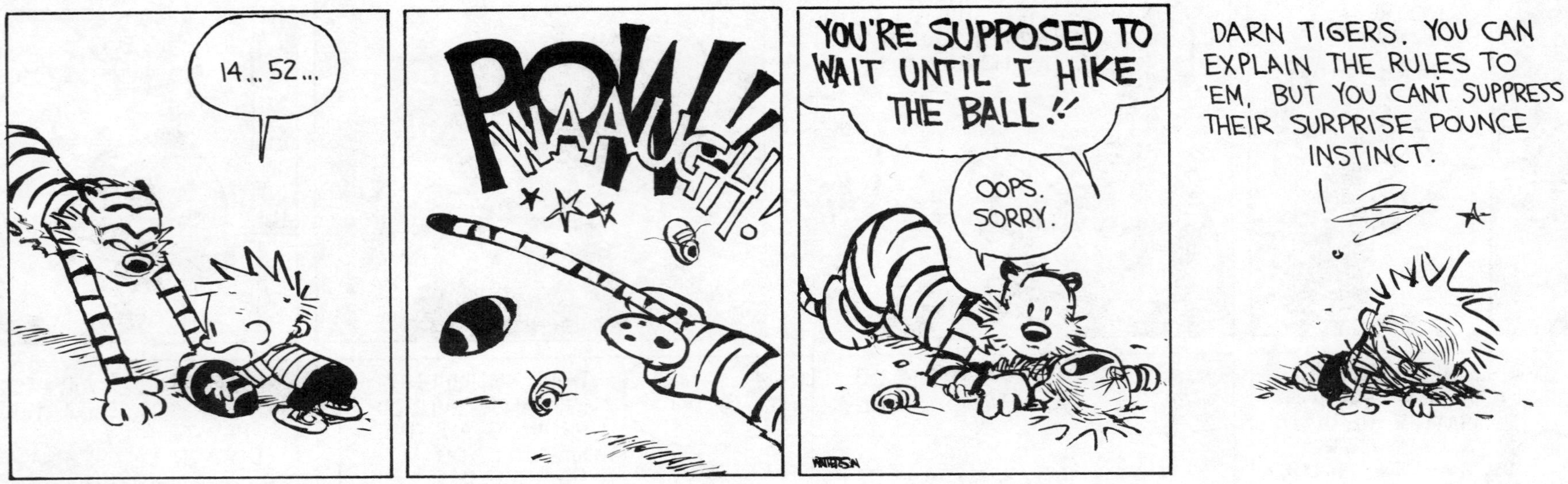
14... 52...
POW
WAAAUGH!!
YOU'RE SUPPOSED TO WAIT UNTIL I HIKE THE BALL!!
OOPS. SORRY.
DARN TIGERS. YOU CAN EXPLAIN THE RULES TO 'EM, BUT YOU CAN'T SUPPRESS THEIR SURPRISE POUNCE INSTINCT.

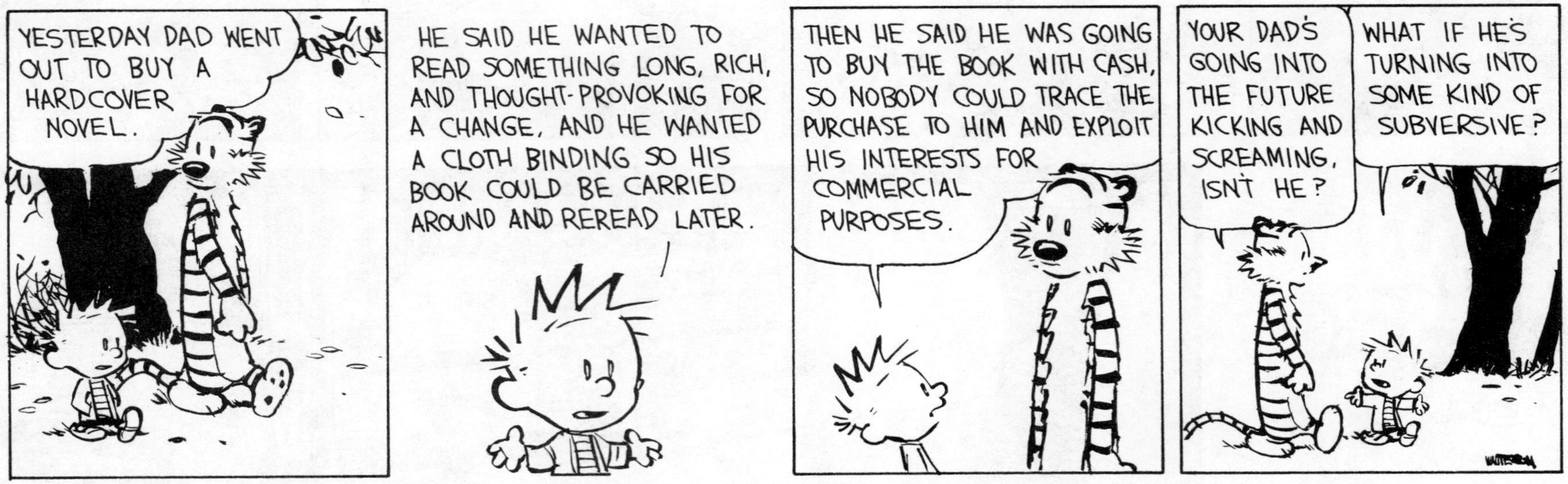
YESTERDAY DAD WENT OUT TO BUY A HARDCOVER NOVEL.
HE SAID HE WANTED TO READ SOMETHING LONG, RICH, AND THOUGHT-PROVOKING FOR A CHANGE, AND HE WANTED A CLOTH BINDING SO HIS BOOK COULD BE CARRIED AROUND AND REREAD LATER.
THEN HE SAID HE WAS GOING TO BUY THE BOOK WITH CASH, SO NOBODY COULD TRACE THE PURCHASE TO HIM AND EXPLOIT HIS INTERESTS FOR COMMERCIAL PURPOSES.
YOUR DAD'S GOING INTO THE FUTURE KICKING AND SCREAMING, ISN'T HE?
WHAT IF HE'S TURNING INTO SOME KIND OF SUBVERSIVE?

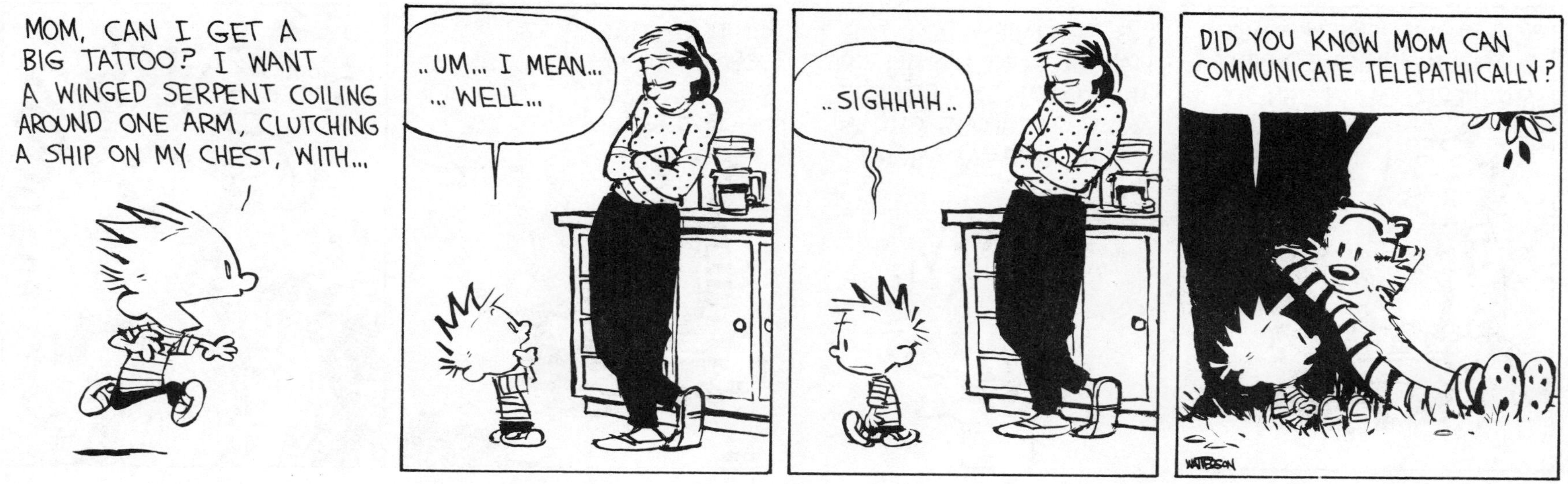
MOM, CAN I GET A BIG TATTOO? I WANT A WINGED SERPENT COILING AROUND ONE ARM, CLUTCHING A SHIP ON MY CHEST, WITH...
..UM... I MEAN... ...WELL...
..SIGHHHH..
DID YOU KNOW MOM CAN COMMUNICATE TELEPATHICALLY?

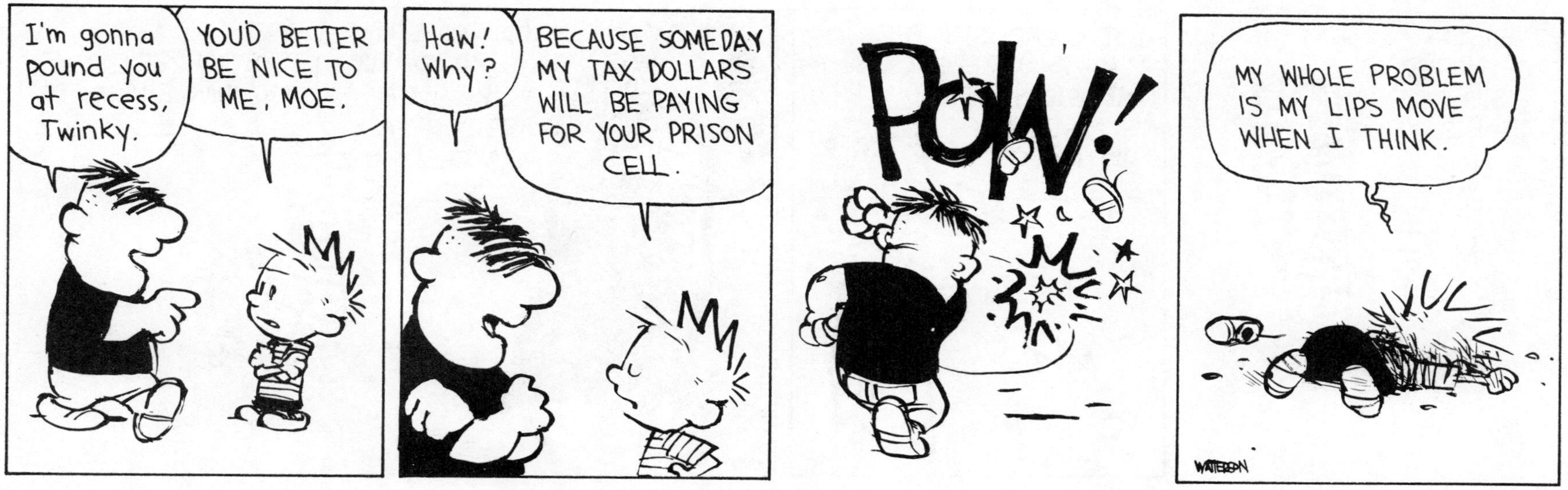
I'm gonna pound you at recess, Twinky.
YOU'D BETTER BE NICE TO ME, MOE.
Haw! Why?
BECAUSE SOMEDAY MY TAX DOLLARS WILL BE PAYING FOR YOUR PRISON CELL.
POW!
MY WHOLE PROBLEM IS MY LIPS MOVE WHEN I THINK.

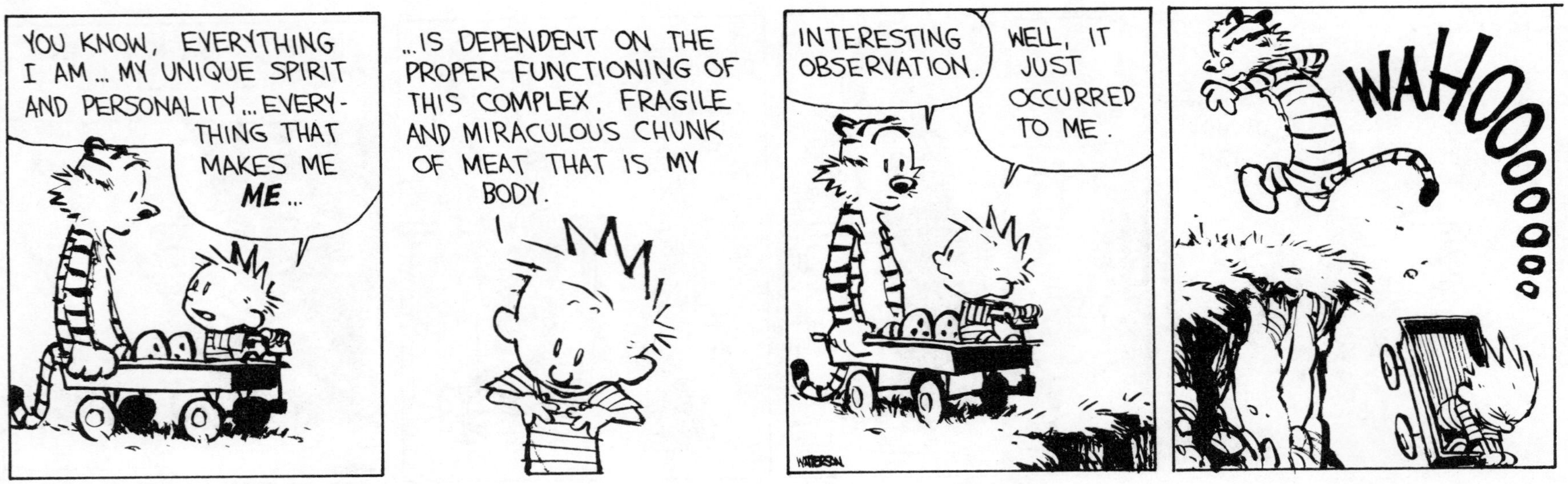
YOU KNOW, EVERYTHING I AM... MY UNIQUE SPIRIT AND PERSONALITY... EVERY-THING THAT MAKES ME **ME**...
...IS DEPENDENT ON THE PROPER FUNCTIONING OF THIS COMPLEX, FRAGILE AND MIRACULOUS CHUNK OF MEAT THAT IS MY BODY.
INTERESTING OBSERVATION.
WELL, IT JUST OCCURRED TO ME.
WAHOOOOOOOO

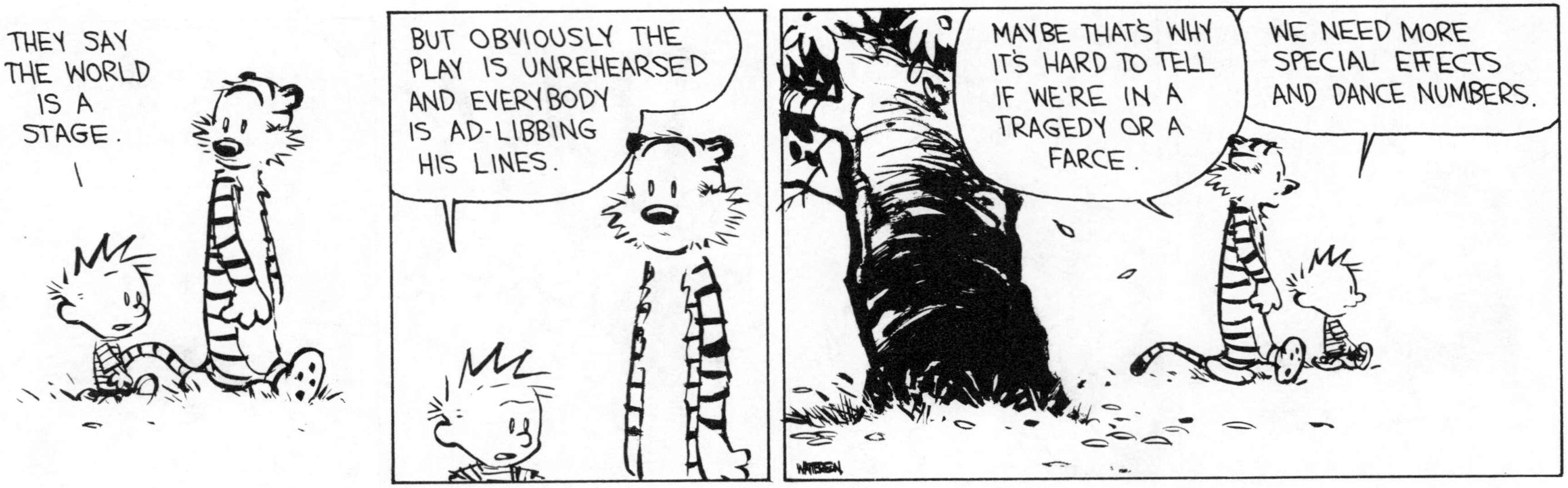
THEY SAY THE WORLD IS A STAGE.
BUT OBVIOUSLY THE PLAY IS UNREHEARSED AND EVERYBODY IS AD-LIBBING HIS LINES.
MAYBE THAT'S WHY IT'S HARD TO TELL IF WE'RE IN A TRAGEDY OR A FARCE.
WE NEED MORE SPECIAL EFFECTS AND DANCE NUMBERS.

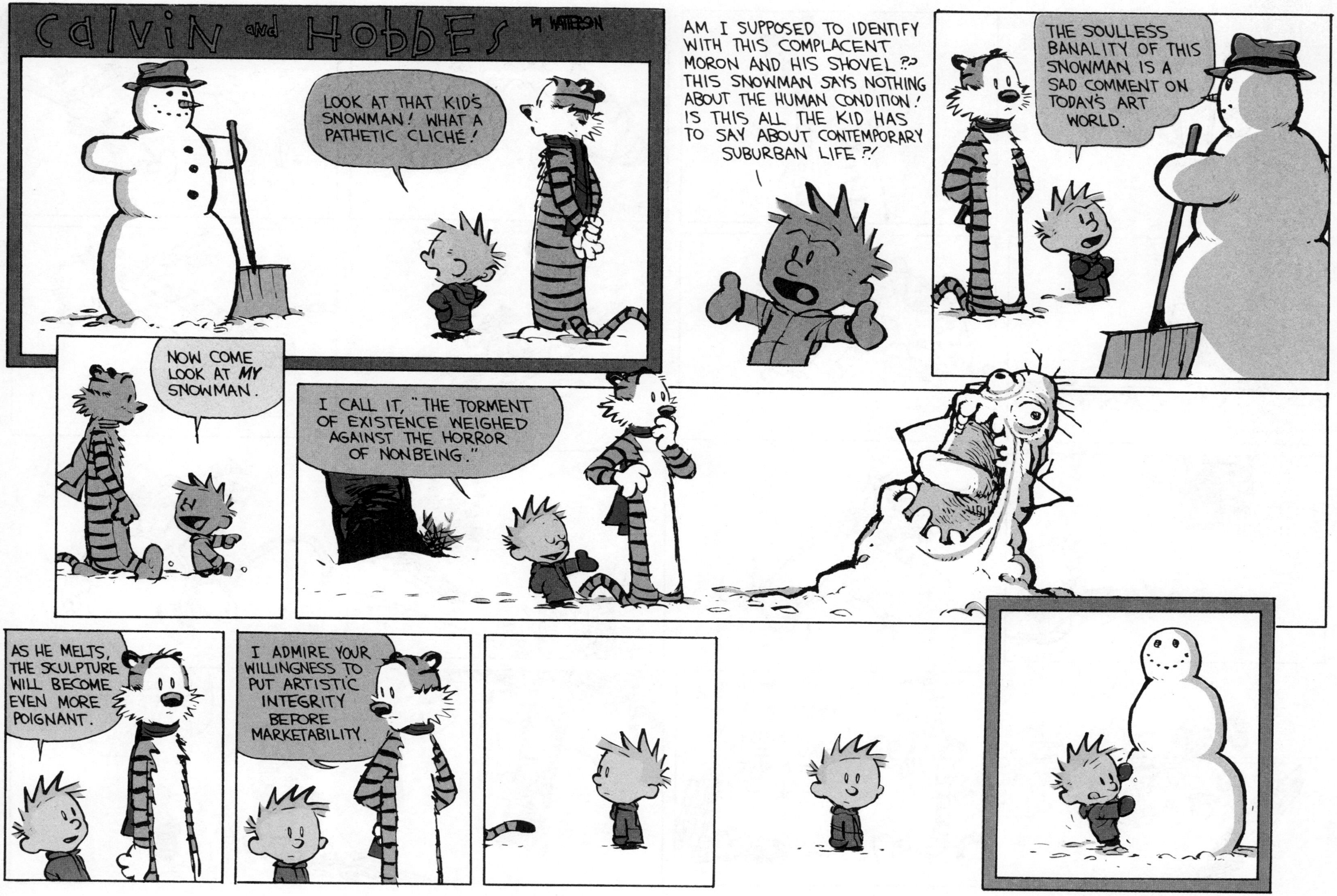
Calvin and Hobbes
by WATTERSON
LOOK AT THAT KID'S SNOWMAN! WHAT A PATHETIC CLICHÉ!
AM I SUPPOSED TO IDENTIFY WITH THIS COMPLACENT MORON AND HIS SHOVEL?? THIS SNOWMAN SAYS NOTHING ABOUT THE HUMAN CONDITION! IS THIS ALL THE KID HAS TO SAY ABOUT CONTEMPORARY SUBURBAN LIFE?!
THE SOULLESS BANALITY OF THIS SNOWMAN IS A SAD COMMENT ON TODAY'S ART WORLD.
NOW COME LOOK AT MY SNOWMAN.
I CALL IT, "THE TORMENT OF EXISTENCE WEIGHED AGAINST THE HORROR OF NONBEING."
AS HE MELTS, THE SCULPTURE WILL BECOME EVEN MORE POIGNANT.
I ADMIRE YOUR WILLINGNESS TO PUT ARTISTIC INTEGRITY BEFORE MARKETABILITY.

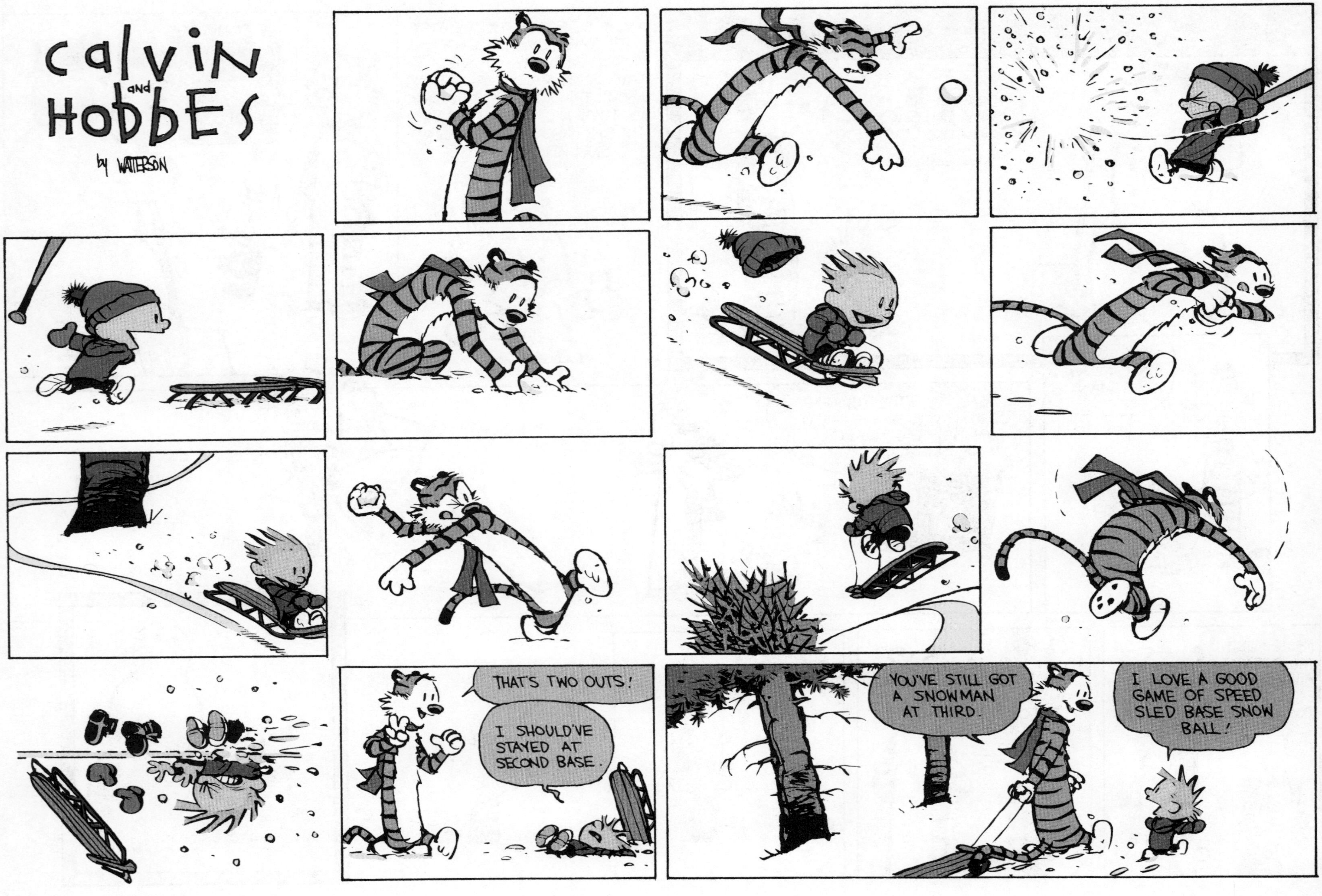
Calvin and HOBBES
by WATTERSON
THAT'S TWO OUTS!
I SHOULD'VE STAYED AT SECOND BASE.
YOU'VE STILL GOT A SNOWMAN AT THIRD.
I LOVE A GOOD GAME OF SPEED SLED BASE SNOW BALL!

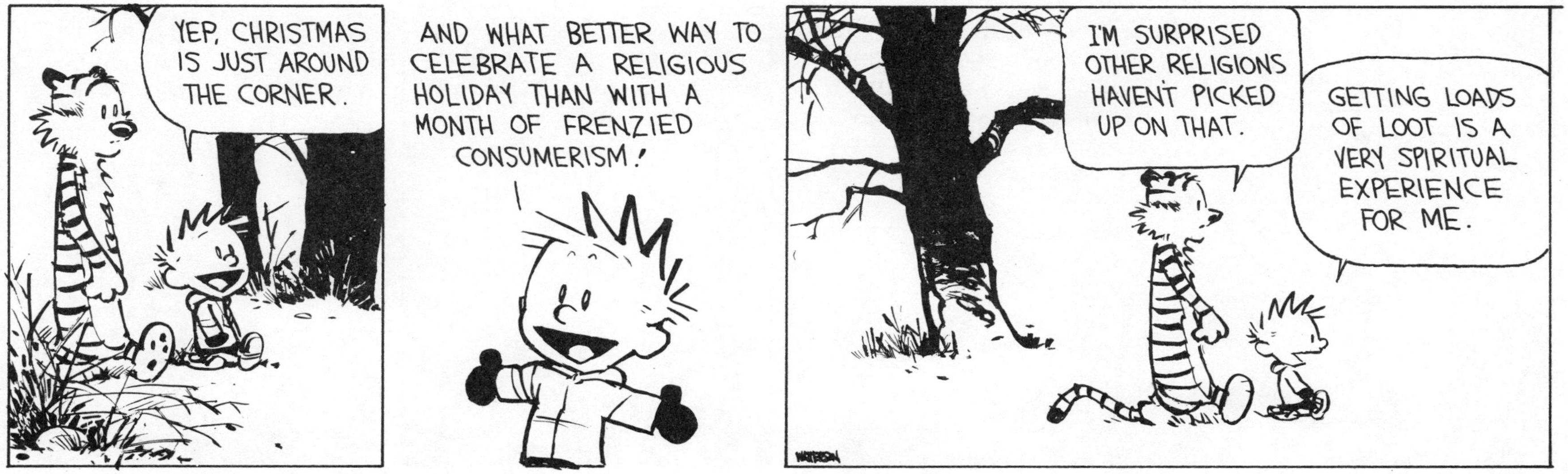
YEP, CHRISTMAS IS JUST AROUND THE CORNER.
AND WHAT BETTER WAY TO CELEBRATE A RELIGIOUS HOLIDAY THAN WITH A MONTH OF FRENZIED CONSUMERISM!
I'M SURPRISED OTHER RELIGIONS HAVEN'T PICKED UP ON THAT.
GETTING LOADS OF LOOT IS A VERY SPIRITUAL EXPERIENCE FOR ME.

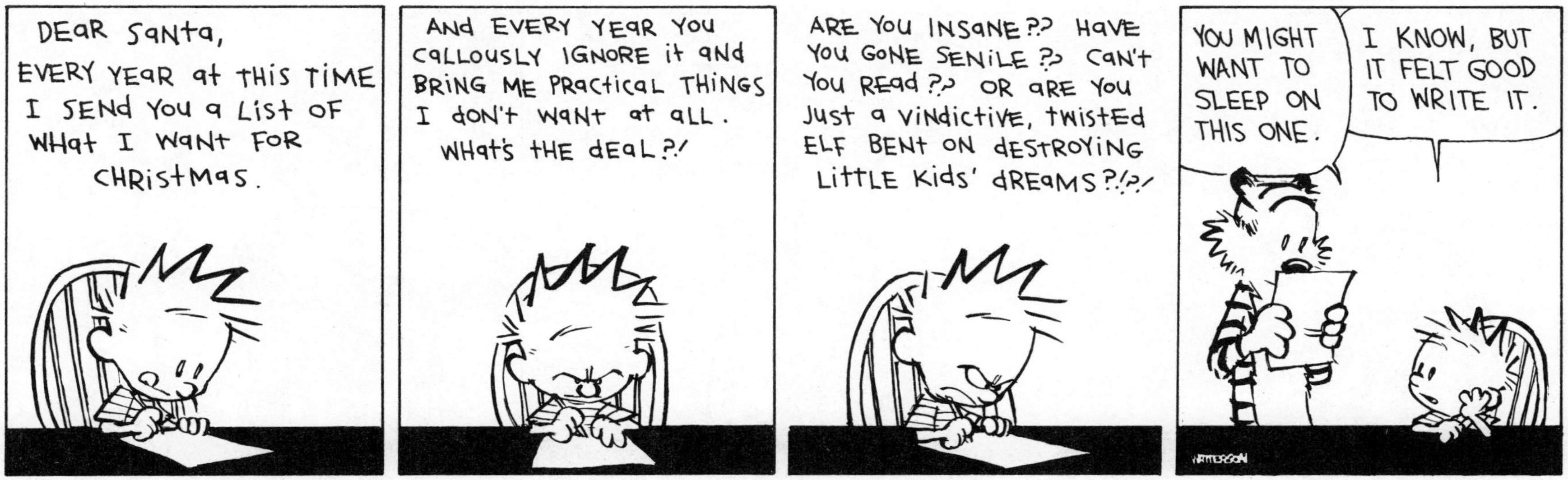
DEAR SANTA, EVERY YEAR AT THIS TIME I SEND YOU A LIST OF WHAT I WANT FOR CHRISTMAS.
AND EVERY YEAR YOU CALLOUSLY IGNORE IT AND BRING ME PRACTICAL THINGS I DON'T WANT AT ALL. WHAT'S THE DEAL?!
ARE YOU INSANE?? HAVE YOU GONE SENILE?? CAN'T YOU READ?? OR ARE YOU JUST A VINDICTIVE, TWISTED ELF BENT ON DESTROYING LITTLE KIDS' DREAMS?!?!
YOU MIGHT WANT TO SLEEP ON THIS ONE.
I KNOW, BUT IT FELT GOOD TO WRITE IT.

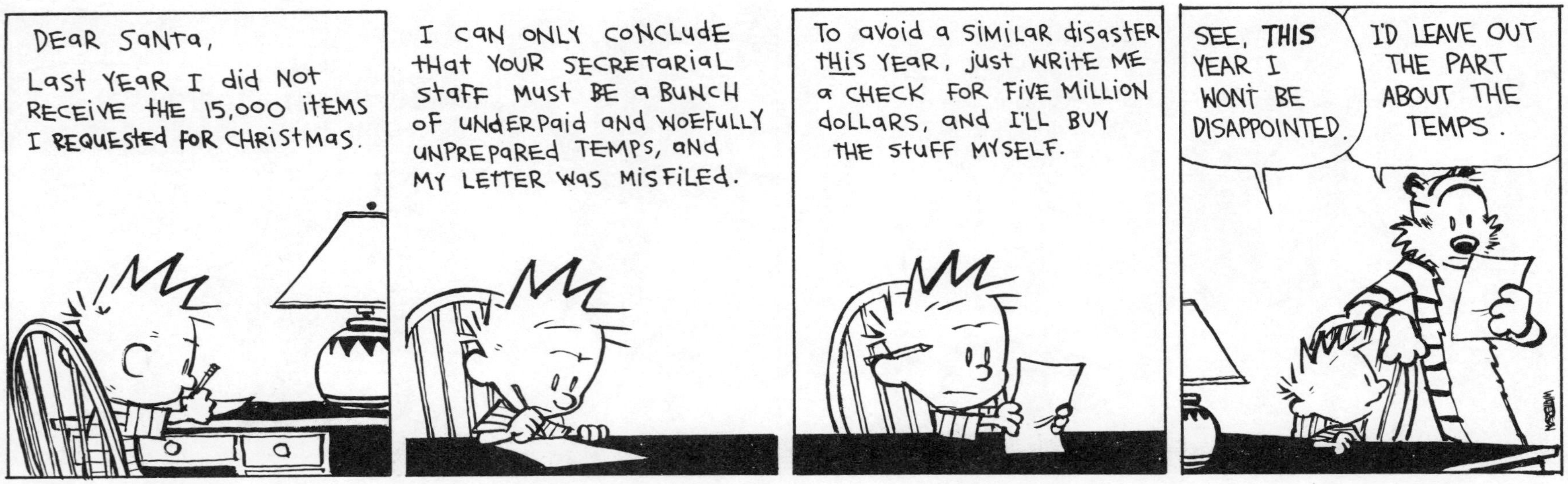
DEAR SANTA,
LAST YEAR I DID NOT RECEIVE THE 15,000 ITEMS I REQUESTED FOR CHRISTMAS.
I CAN ONLY CONCLUDE THAT YOUR SECRETARIAL STAFF MUST BE A BUNCH OF UNDERPAID AND WOEFULLY UNPREPARED TEMPS, AND MY LETTER WAS MISFILED.
TO AVOID A SIMILAR DISASTER THIS YEAR, JUST WRITE ME A CHECK FOR FIVE MILLION DOLLARS, AND I'LL BUY THE STUFF MYSELF.
SEE, THIS YEAR I WON'T BE DISAPPOINTED.
I'D LEAVE OUT THE PART ABOUT THE TEMPS.

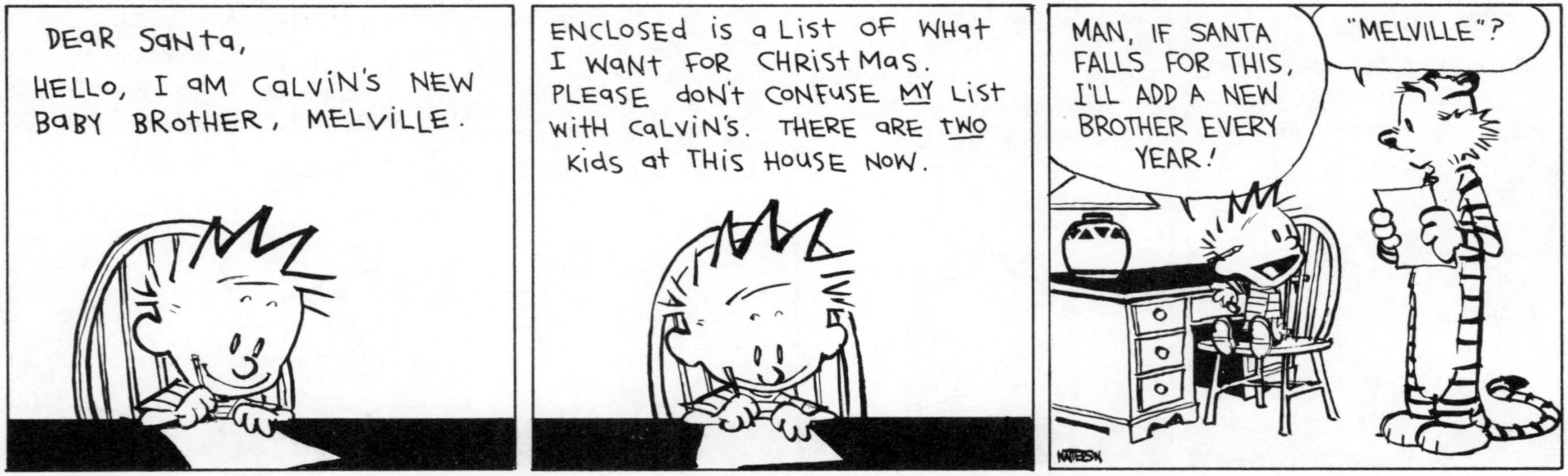
DEAR SANTA,
HELLO, I AM CALVIN'S NEW BABY BROTHER, MELVILLE.
ENCLOSED IS A LIST OF WHAT I WANT FOR CHRISTMAS. PLEASE DON'T CONFUSE MY LIST WITH CALVIN'S. THERE ARE TWO KIDS AT THIS HOUSE NOW.
MAN, IF SANTA FALLS FOR THIS, I'LL ADD A NEW BROTHER EVERY YEAR!
"MELVILLE"?

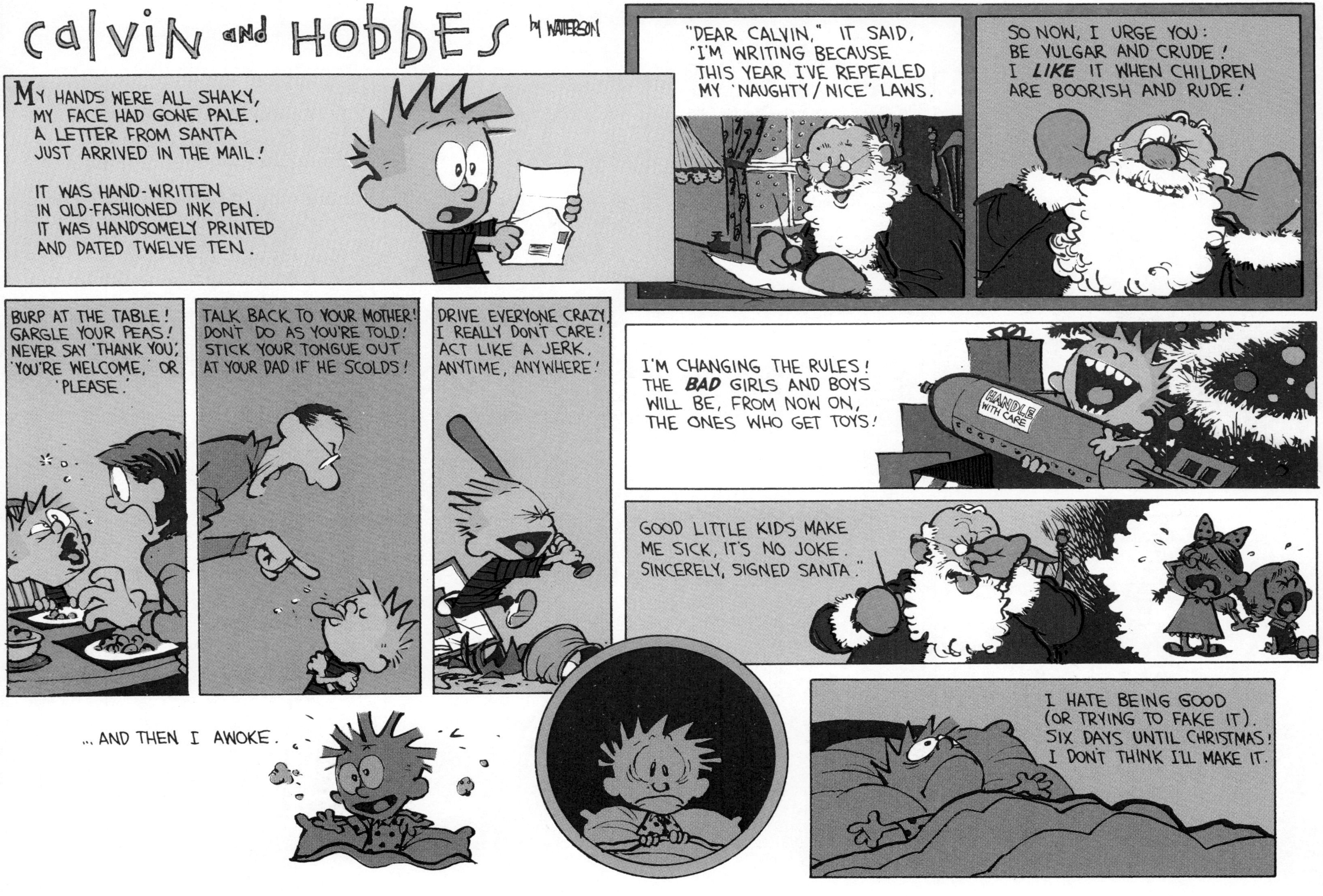
Calvin and HOBBES by WATTERSON
MY HANDS WERE ALL SHAKY, MY FACE HAD GONE PALE. A LETTER FROM SANTA JUST ARRIVED IN THE MAIL!
IT WAS HAND-WRITTEN IN OLD-FASHIONED INK PEN. IT WAS HANDSOMELY PRINTED AND DATED TWELVE TEN.
"DEAR CALVIN," IT SAID, "I'M WRITING BECAUSE THIS YEAR I'VE REPEALED MY 'NAUGHTY / NICE' LAWS.
SO NOW, I URGE YOU: BE VULGAR AND CRUDE! I LIKE IT WHEN CHILDREN ARE BOORISH AND RUDE!
BURP AT THE TABLE! GARGLE YOUR PEAS! NEVER SAY 'THANK YOU,' 'YOU'RE WELCOME,' OR 'PLEASE.'
TALK BACK TO YOUR MOTHER! DON'T DO AS YOU'RE TOLD! STICK YOUR TONGUE OUT AT YOUR DAD IF HE SCOLDS!
DRIVE EVERYONE CRAZY, I REALLY DON'T CARE! ACT LIKE A JERK, ANYTIME, ANYWHERE!
I'M CHANGING THE RULES! THE BAD GIRLS AND BOYS WILL BE, FROM NOW ON, THE ONES WHO GET TOYS!
HANDLE WITH CARE
GOOD LITTLE KIDS MAKE ME SICK, IT'S NO JOKE. SINCERELY, SIGNED SANTA."
... AND THEN I AWOKE.
I HATE BEING GOOD (OR TRYING TO FAKE IT). SIX DAYS UNTIL CHRISTMAS! I DON'T THINK I'LL MAKE IT.

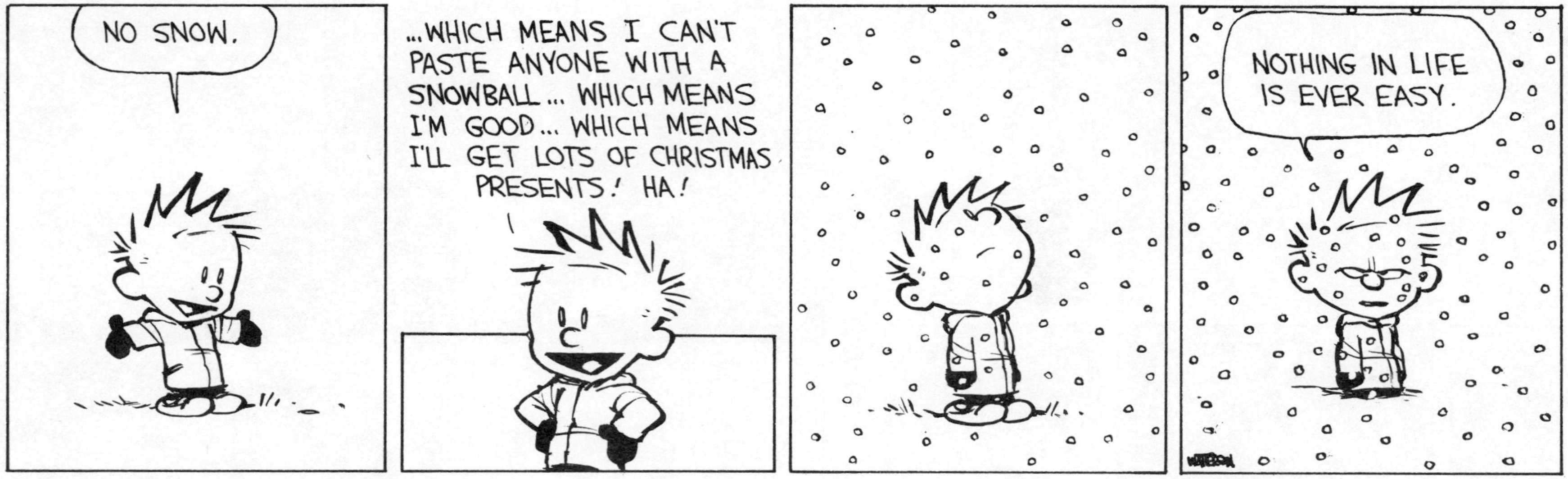
NO SNOW.
...WHICH MEANS I CAN'T PASTE ANYONE WITH A SNOWBALL... WHICH MEANS I'M GOOD... WHICH MEANS I'LL GET LOTS OF CHRISTMAS PRESENTS! HA!
NOTHING IN LIFE IS EVER EASY.

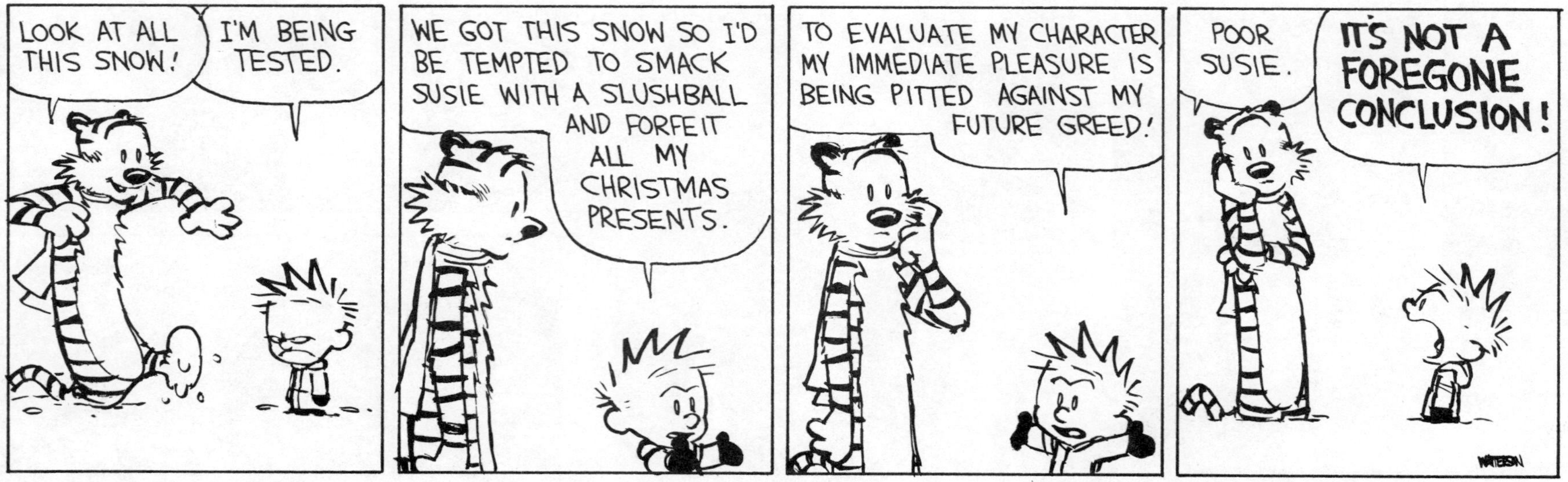
LOOK AT ALL THIS SNOW!
I'M BEING TESTED.
WE GOT THIS SNOW SO I'D BE TEMPTED TO SMACK SUSIE WITH A SLUSHBALL AND FORFEIT ALL MY CHRISTMAS PRESENTS.
TO EVALUATE MY CHARACTER, MY IMMEDIATE PLEASURE IS BEING PITTED AGAINST MY FUTURE GREED!
POOR SUSIE.
IT'S NOT A FOREGONE CONCLUSION!

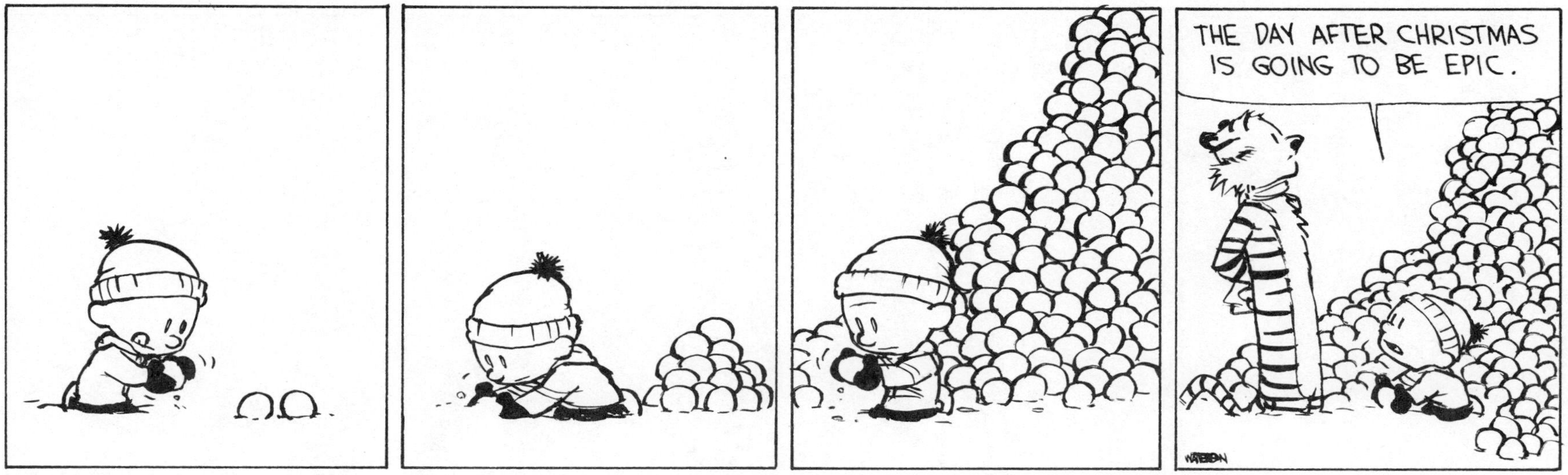
THE DAY AFTER CHRISTMAS IS GOING TO BE EPIC.
WATTERSON

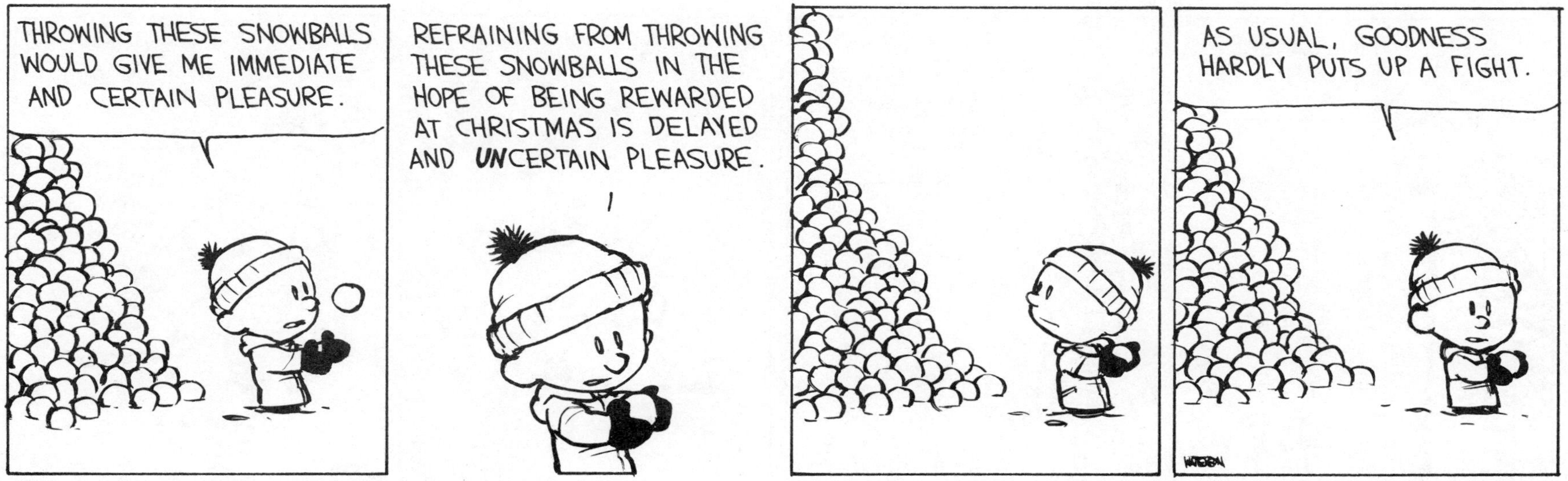
THROWING THESE SNOWBALLS WOULD GIVE ME IMMEDIATE AND CERTAIN PLEASURE.
REFRAINING FROM THROWING THESE SNOWBALLS IN THE HOPE OF BEING REWARDED AT CHRISTMAS IS DELAYED AND **UN**CERTAIN PLEASURE.
AS USUAL, GOODNESS HARDLY PUTS UP A FIGHT.
WATTERSON

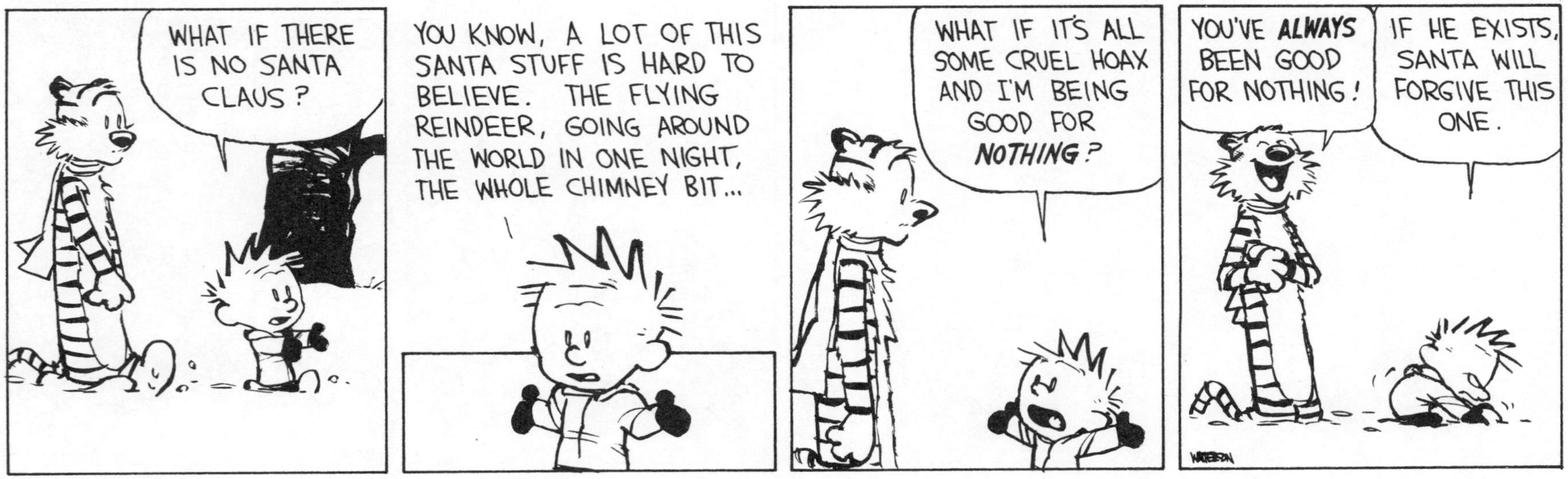
WHAT IF THERE IS NO SANTA CLAUS?
YOU KNOW, A LOT OF THIS SANTA STUFF IS HARD TO BELIEVE. THE FLYING REINDEER, GOING AROUND THE WORLD IN ONE NIGHT, THE WHOLE CHIMNEY BIT...
WHAT IF IT'S ALL SOME CRUEL HOAX AND I'M BEING GOOD FOR NOTHING?
YOU'VE ALWAYS BEEN GOOD FOR NOTHING!
IF HE EXISTS, SANTA WILL FORGIVE THIS ONE.
WATTERSON

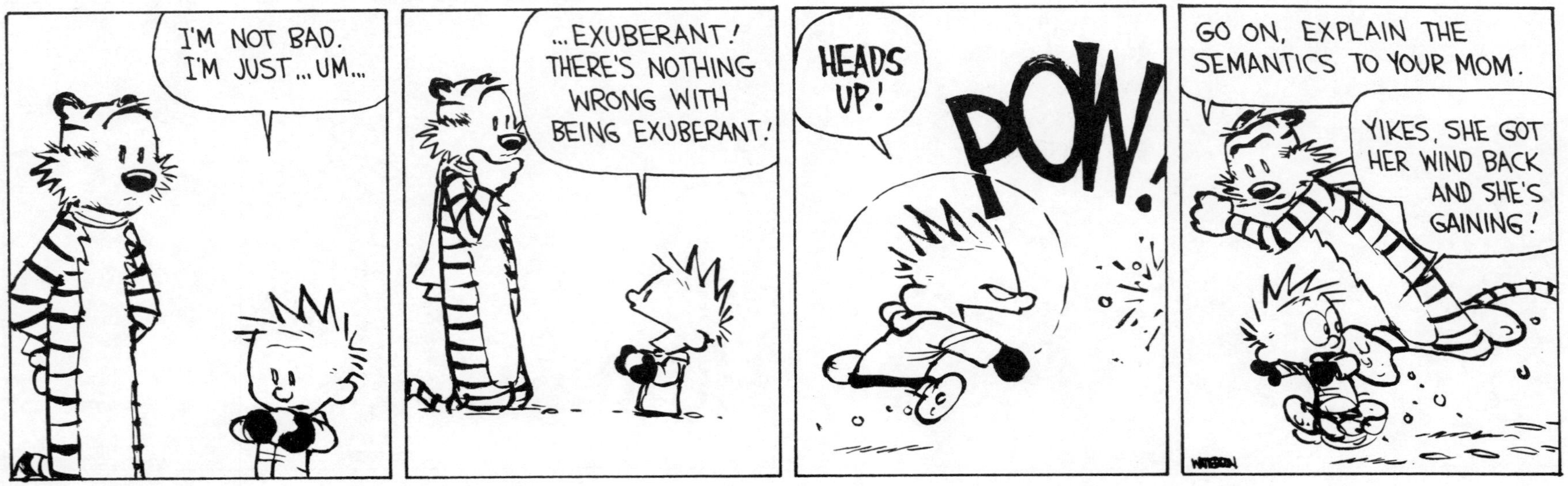
I'M NOT BAD. I'M JUST... UM...
...EXUBERANT! THERE'S NOTHING WRONG WITH BEING EXUBERANT!
HEADS UP!
POW!
GO ON, EXPLAIN THE SEMANTICS TO YOUR MOM.
YIKES, SHE GOT HER WIND BACK AND SHE'S GAINING!
WATTERSON

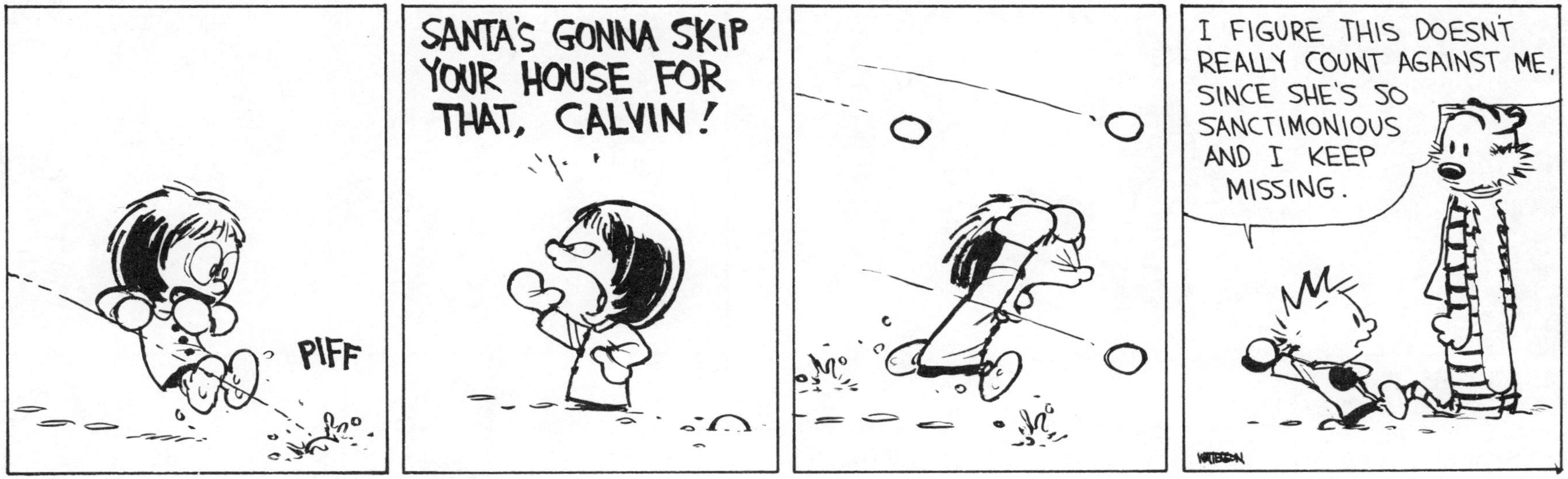
PIFF
SANTA'S GONNA SKIP YOUR HOUSE FOR THAT, CALVIN!
I FIGURE THIS DOESN'T REALLY COUNT AGAINST ME, SINCE SHE'S SO SANCTIMONIOUS AND I KEEP MISSING.

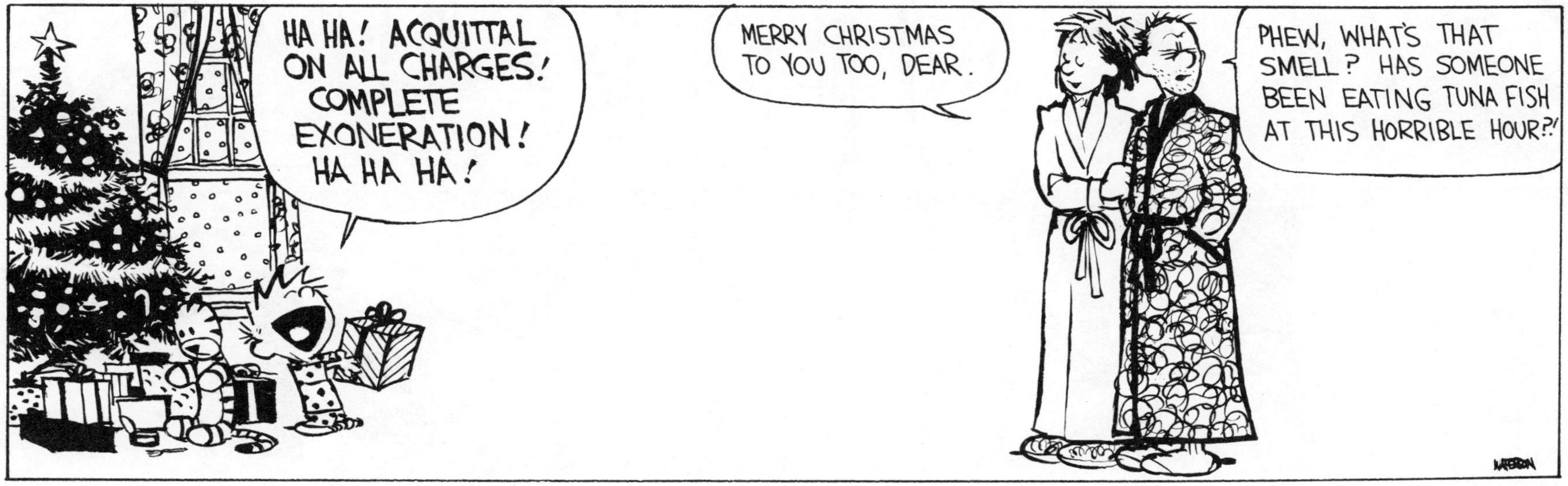
HA HA! ACQUITTAL ON ALL CHARGES! COMPLETE EXONERATION! HA HA HA!
MERRY CHRISTMAS TO YOU TOO, DEAR.
PHEW, WHAT'S THAT SMELL? HAS SOMEONE BEEN EATING TUNA FISH AT THIS HORRIBLE HOUR?!

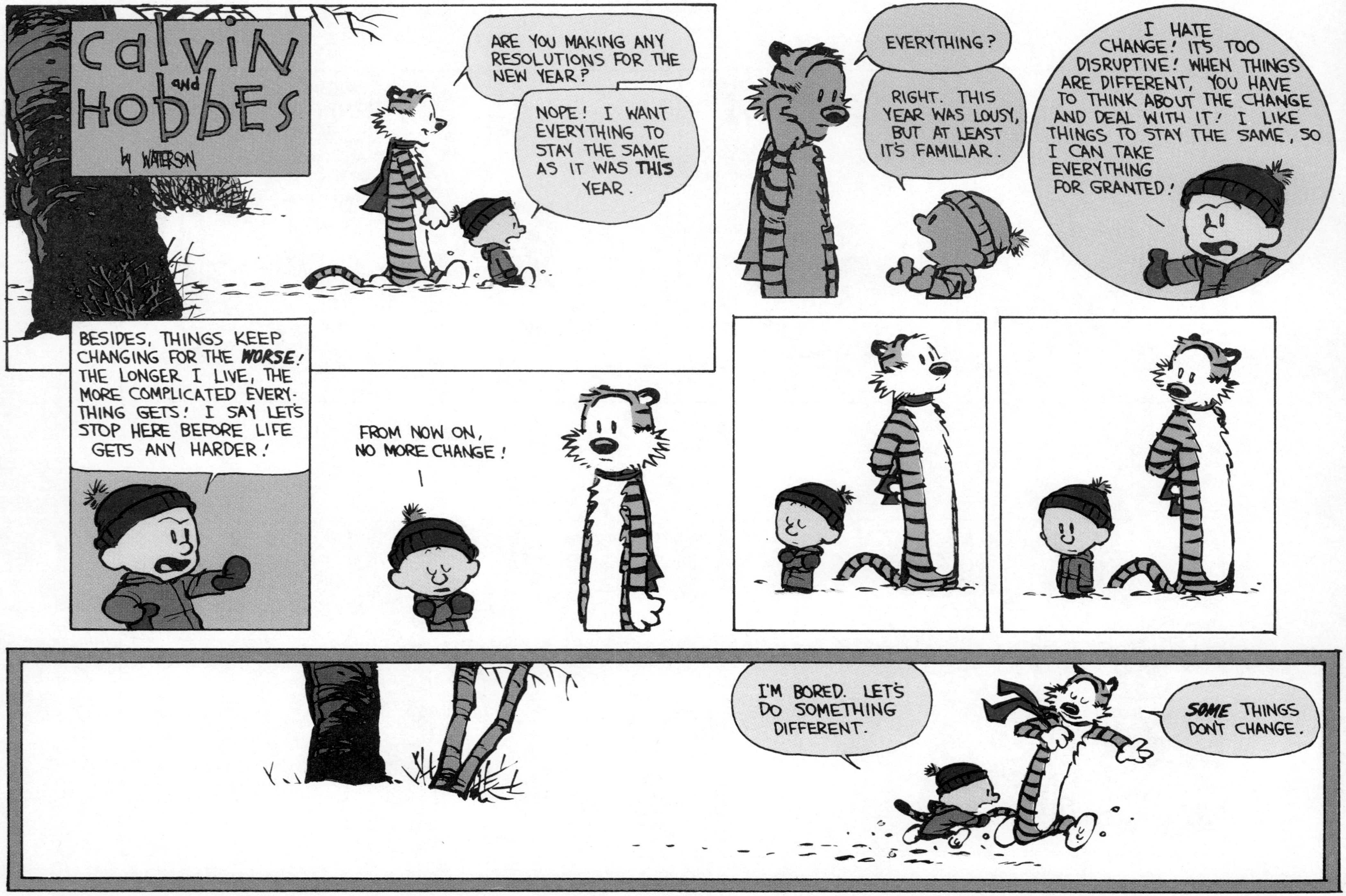
Calvin and Hobbes
by WATTERSON
ARE YOU MAKING ANY RESOLUTIONS FOR THE NEW YEAR?
NOPE! I WANT EVERYTHING TO STAY THE SAME AS IT WAS **THIS** YEAR.
EVERYTHING?
RIGHT. THIS YEAR WAS LOUSY, BUT AT LEAST IT'S FAMILIAR.
I HATE CHANGE! IT'S TOO DISRUPTIVE! WHEN THINGS ARE DIFFERENT, YOU HAVE TO THINK ABOUT THE CHANGE AND DEAL WITH IT! I LIKE THINGS TO STAY THE SAME, SO I CAN TAKE EVERYTHING FOR GRANTED!
BESIDES, THINGS KEEP CHANGING FOR THE ***WORSE***! THE LONGER I LIVE, THE MORE COMPLICATED EVERYTHING GETS! I SAY LET'S STOP HERE BEFORE LIFE GETS ANY HARDER!
FROM NOW ON, NO MORE CHANGE!
I'M BORED. LET'S DO SOMETHING DIFFERENT.
SOME THINGS DON'T CHANGE.

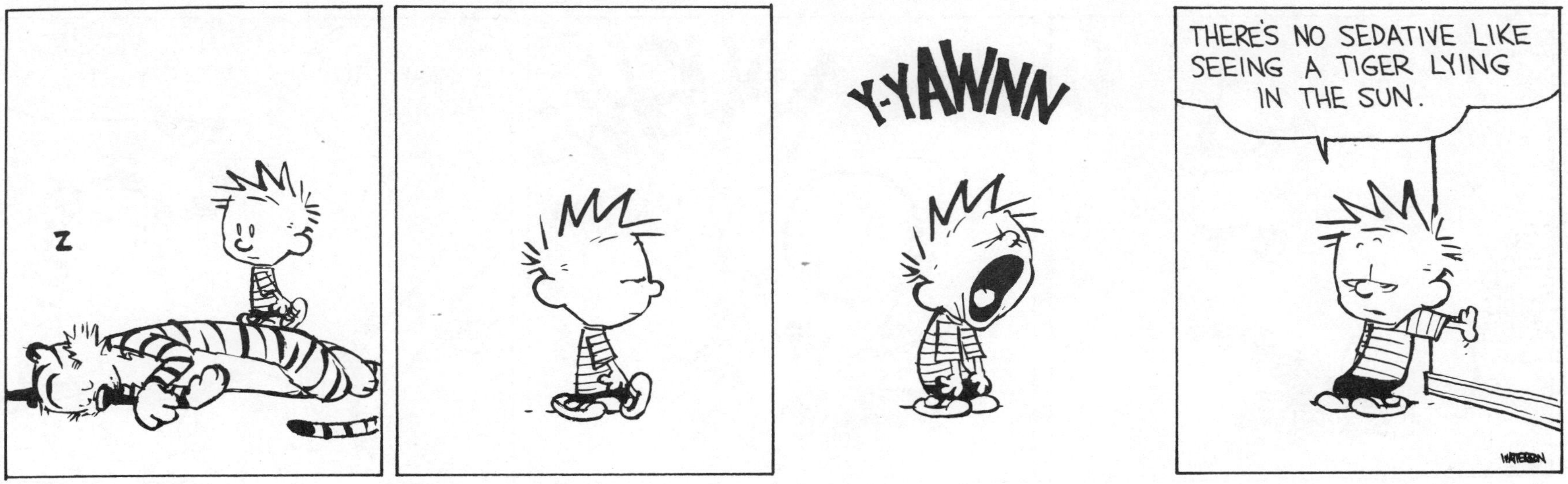
Z
Y-YAWNN
THERE'S NO SEDATIVE LIKE SEEING A TIGER LYING IN THE SUN.
WATTERSON

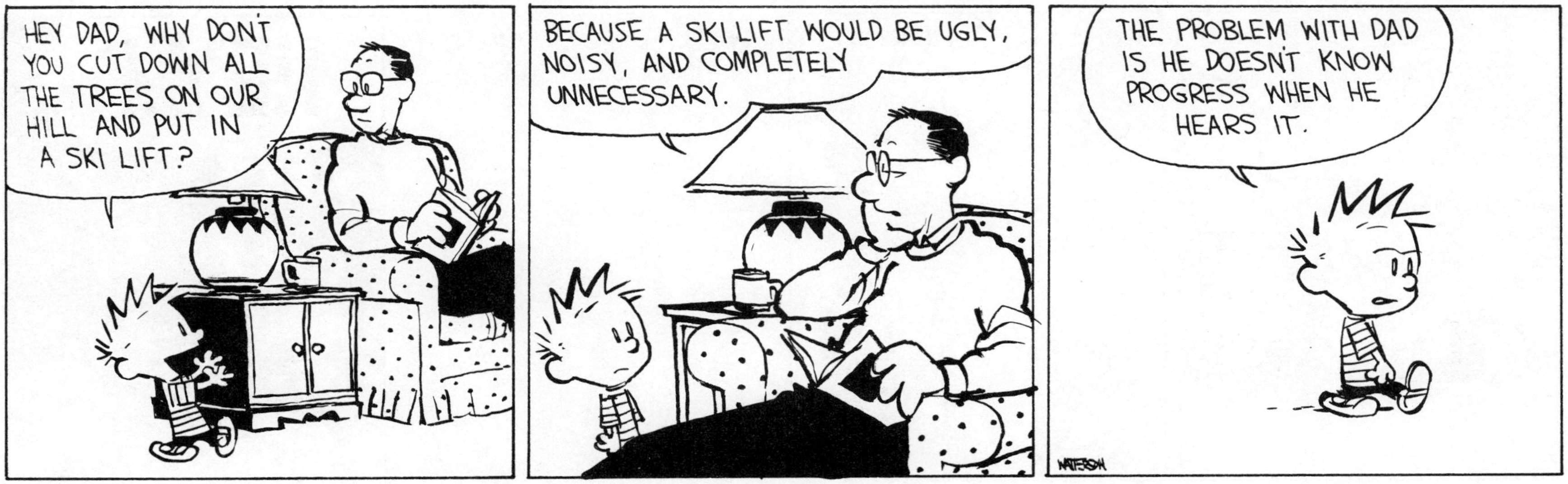
HEY DAD, WHY DON'T YOU CUT DOWN ALL THE TREES ON OUR HILL AND PUT IN A SKI LIFT?
BECAUSE A SKI LIFT WOULD BE UGLY, NOISY, AND COMPLETELY UNNECESSARY.
THE PROBLEM WITH DAD IS HE DOESN'T KNOW PROGRESS WHEN HE HEARS IT.
WATTERSON

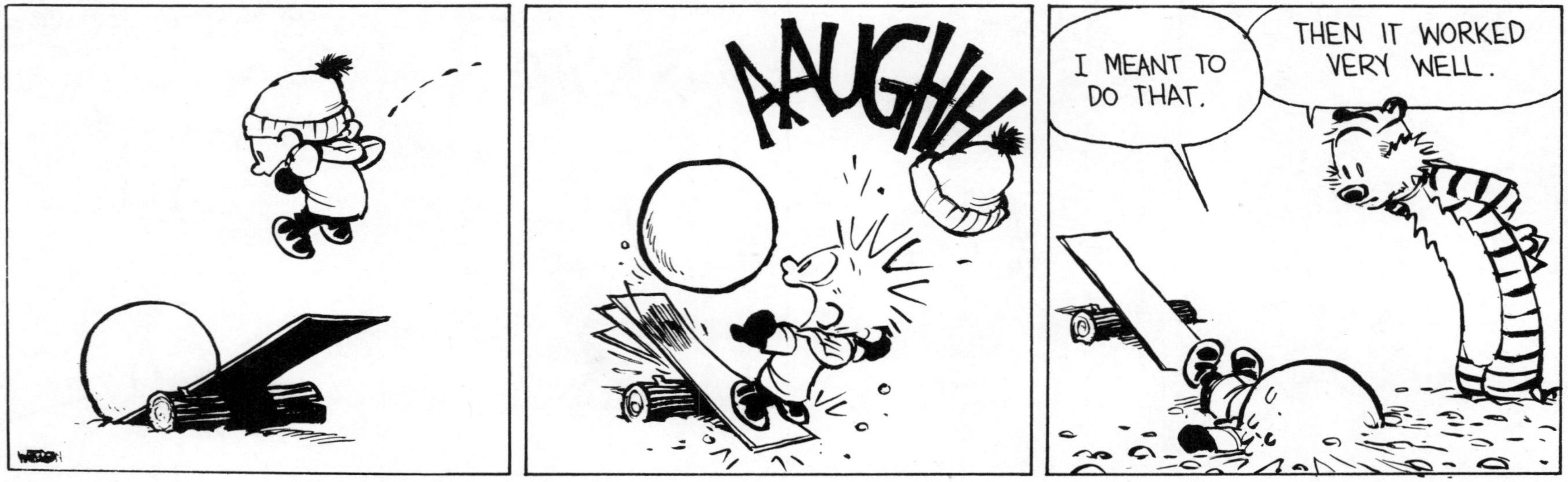
AAUGHH
I MEANT TO DO THAT.
THEN IT WORKED VERY WELL.

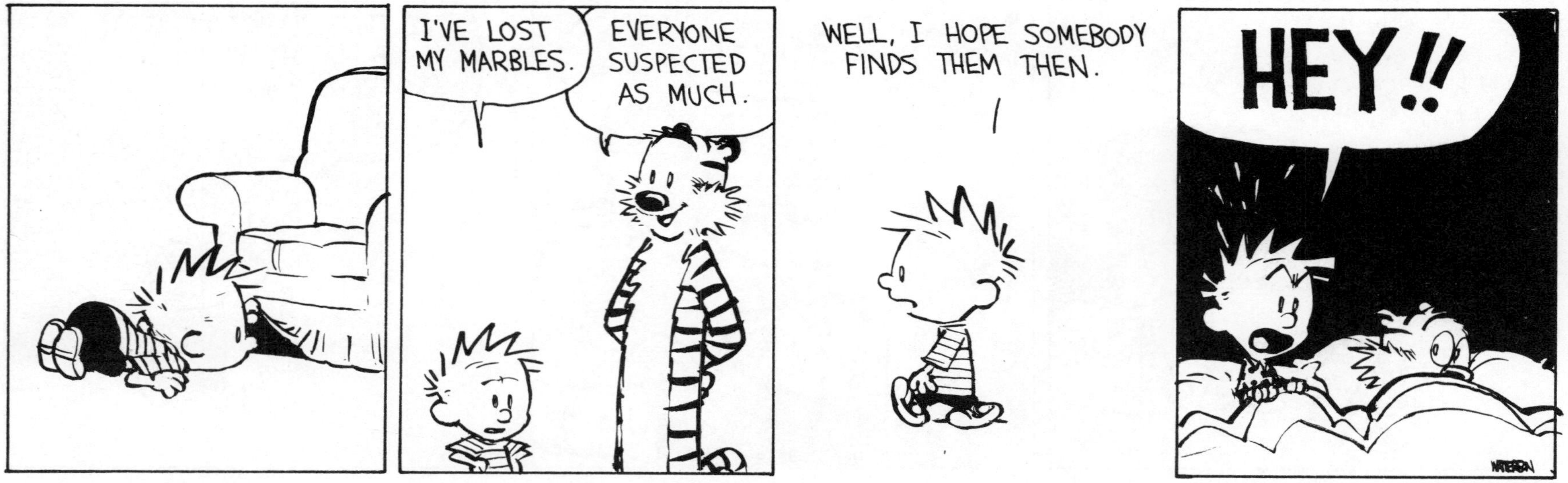
I'VE LOST MY MARBLES.
EVERYONE SUSPECTED AS MUCH.
WELL, I HOPE SOMEBODY FINDS THEM THEN.
HEY!!

I NEED A NEW TOBOGGAN.
WHAT FOR?
MINE IS OUTDATED. I'M SURE THE '94 MODELS HAVE ALL SORTS OF NEW FEATURES, COLORS AND OPTIONS.
TOBOGGANS DON'T COME IN MODEL YEARS.
THEY DON'T??
I TELL YOU, HOBBES, THERE'S A FORTUNE TO BE MADE!
WATTERSON

WHAT THE...??
I'M NOT PLAYING WITH A FULL DECK!
THAT'S WHAT PEOPLE SAY.
REALLY? THEN WHY DIDN'T SOMEBODY GO BUY SOME NEW CARDS?!
HEY!!
WATTERSON

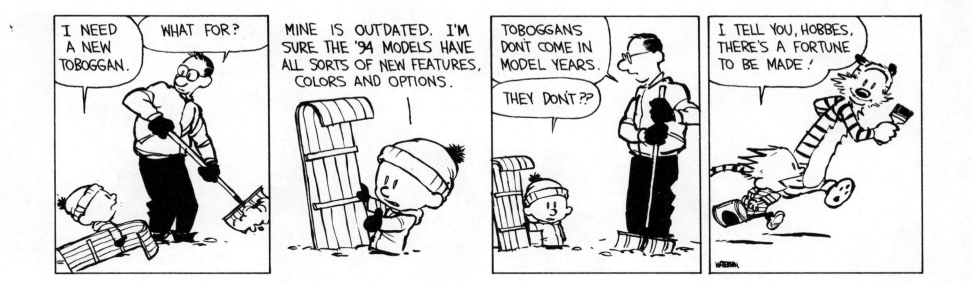

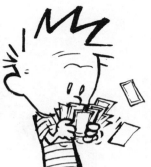

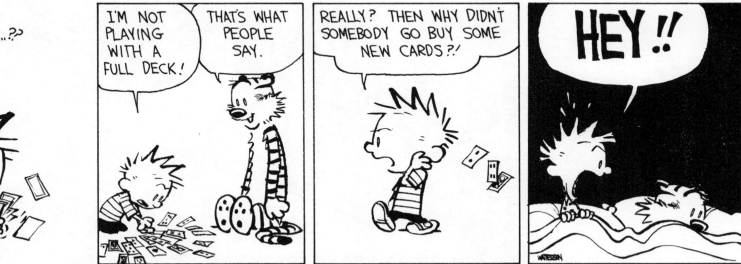

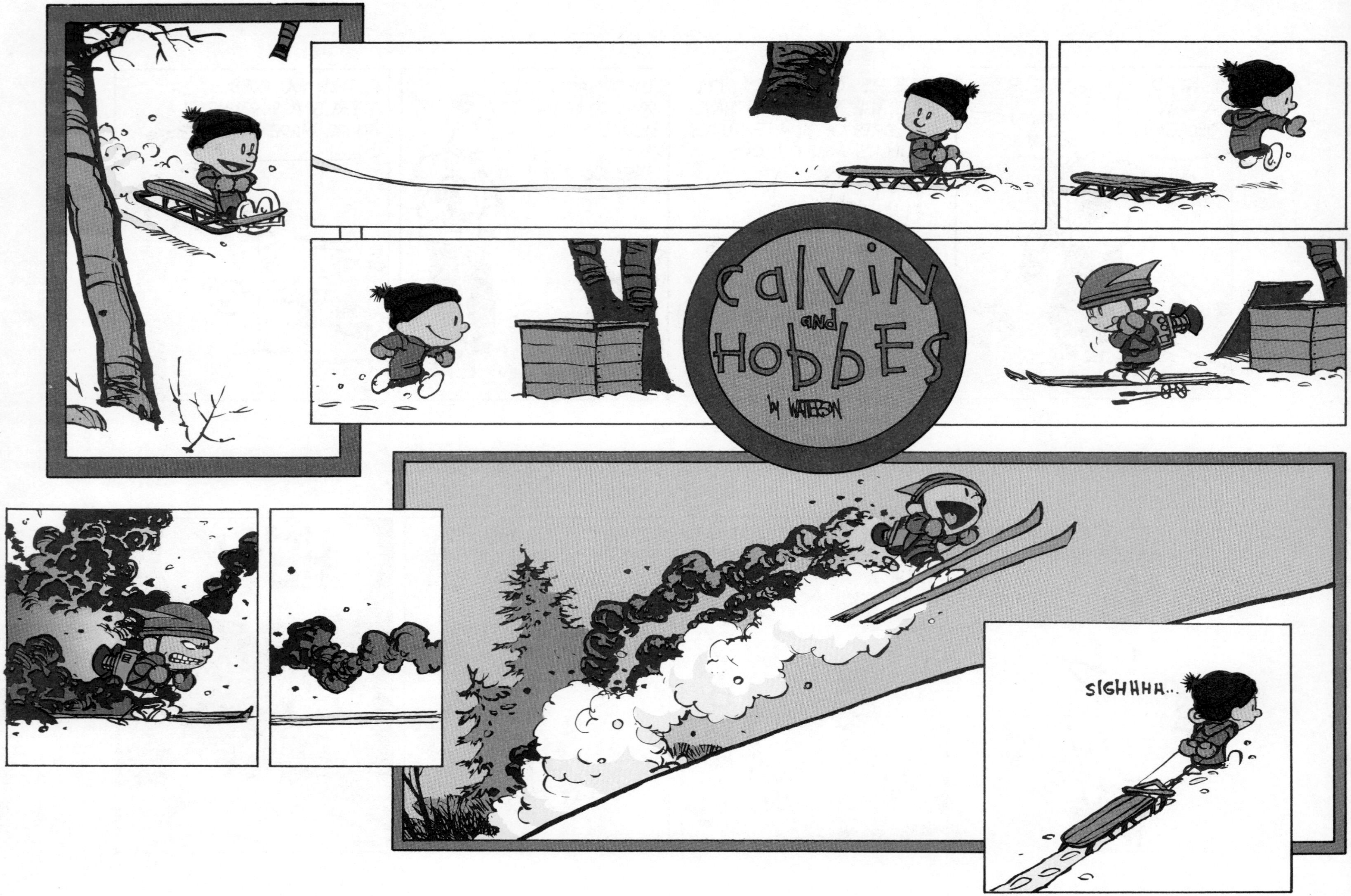
Calvin and HOBBES
by WATTERSON
SIGHHHA...

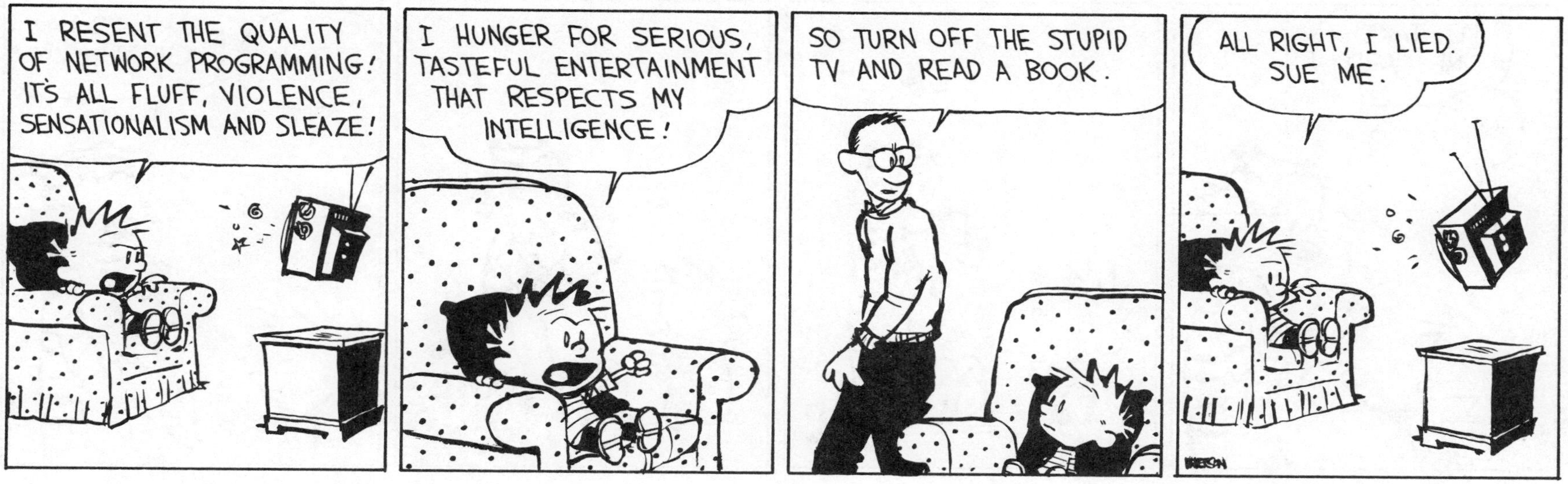
I RESENT THE QUALITY OF NETWORK PROGRAMMING! IT'S ALL FLUFF, VIOLENCE, SENSATIONALISM AND SLEAZE!
I HUNGER FOR SERIOUS, TASTEFUL ENTERTAINMENT THAT RESPECTS MY INTELLIGENCE!
SO TURN OFF THE STUPID TV AND READ A BOOK.
ALL RIGHT, I LIED. SUE ME.

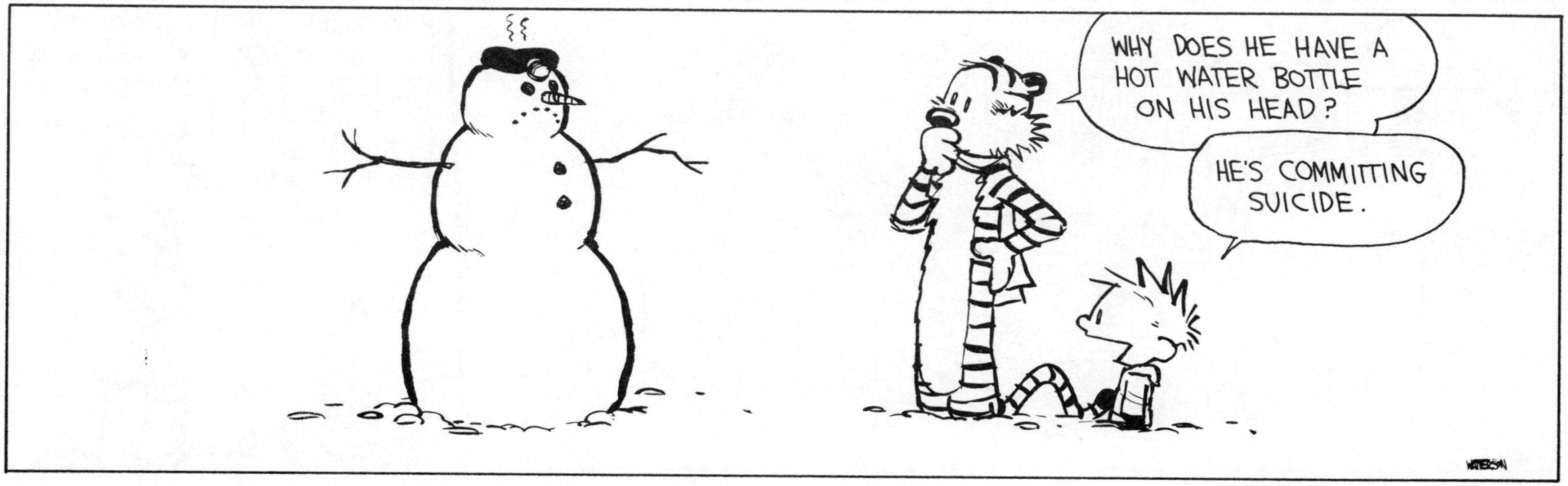
WHY DOES HE HAVE A HOT WATER BOTTLE ON HIS HEAD?
HE'S COMMITTING SUICIDE.

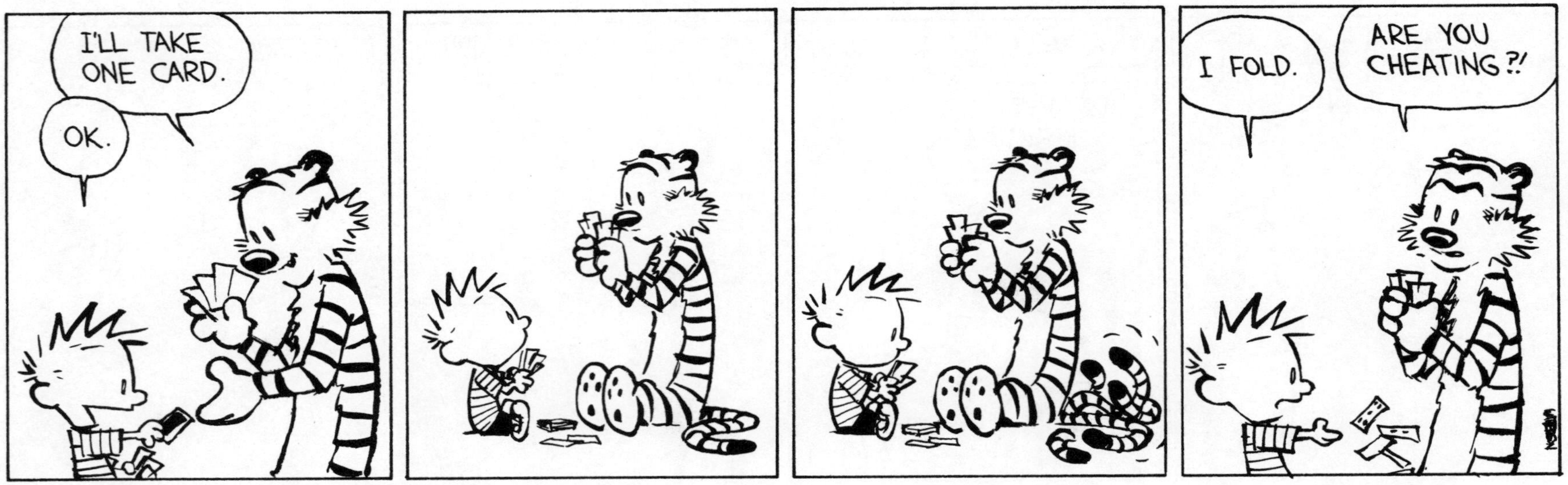
I'LL TAKE ONE CARD.
OK.
I FOLD.
ARE YOU CHEATING?!

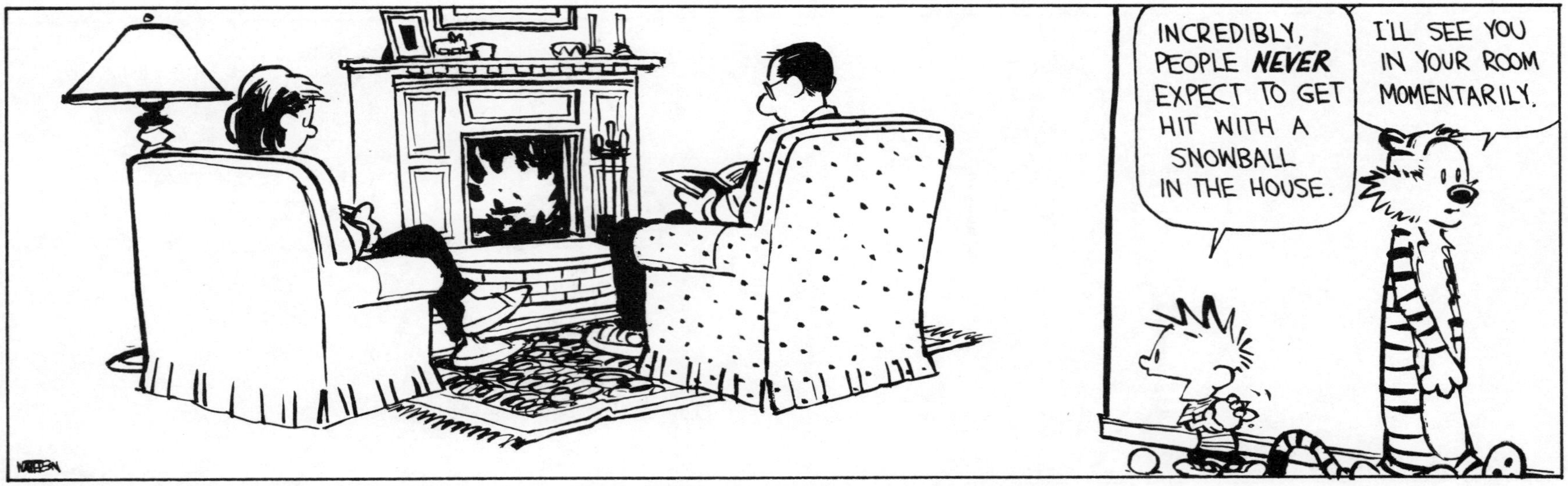
INCREDIBLY, PEOPLE NEVER EXPECT TO GET HIT WITH A SNOWBALL IN THE HOUSE.
I'LL SEE YOU IN YOUR ROOM MOMENTARILY.

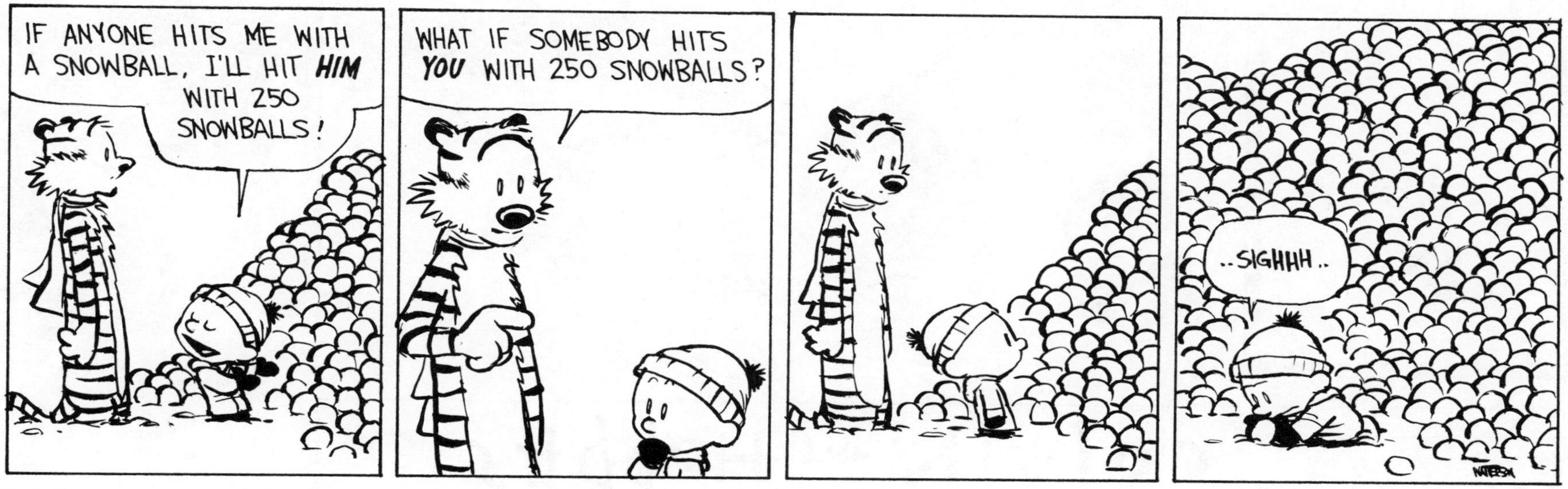
IF ANYONE HITS ME WITH A SNOWBALL, I'LL HIT **HIM** WITH 250 SNOWBALLS!
WHAT IF SOMEBODY HITS **YOU** WITH 250 SNOWBALLS?
..SIGHHH..

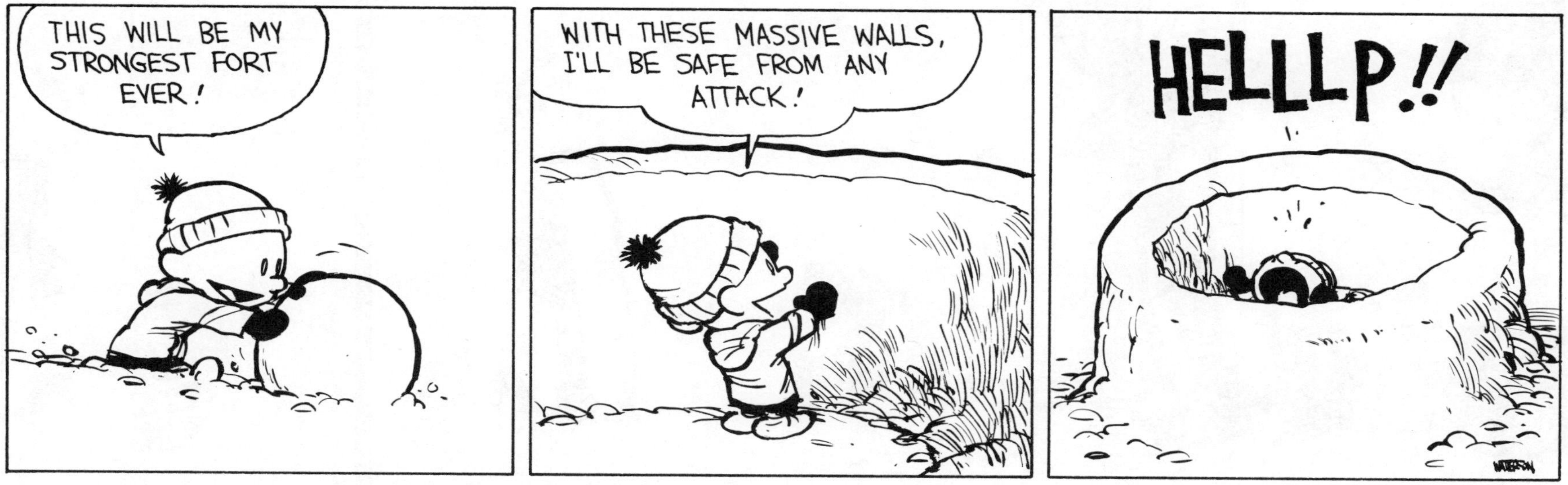
THIS WILL BE MY STRONGEST FORT EVER!
WITH THESE MASSIVE WALLS, I'LL BE SAFE FROM ANY ATTACK!
HELLLP!!

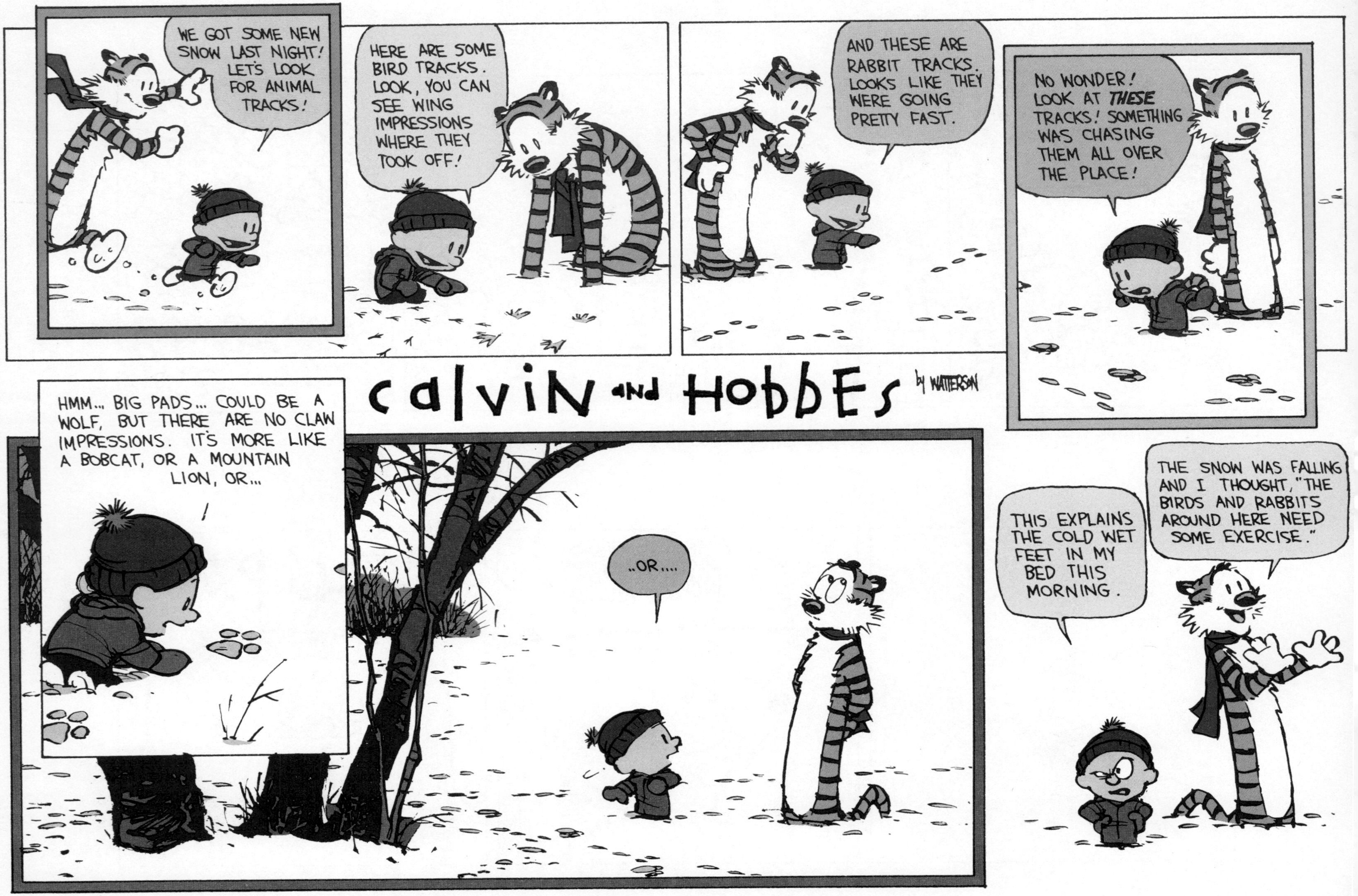

WE GOT SOME NEW SNOW LAST NIGHT! LET'S LOOK FOR ANIMAL TRACKS!
HERE ARE SOME BIRD TRACKS. LOOK, YOU CAN SEE WING IMPRESSIONS WHERE THEY TOOK OFF!
AND THESE ARE RABBIT TRACKS. LOOKS LIKE THEY WERE GOING PRETTY FAST.
NO WONDER! LOOK AT THESE TRACKS! SOMETHING WAS CHASING THEM ALL OVER THE PLACE!
calvin and HOBBES
by WATTERSON
HMM... BIG PADS... COULD BE A WOLF, BUT THERE ARE NO CLAW IMPRESSIONS. IT'S MORE LIKE A BOBCAT, OR A MOUNTAIN LION, OR...
!
..OR....
THIS EXPLAINS THE COLD WET FEET IN MY BED THIS MORNING.
THE SNOW WAS FALLING AND I THOUGHT, "THE BIRDS AND RABBITS AROUND HERE NEED SOME EXERCISE."

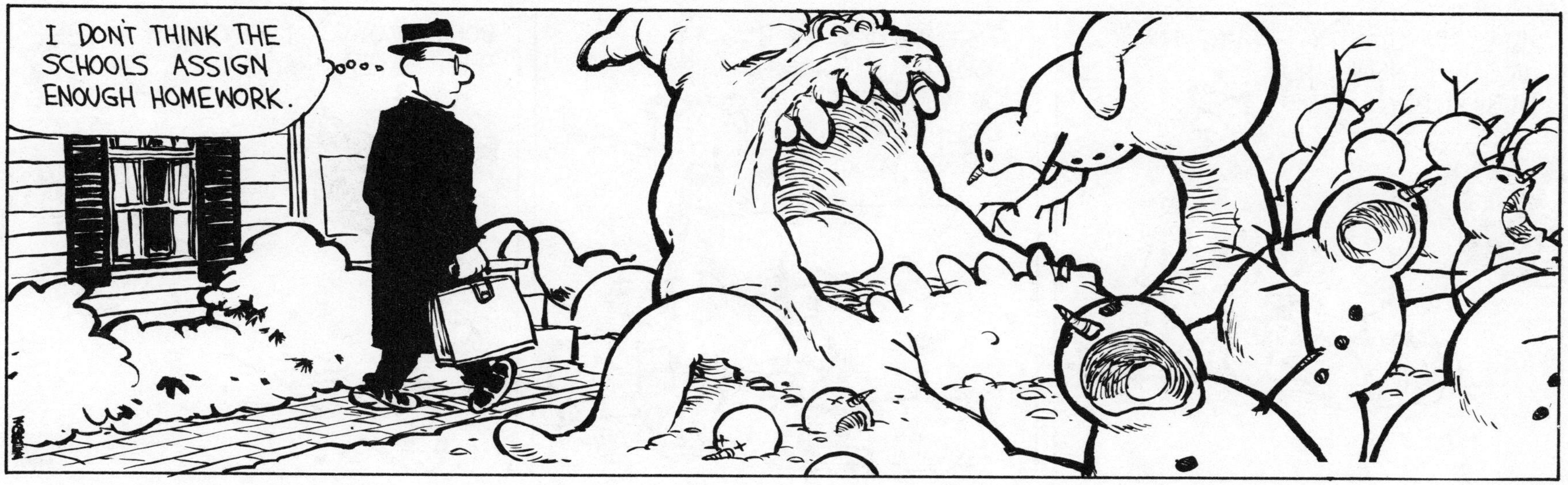
I DON'T THINK THE SCHOOLS ASSIGN ENOUGH HOMEWORK.

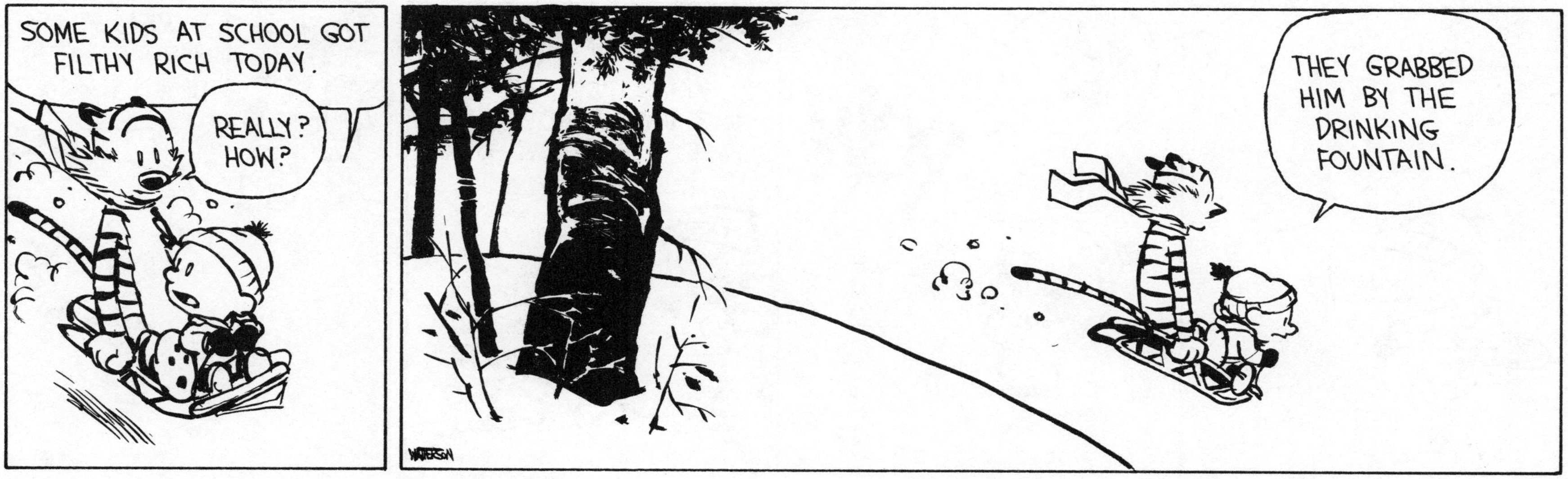
SOME KIDS AT SCHOOL GOT FILTHY RICH TODAY.
REALLY? HOW?
THEY GRABBED HIM BY THE DRINKING FOUNTAIN.

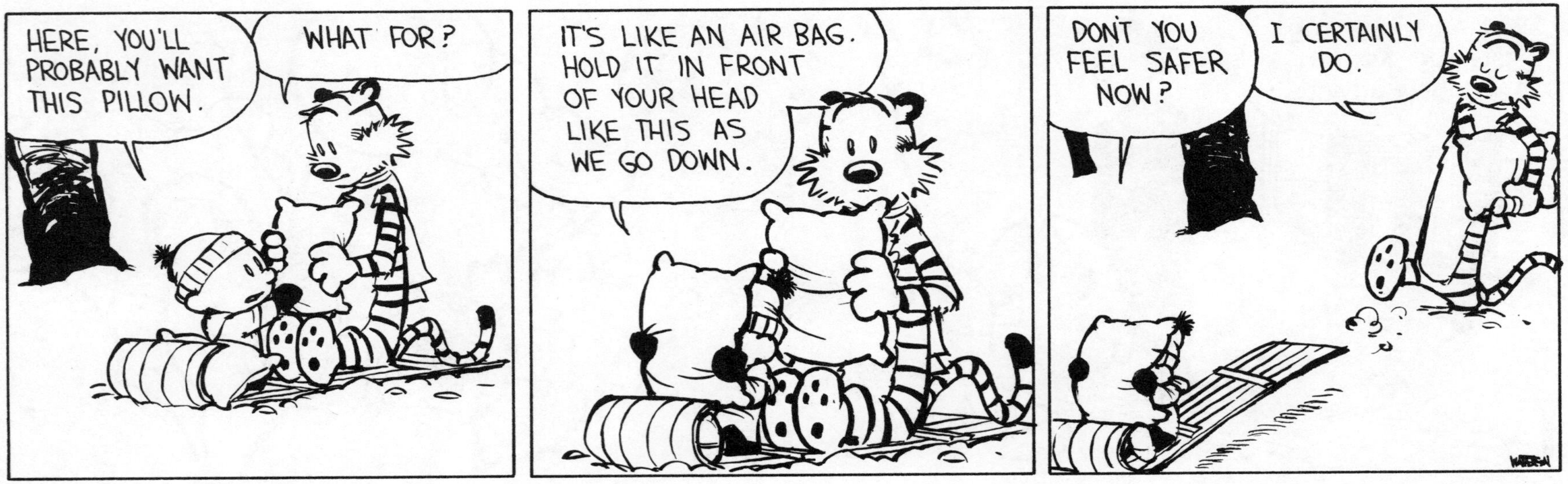
HERE, YOU'LL PROBABLY WANT THIS PILLOW.
WHAT FOR?
IT'S LIKE AN AIR BAG. HOLD IT IN FRONT OF YOUR HEAD LIKE THIS AS WE GO DOWN.
DON'T YOU FEEL SAFER NOW?
I CERTAINLY DO.

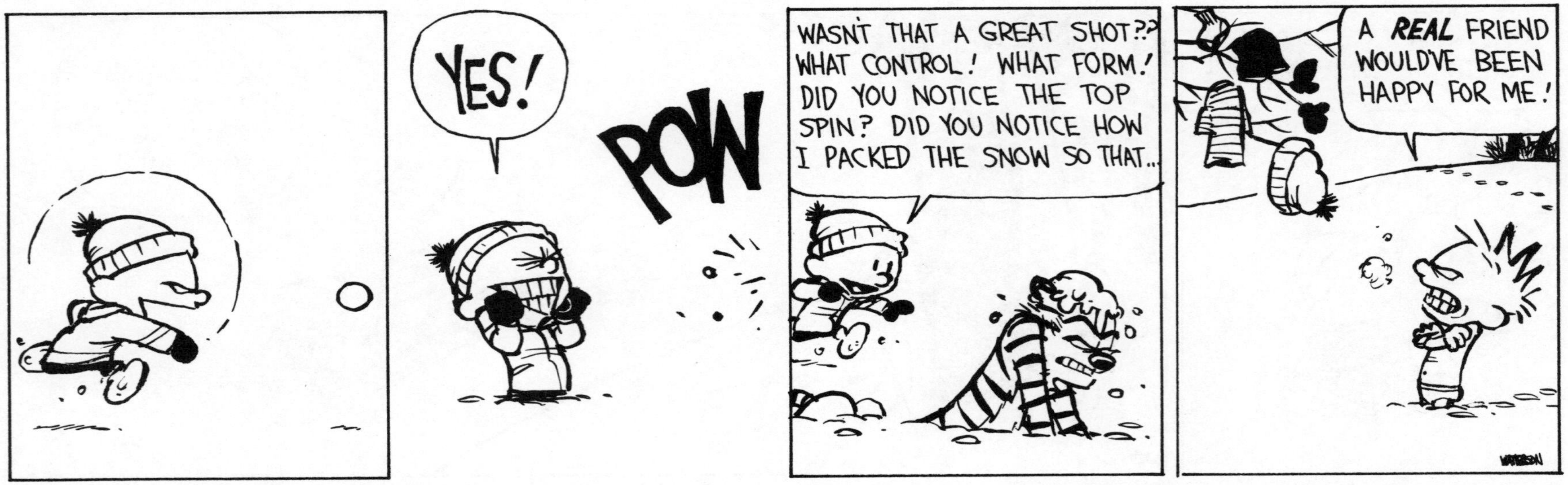
YES!
POW
WASN'T THAT A GREAT SHOT?? WHAT CONTROL! WHAT FORM! DID YOU NOTICE THE TOP SPIN? DID YOU NOTICE HOW I PACKED THE SNOW SO THAT...
A REAL FRIEND WOULD'VE BEEN HAPPY FOR ME!

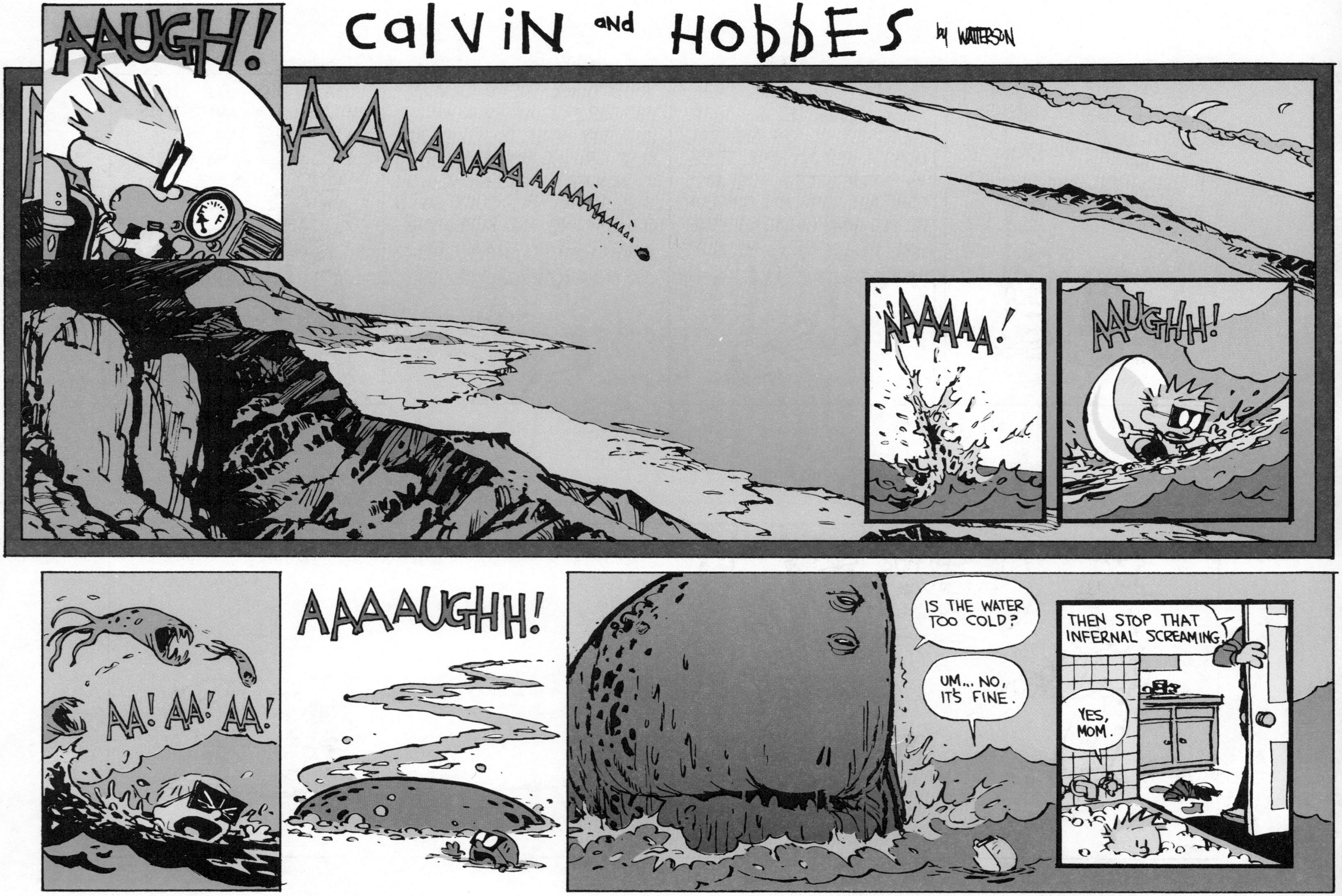
Calvin and Hobbes
by WATTERSON
AAUGH!
AAAAAAAAAAAAAAAAAA
AAAAAA!
AAUGHHH!
AA! AA! AA!
AAAAUGHH!
IS THE WATER TOO COLD?
UM... NO, IT'S FINE.
THEN STOP THAT INFERNAL SCREAMING.
YES, MOM.

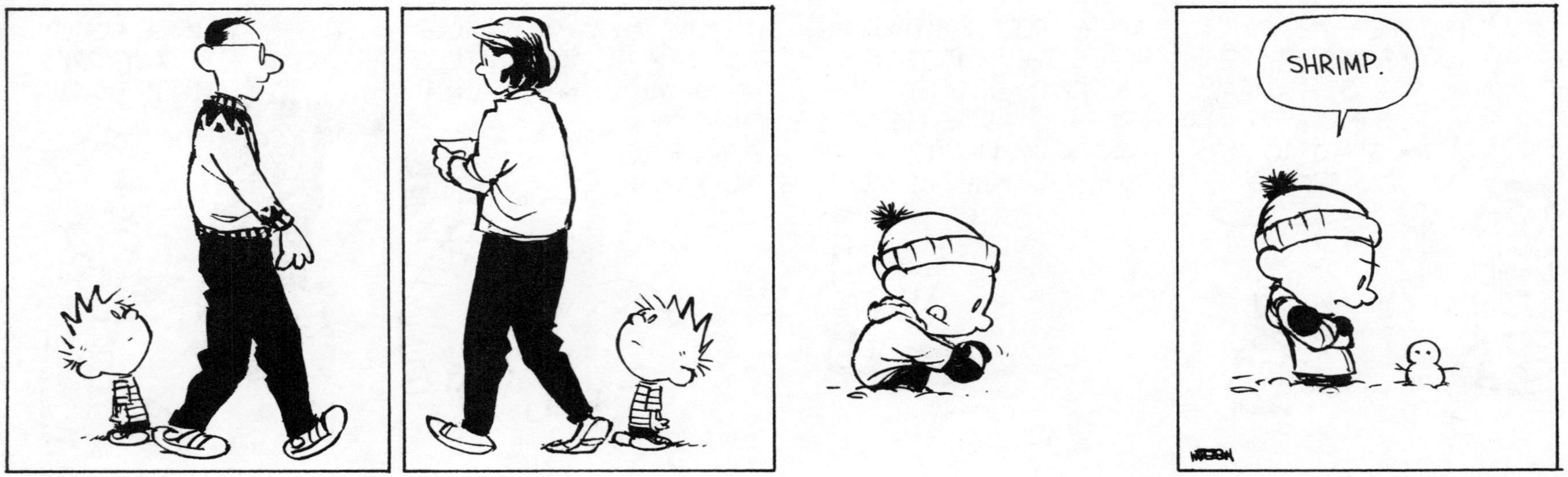
SHRIMP.

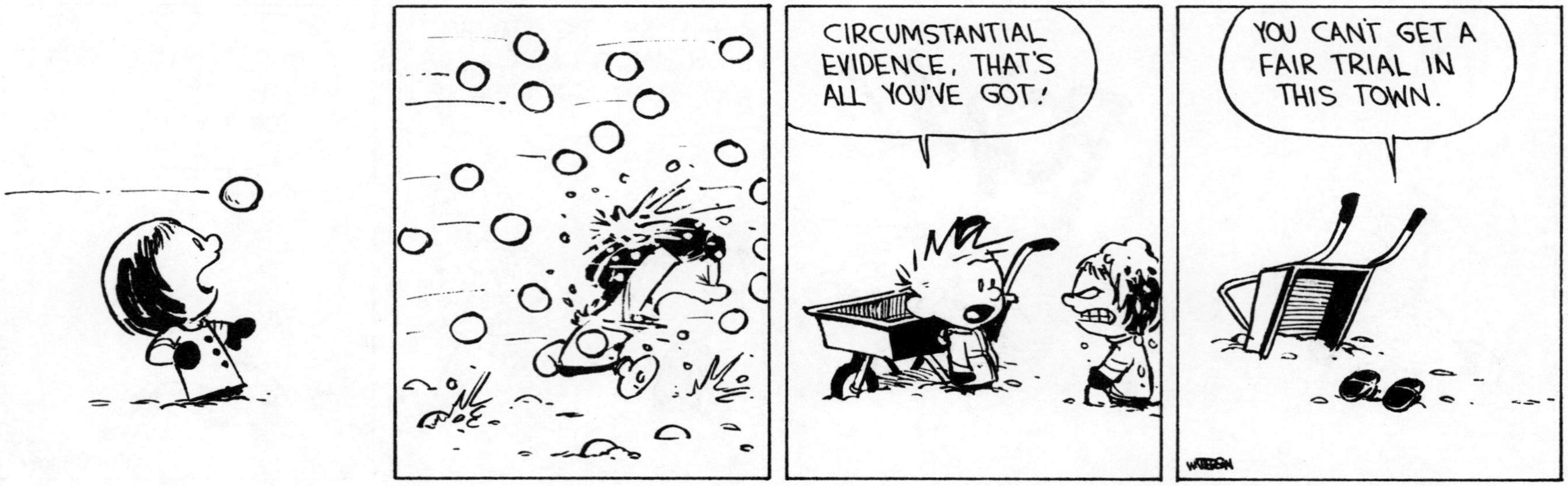
CIRCUMSTANTIAL EVIDENCE, THAT'S ALL YOU'VE GOT!
YOU CAN'T GET A FAIR TRIAL IN THIS TOWN.

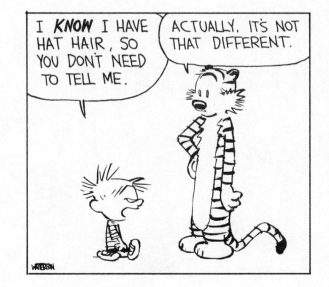

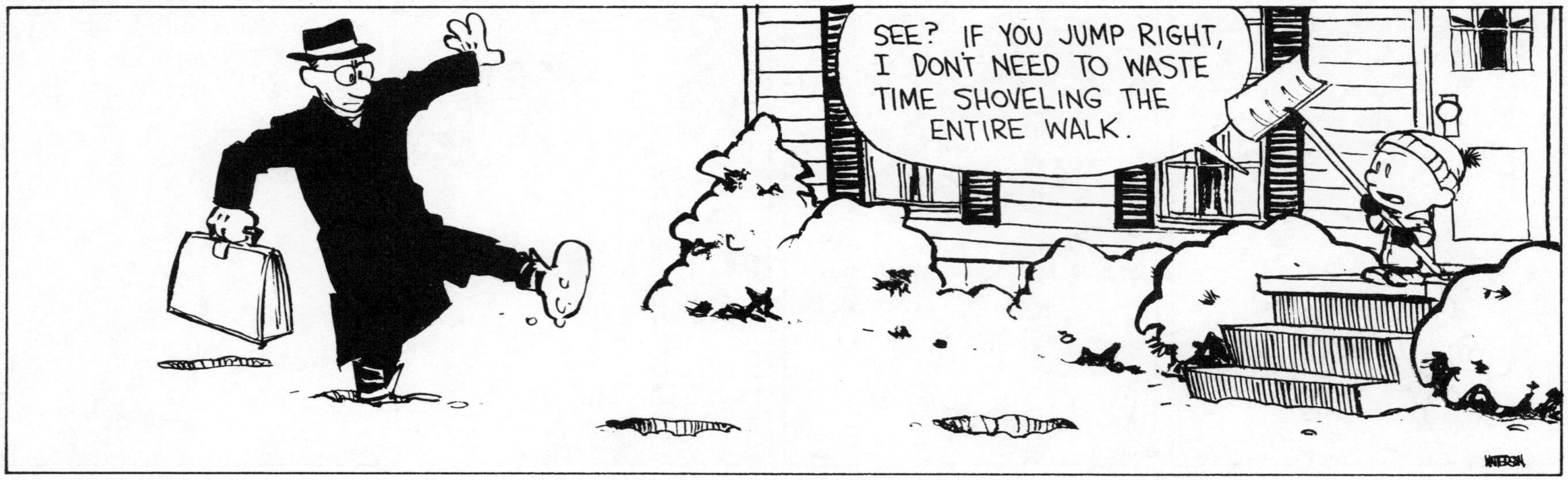
SEE? IF YOU JUMP RIGHT, I DON'T NEED TO WASTE TIME SHOVELING THE ENTIRE WALK.

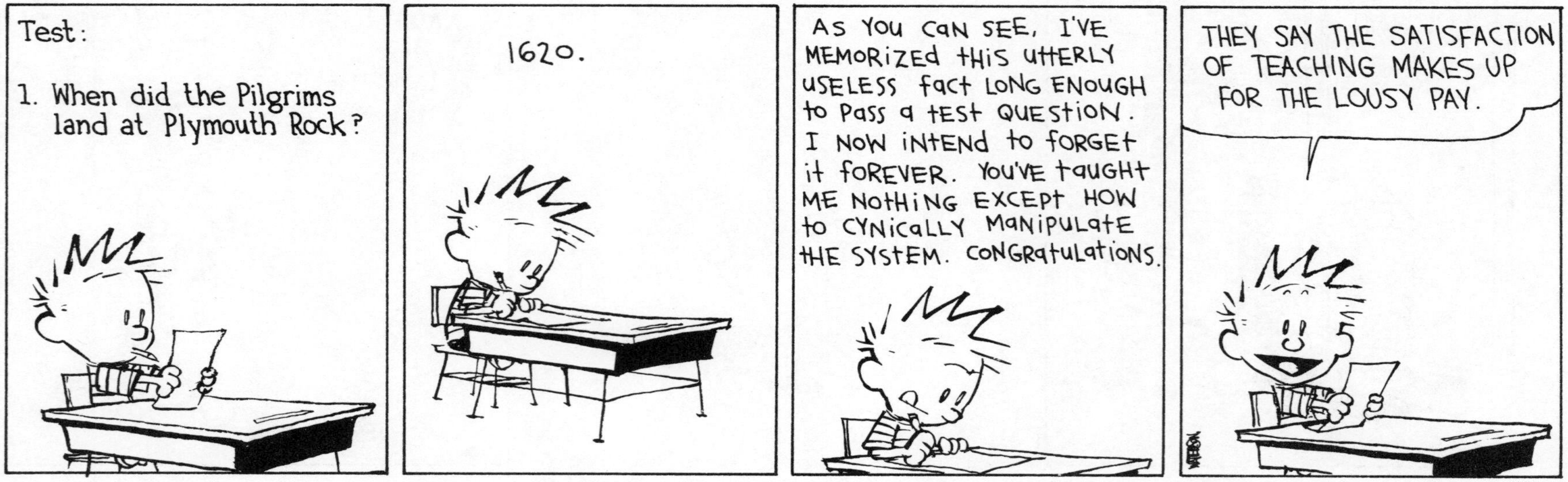
Test:
1. When did the Pilgrims land at Plymouth Rock?
1620.
AS YOU CAN SEE, I'VE MEMORIZED THIS UTTERLY USELESS FACT LONG ENOUGH TO PASS A TEST QUESTION. I NOW INTEND TO FORGET IT FOREVER. YOU'VE TAUGHT ME NOTHING EXCEPT HOW TO CYNICALLY MANIPULATE THE SYSTEM. CONGRATULATIONS.
THEY SAY THE SATISFACTION OF TEACHING MAKES UP FOR THE LOUSY PAY.

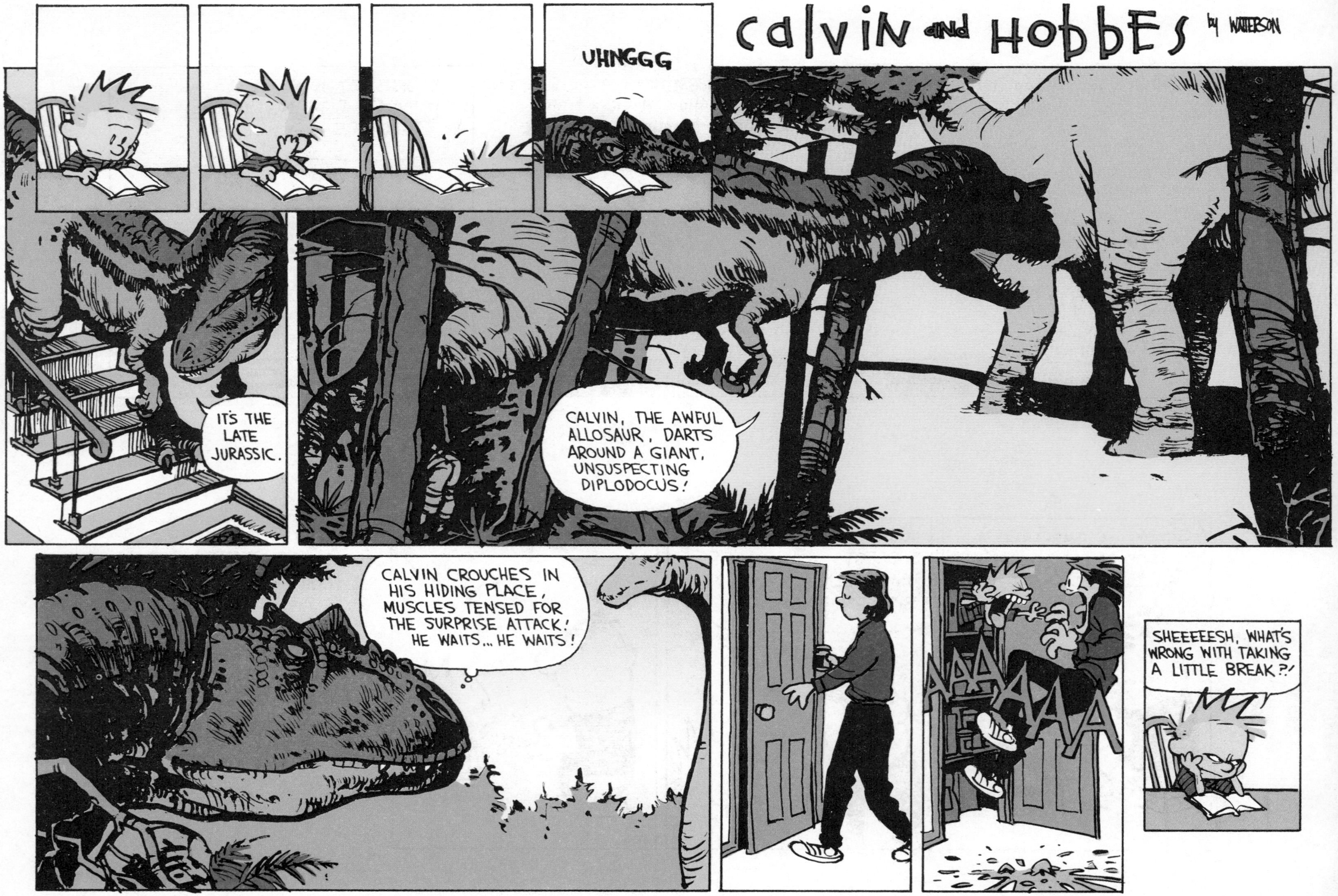
Calvin and HobbEs by WATTERSON
UHNGGG
IT'S THE LATE JURASSIC.
CALVIN, THE AWFUL ALLOSAUR, DARTS AROUND A GIANT, UNSUSPECTING DIPLODOCUS!
CALVIN CROUCHES IN HIS HIDING PLACE, MUSCLES TENSED FOR THE SURPRISE ATTACK! HE WAITS... HE WAITS!
AAAAAAA
SHEEEEESH, WHAT'S WRONG WITH TAKING A LITTLE BREAK?!

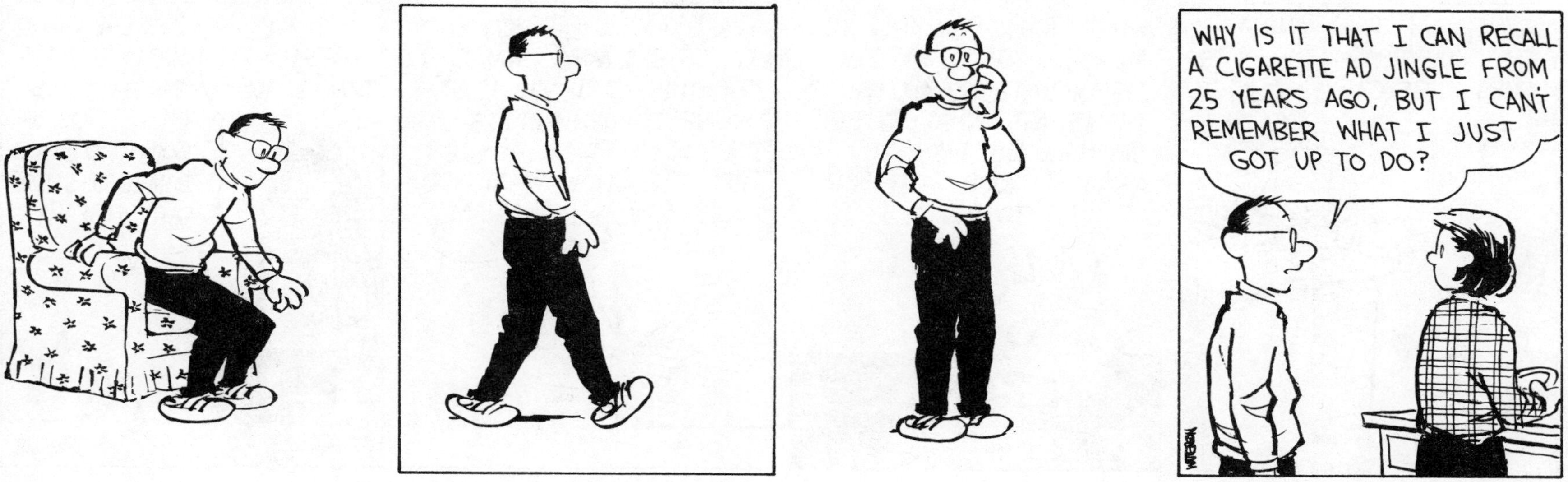
WHY IS IT THAT I CAN RECALL A CIGARETTE AD JINGLE FROM 25 YEARS AGO, BUT I CAN'T REMEMBER WHAT I JUST GOT UP TO DO?

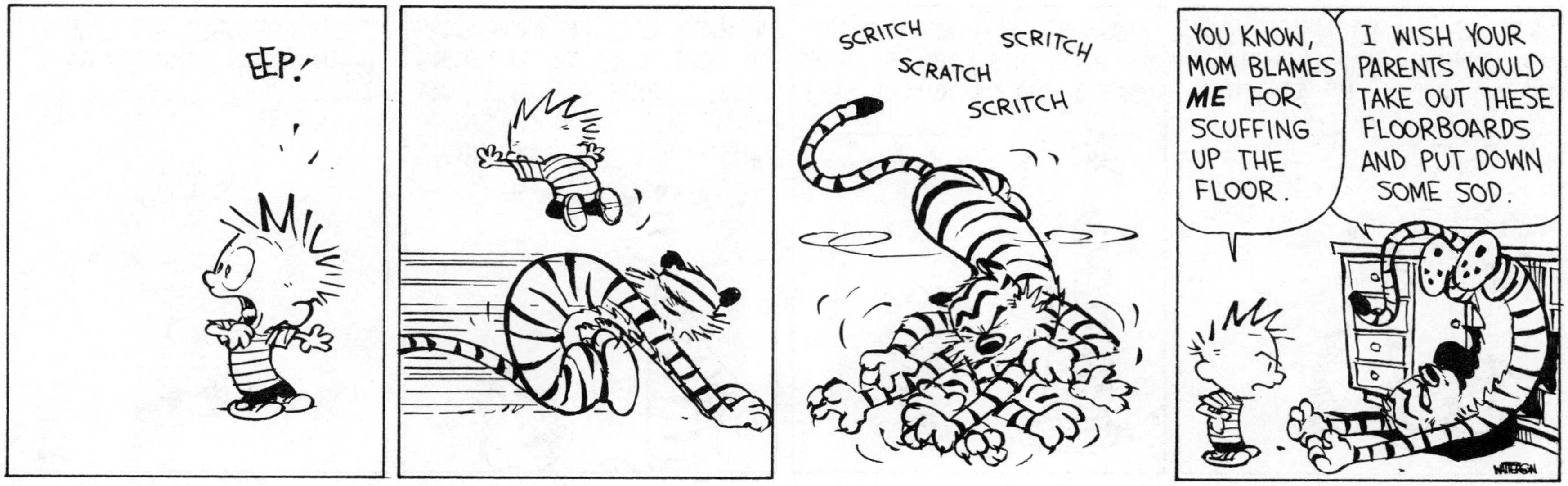
EEP!
SCRITCH
SCRATCH
SCRITCH
SCRITCH
YOU KNOW, MOM BLAMES **ME** FOR SCUFFING UP THE FLOOR.
I WISH YOUR PARENTS WOULD TAKE OUT THESE FLOORBOARDS AND PUT DOWN SOME SOD.

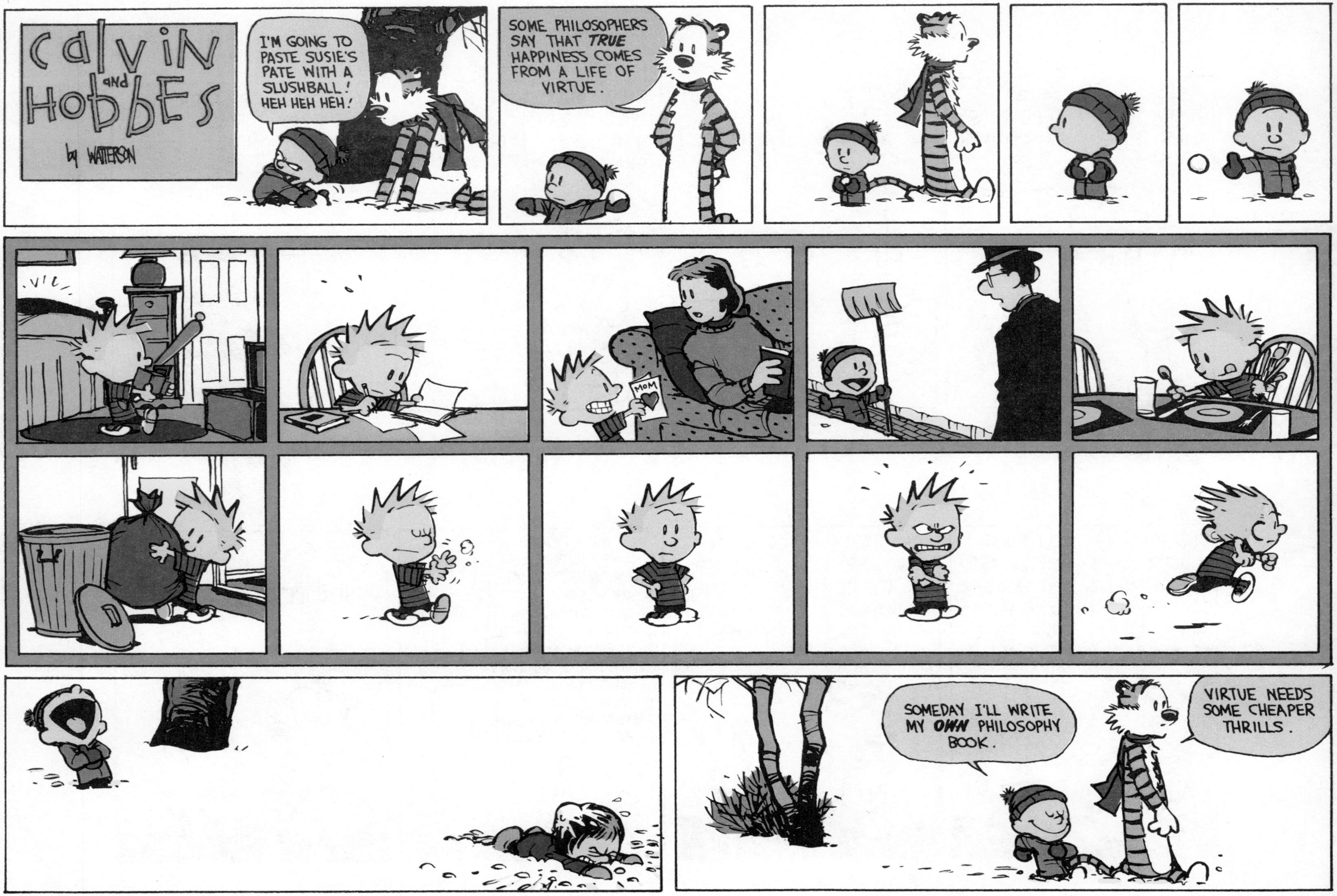

Calvin and Hobbes
by WATTERSON
I'M GOING TO PASTE SUSIE'S PATE WITH A SLUSHBALL! HEH HEH HEH!
SOME PHILOSOPHERS SAY THAT *TRUE* HAPPINESS COMES FROM A LIFE OF VIRTUE.
SOMEDAY I'LL WRITE MY *OWN* PHILOSOPHY BOOK.
VIRTUE NEEDS SOME CHEAPER THRILLS.
MOM

99

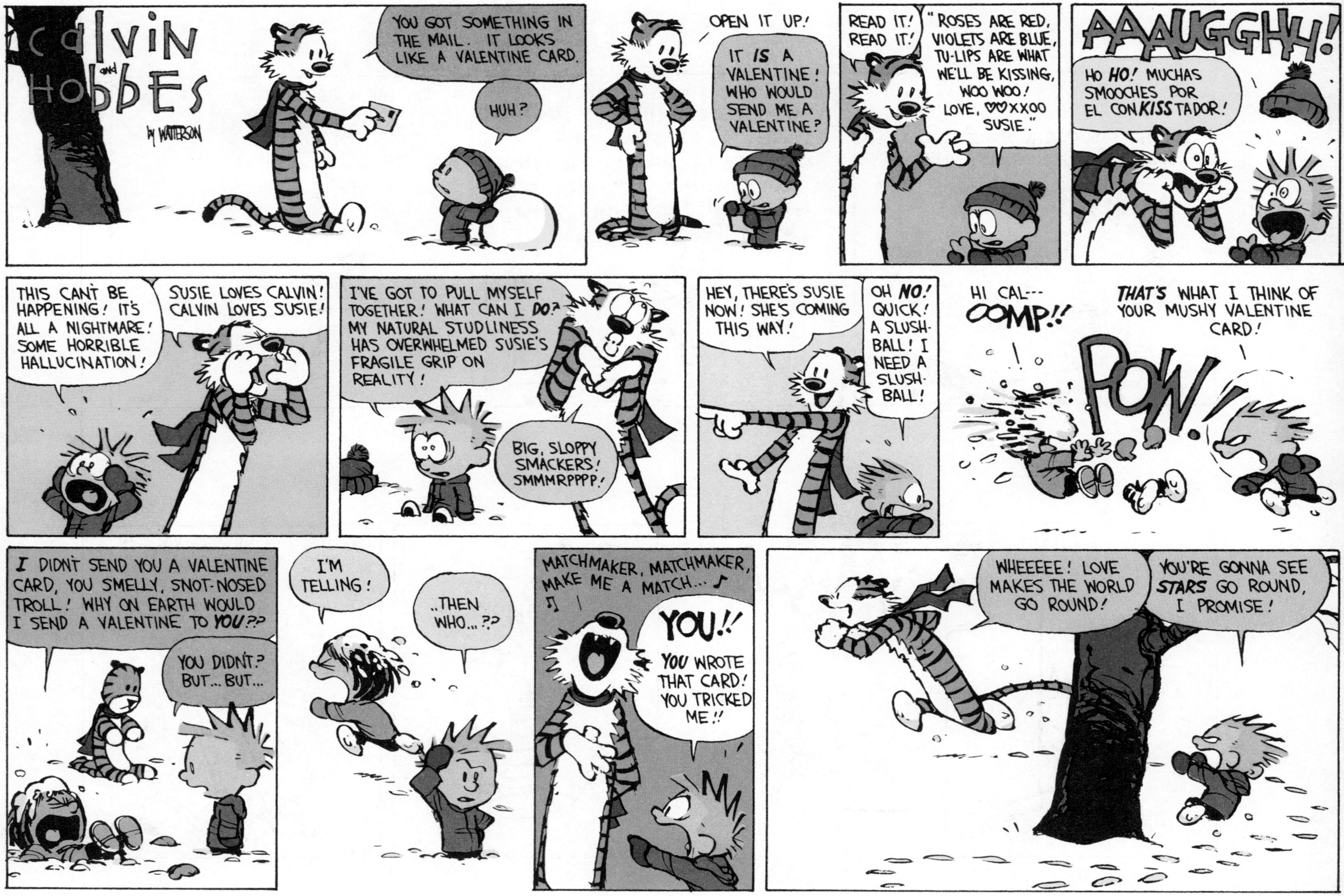
Calvin and Hobbes
by WATTERSON
YOU GOT SOMETHING IN THE MAIL. IT LOOKS LIKE A VALENTINE CARD.
HUH?
OPEN IT UP!
IT IS A VALENTINE! WHO WOULD SEND ME A VALENTINE?
READ IT! READ IT!
"ROSES ARE RED, VIOLETS ARE BLUE, TU-LIPS ARE WHAT WE'LL BE KISSING, WOO WOO! LOVE, ♡♡XXOO SUSIE."
AAAUGGHH!
HO HO! MUCHAS SMOOCHES POR EL CONKISSTADOR!
THIS CAN'T BE HAPPENING! IT'S ALL A NIGHTMARE! SOME HORRIBLE HALLUCINATION!
SUSIE LOVES CALVIN! CALVIN LOVES SUSIE!
I'VE GOT TO PULL MYSELF TOGETHER! WHAT CAN I DO? MY NATURAL STUDLINESS HAS OVERWHELMED SUSIE'S FRAGILE GRIP ON REALITY!
BIG, SLOPPY SMACKERS! SMMMRPPPP!
HEY, THERE'S SUSIE NOW! SHE'S COMING THIS WAY!
OH NO! QUICK! A SLUSH-BALL! I NEED A SLUSH-BALL!
HI CAL---
OOMP!!
POW!!
THAT'S WHAT I THINK OF YOUR MUSHY VALENTINE CARD!
I DIDN'T SEND YOU A VALENTINE CARD, YOU SMELLY, SNOT-NOSED TROLL! WHY ON EARTH WOULD I SEND A VALENTINE TO YOU??
YOU DIDN'T? BUT... BUT...
I'M TELLING!
..THEN WHO...??
MATCHMAKER, MATCHMAKER, MAKE ME A MATCH... ♪ ♫
YOU!!
YOU WROTE THAT CARD! YOU TRICKED ME!!
WHEEEEE! LOVE MAKES THE WORLD GO ROUND!
YOU'RE GONNA SEE STARS GO ROUND, I PROMISE!

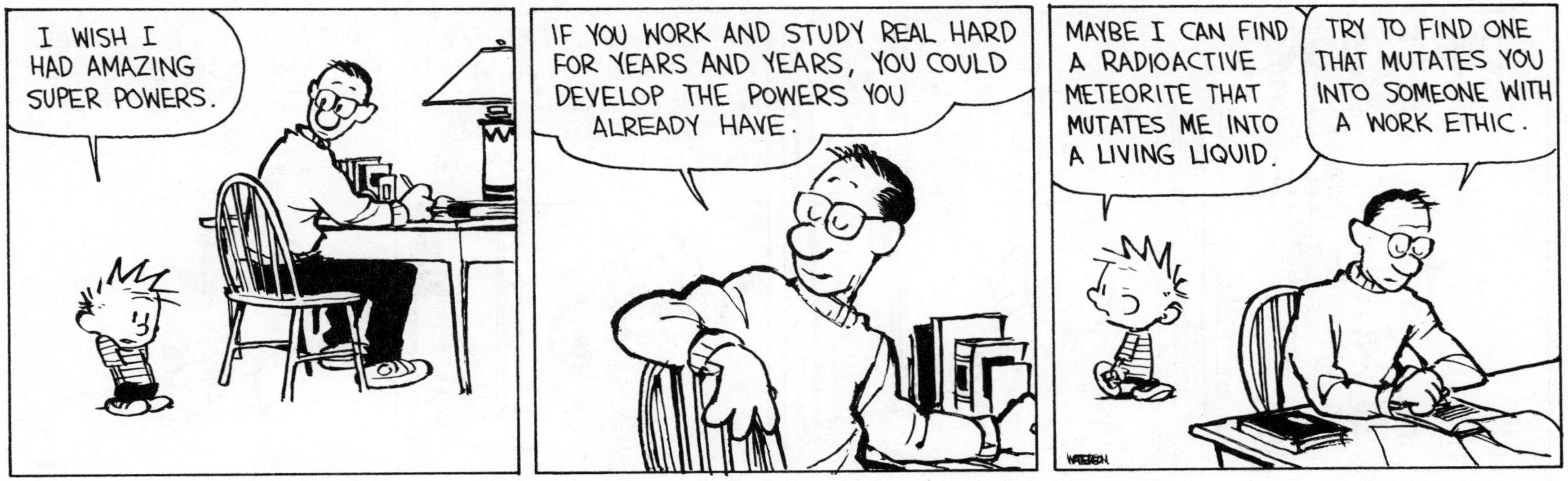
I WISH I HAD AMAZING SUPER POWERS.
IF YOU WORK AND STUDY REAL HARD FOR YEARS AND YEARS, YOU COULD DEVELOP THE POWERS YOU ALREADY HAVE.
MAYBE I CAN FIND A RADIOACTIVE METEORITE THAT MUTATES ME INTO A LIVING LIQUID.
TRY TO FIND ONE THAT MUTATES YOU INTO SOMEONE WITH A WORK ETHIC.
WATERSON

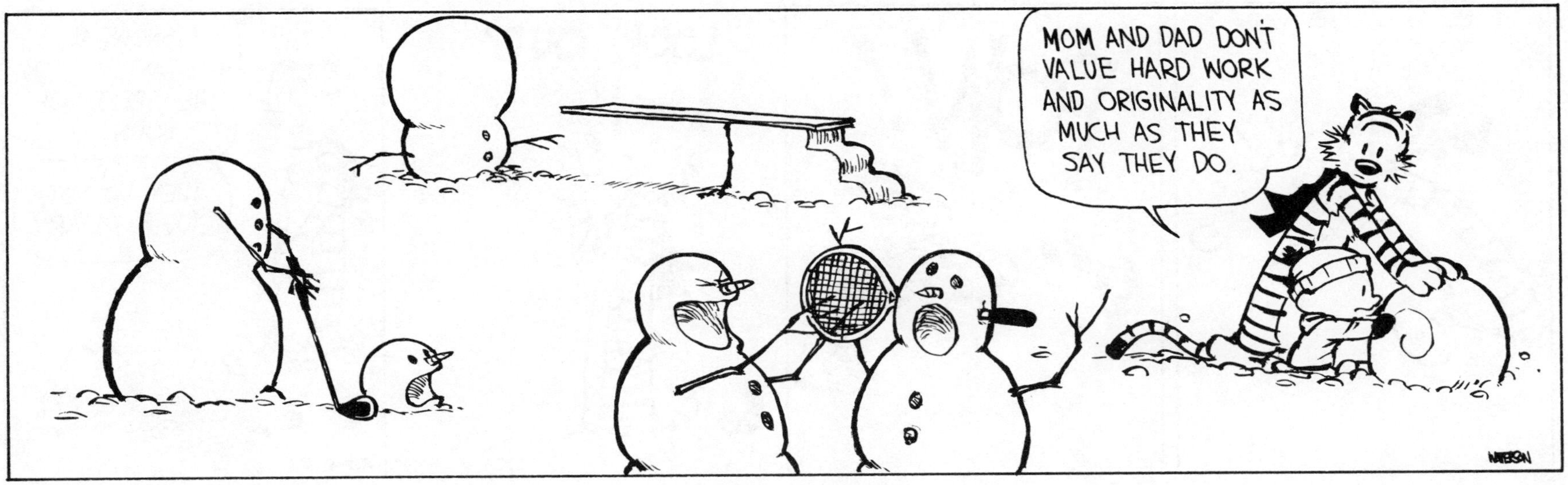
MOM AND DAD DON'T VALUE HARD WORK AND ORIGINALITY AS MUCH AS THEY SAY THEY DO.
WATERSON

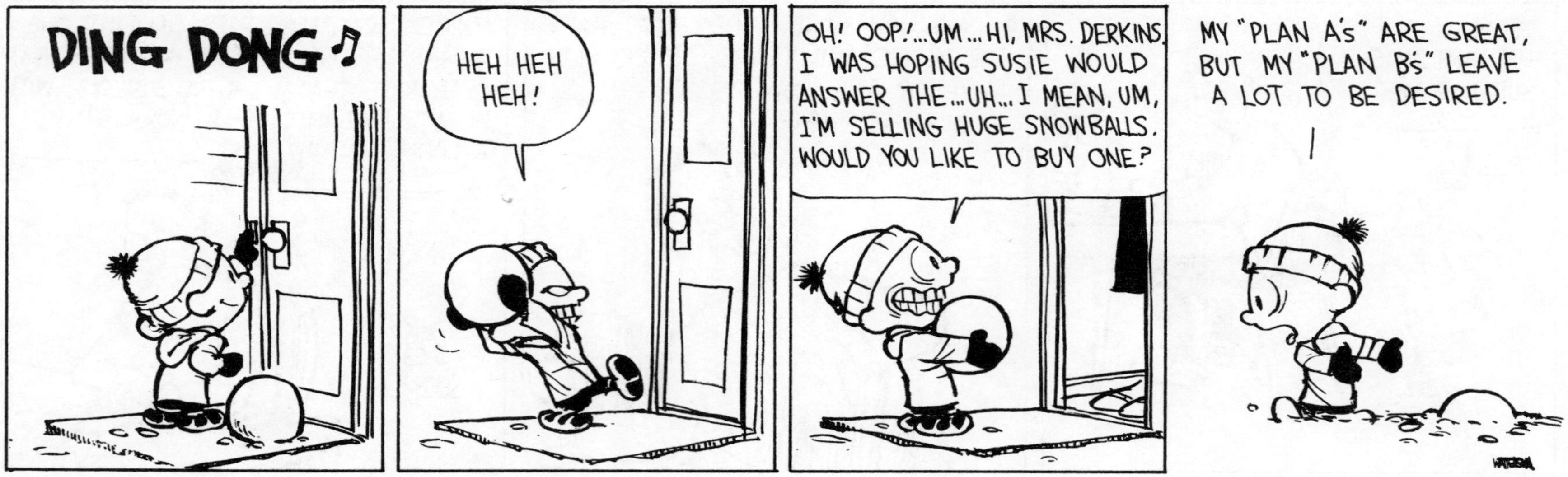
DING DONG ♫
HEH HEH HEH!
OH! OOP!...UM...HI, MRS. DERKINS. I WAS HOPING SUSIE WOULD ANSWER THE...UH...I MEAN, UM, I'M SELLING HUGE SNOWBALLS. WOULD YOU LIKE TO BUY ONE?
MY "PLAN A's" ARE GREAT, BUT MY "PLAN B's" LEAVE A LOT TO BE DESIRED.

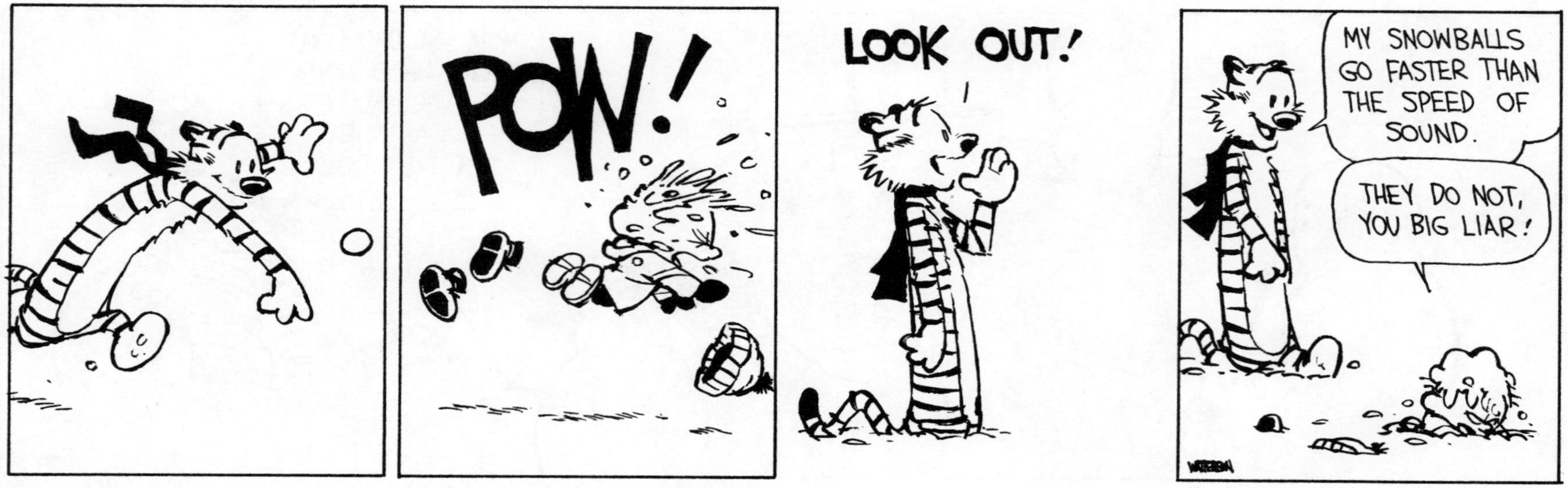
POW!
LOOK OUT!
MY SNOWBALLS GO FASTER THAN THE SPEED OF SOUND.
THEY DO NOT, YOU BIG LIAR!

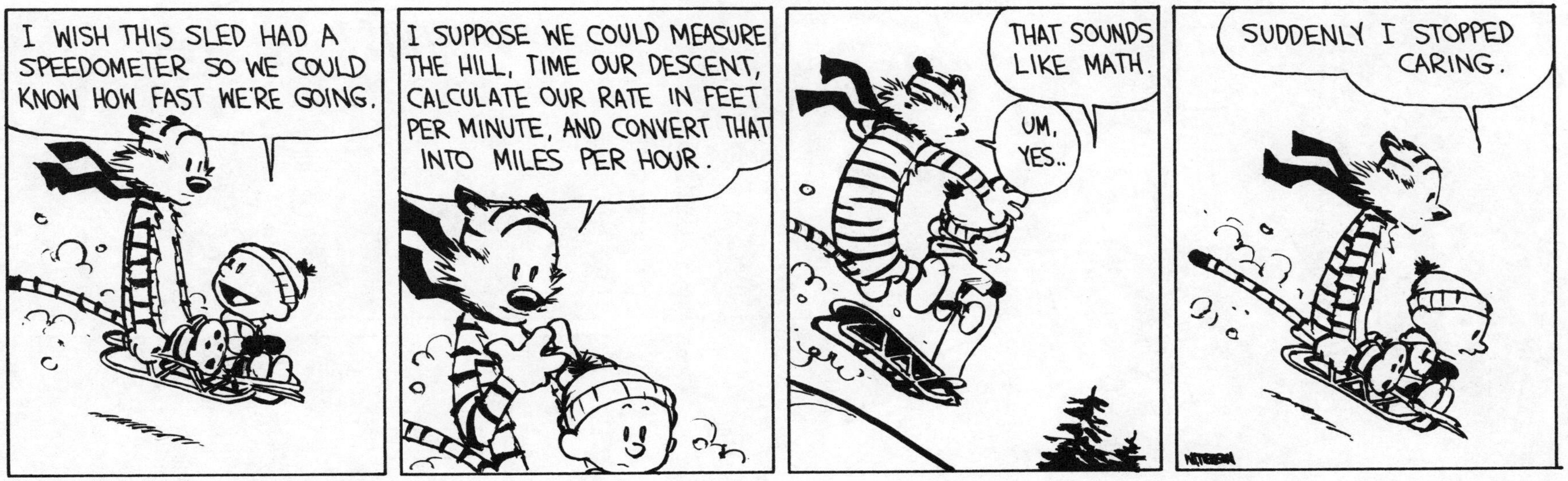
I WISH THIS SLED HAD A SPEEDOMETER SO WE COULD KNOW HOW FAST WE'RE GOING.
I SUPPOSE WE COULD MEASURE THE HILL, TIME OUR DESCENT, CALCULATE OUR RATE IN FEET PER MINUTE, AND CONVERT THAT INTO MILES PER HOUR.
THAT SOUNDS LIKE MATH.
UM, YES..
SUDDENLY I STOPPED CARING.

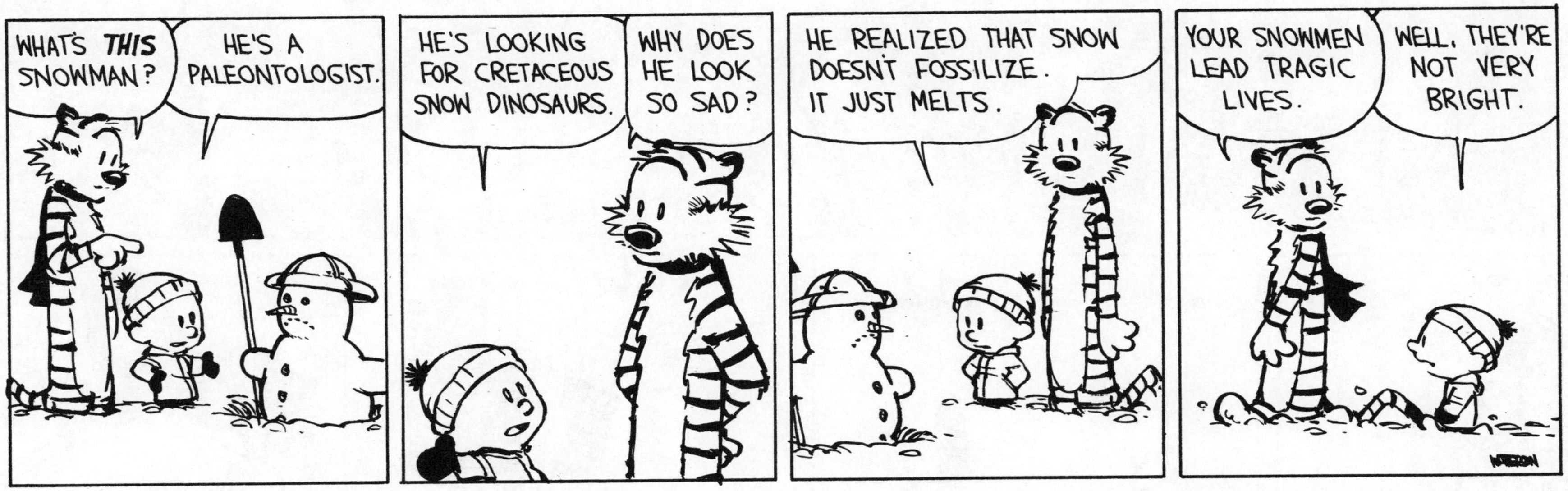
WHAT'S **THIS** SNOWMAN?
HE'S A PALEONTOLOGIST.
HE'S LOOKING FOR CRETACEOUS SNOW DINOSAURS.
WHY DOES HE LOOK SO SAD?
HE REALIZED THAT SNOW DOESN'T FOSSILIZE. IT JUST MELTS.
YOUR SNOWMEN LEAD TRAGIC LIVES.
WELL, THEY'RE NOT VERY BRIGHT.

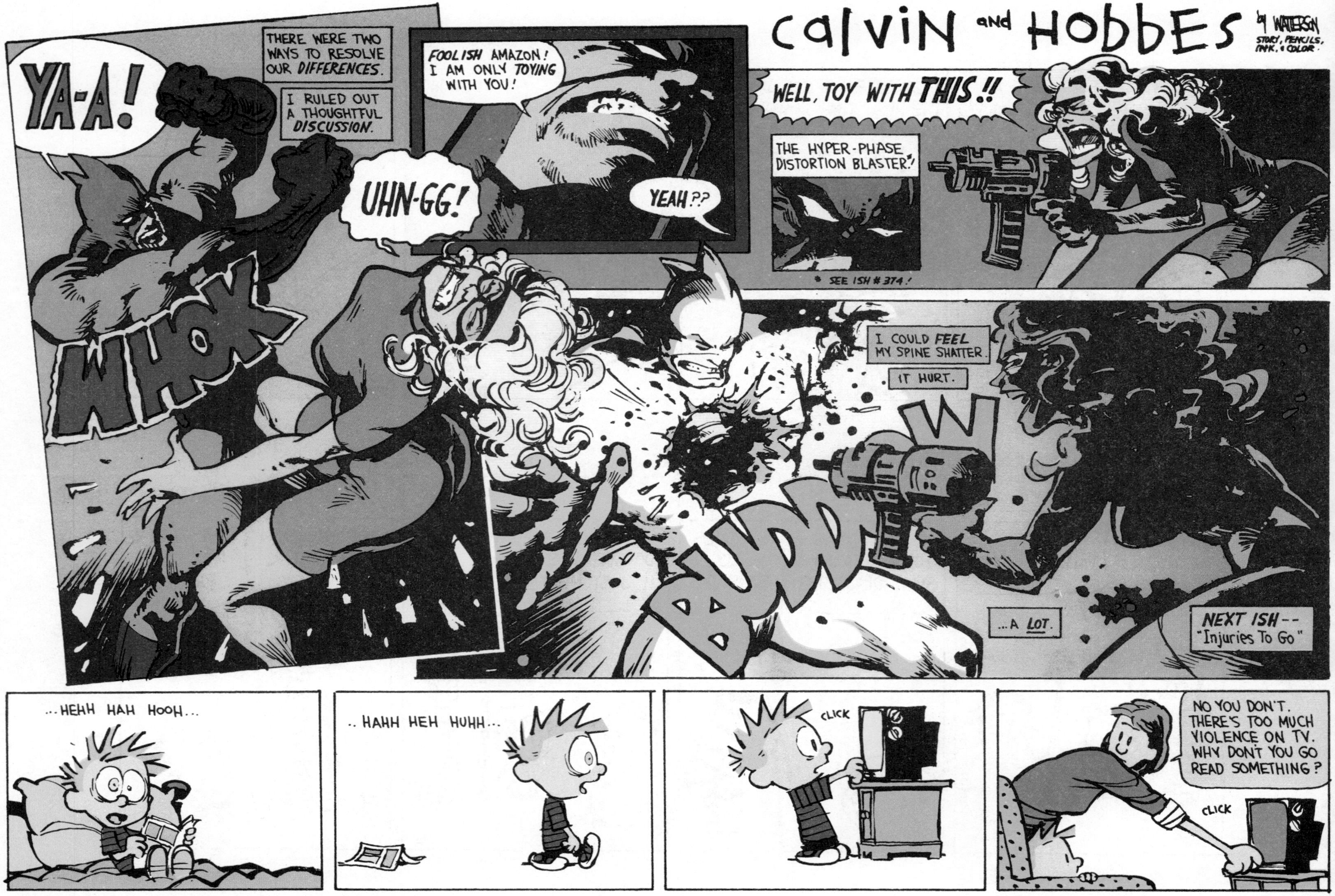
Calvin and HOBBES
by WATTERSON
STORY, PENCILS, INK, & COLOR
YA-A!
THERE WERE TWO WAYS TO RESOLVE OUR DIFFERENCES.
I RULED OUT A THOUGHTFUL DISCUSSION.
FOOLISH AMAZON! I AM ONLY TOYING WITH YOU!
UHN-GG!
YEAH??
WELL, TOY WITH THIS!!
THE HYPER-PHASE DISTORTION BLASTER*!
* SEE ISH # 374!
WHOK
I COULD FEEL MY SPINE SHATTER.
IT HURT.
BUDOOW
...A LOT.
NEXT ISH--
"Injuries To Go"
...HEHH HAH HOOH...
.. HAHH HEH HUHH...
CLICK
NO YOU DON'T. THERE'S TOO MUCH VIOLENCE ON TV. WHY DON'T YOU GO READ SOMETHING?
CLICK

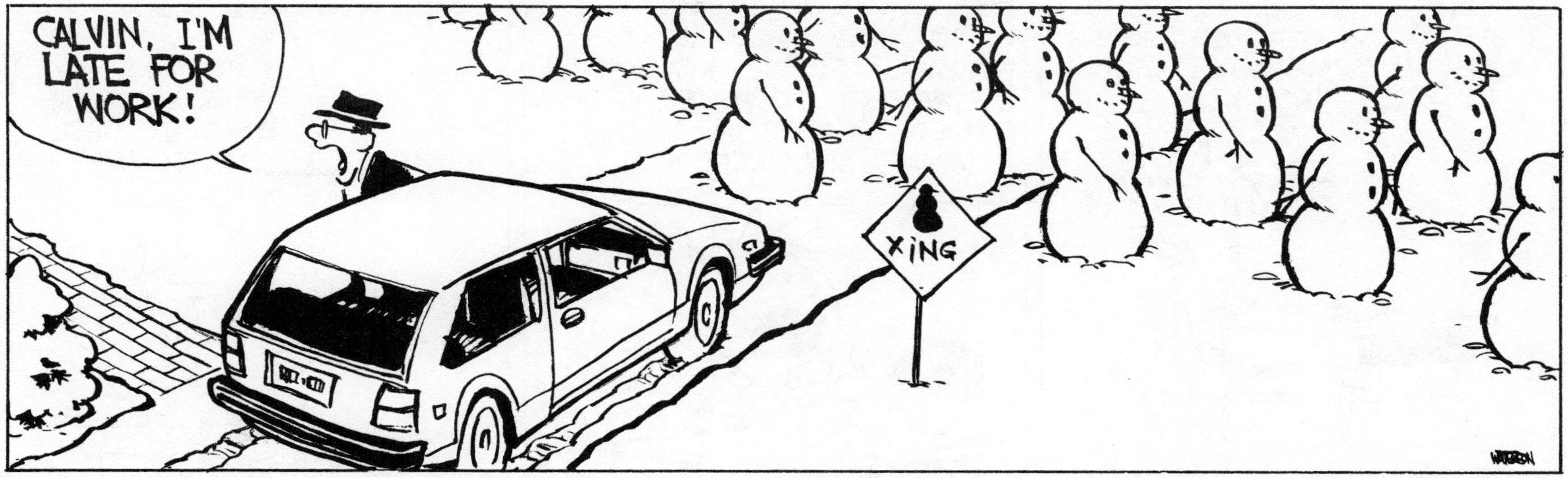
CALVIN, I'M LATE FOR WORK!
XING

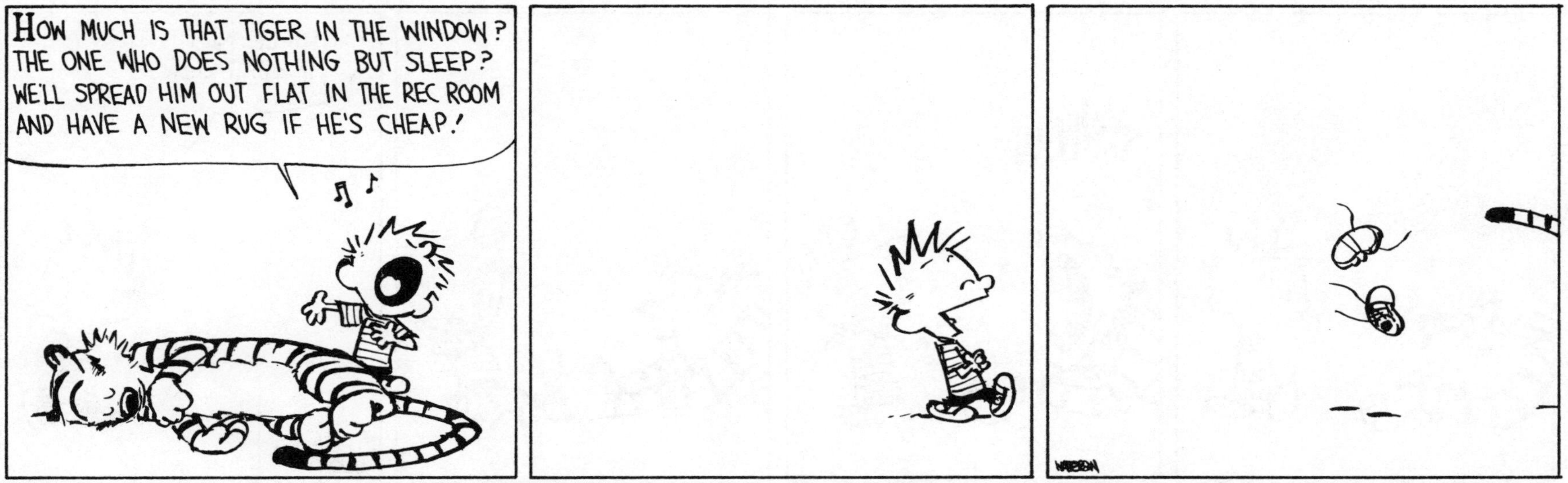
HOW MUCH IS THAT TIGER IN THE WINDOW? THE ONE WHO DOES NOTHING BUT SLEEP? WE'LL SPREAD HIM OUT FLAT IN THE REC ROOM AND HAVE A NEW RUG IF HE'S CHEAP!

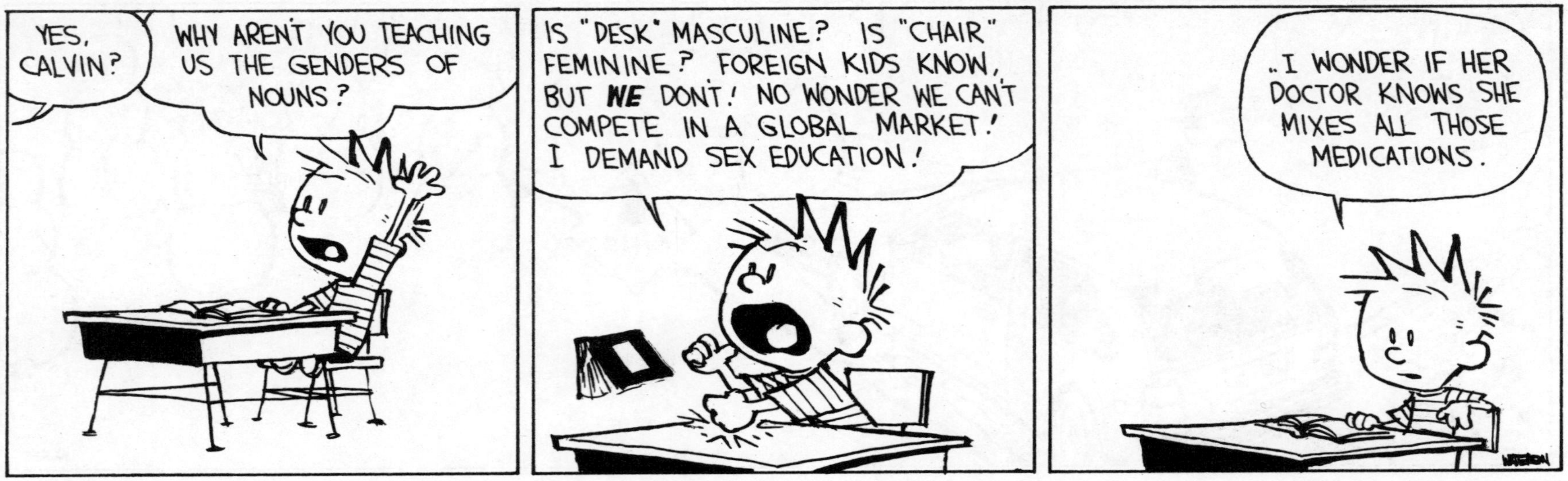
YES, CALVIN?
WHY AREN'T YOU TEACHING US THE GENDERS OF NOUNS?
IS "DESK" MASCULINE? IS "CHAIR" FEMININE? FOREIGN KIDS KNOW, BUT WE DON'T! NO WONDER WE CAN'T COMPETE IN A GLOBAL MARKET! I DEMAND SEX EDUCATION!
..I WONDER IF HER DOCTOR KNOWS SHE MIXES ALL THOSE MEDICATIONS.

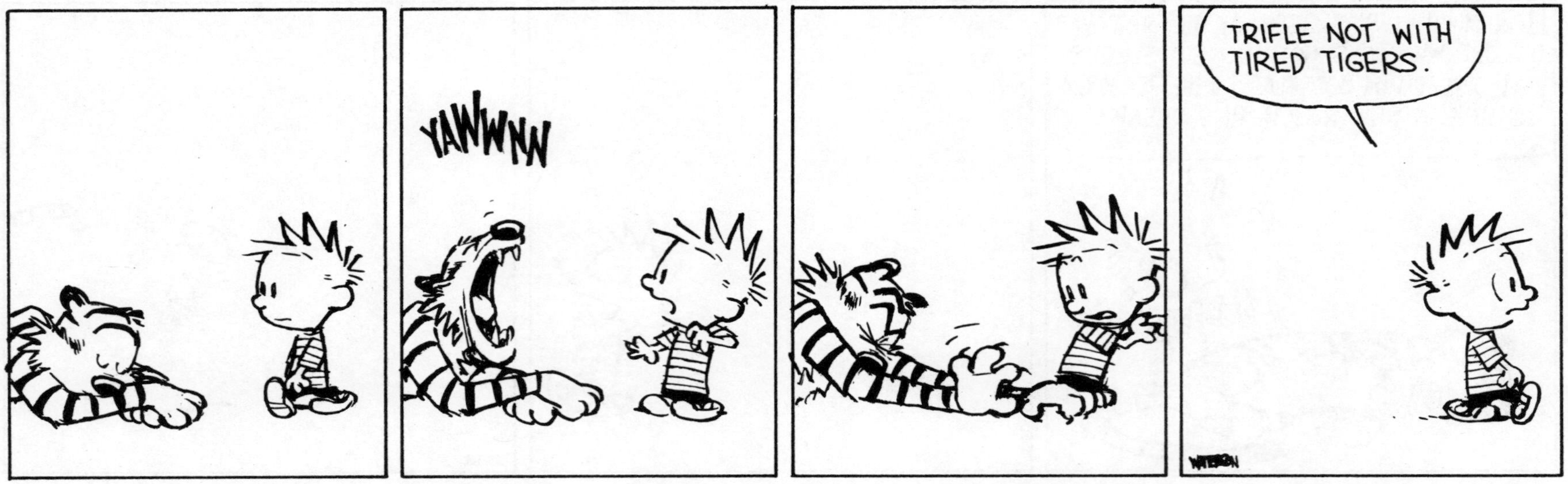
YAWWNN
TRIFLE NOT WITH TIRED TIGERS.

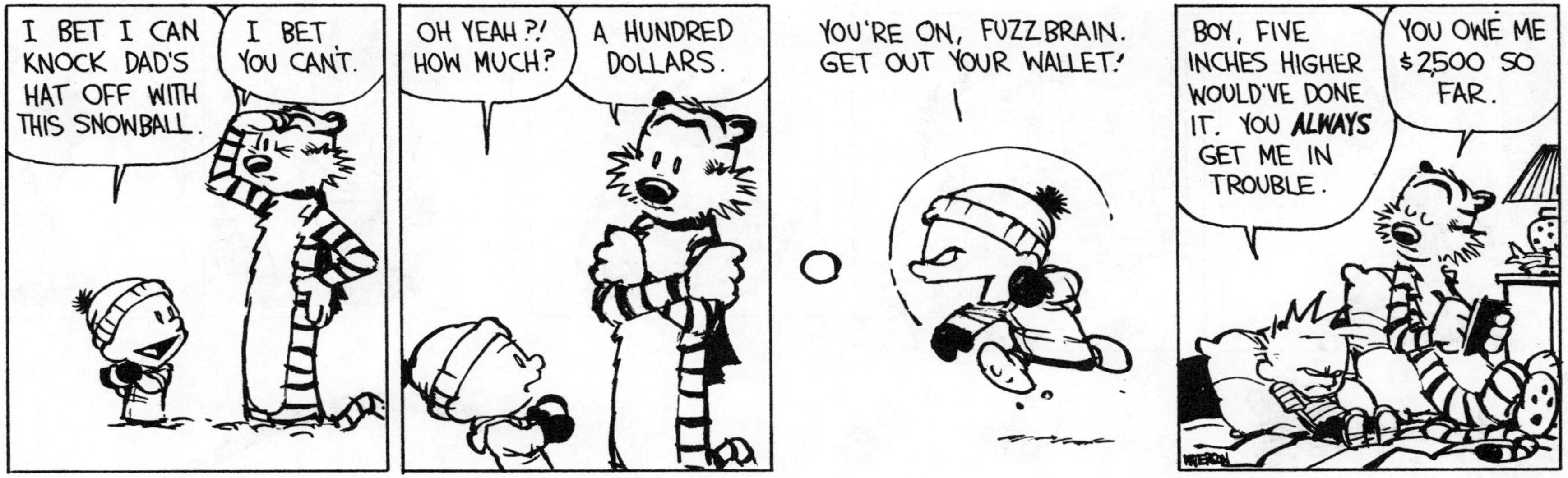
I BET I CAN KNOCK DAD'S HAT OFF WITH THIS SNOWBALL.
I BET YOU CAN'T.
OH YEAH ?! HOW MUCH?
A HUNDRED DOLLARS.
YOU'RE ON, FUZZBRAIN. GET OUT YOUR WALLET!
BOY, FIVE INCHES HIGHER WOULD'VE DONE IT. YOU **ALWAYS** GET ME IN TROUBLE.
YOU OWE ME $2,500 SO FAR.

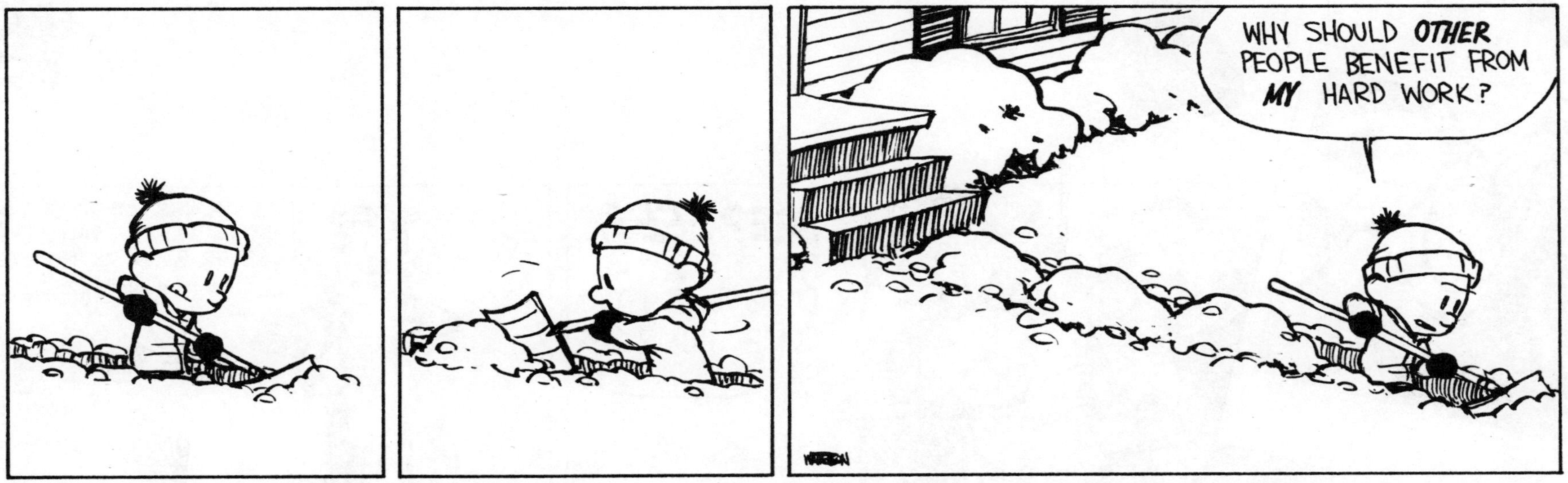
WHY SHOULD **OTHER** PEOPLE BENEFIT FROM **MY** HARD WORK?

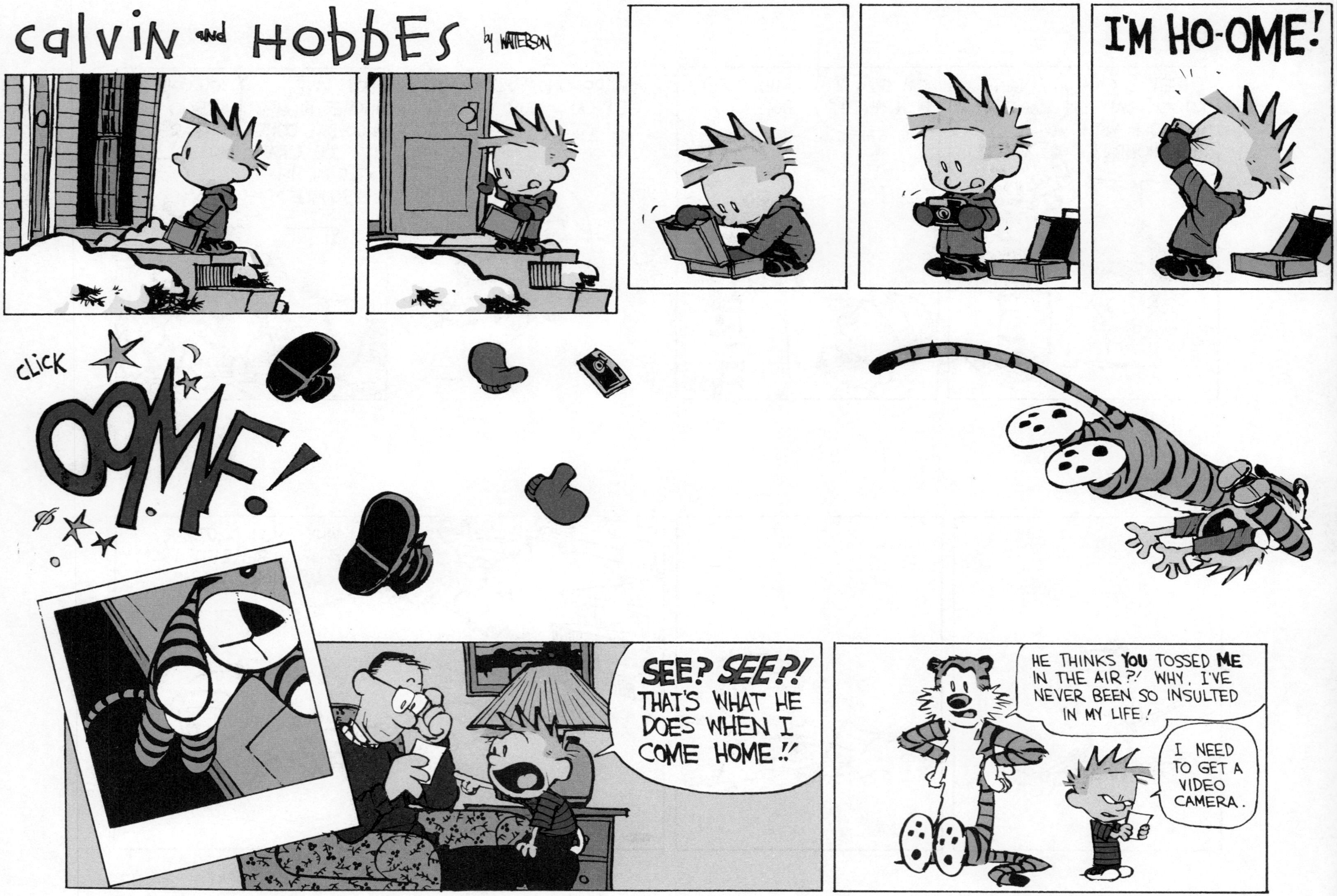
calvin and HOBBES by WATTERSON
I'M HO-OME!
CLICK
OOMF!
SEE? SEE?! THAT'S WHAT HE DOES WHEN I COME HOME!!
HE THINKS YOU TOSSED ME IN THE AIR?! WHY, I'VE NEVER BEEN SO INSULTED IN MY LIFE!
I NEED TO GET A VIDEO CAMERA.

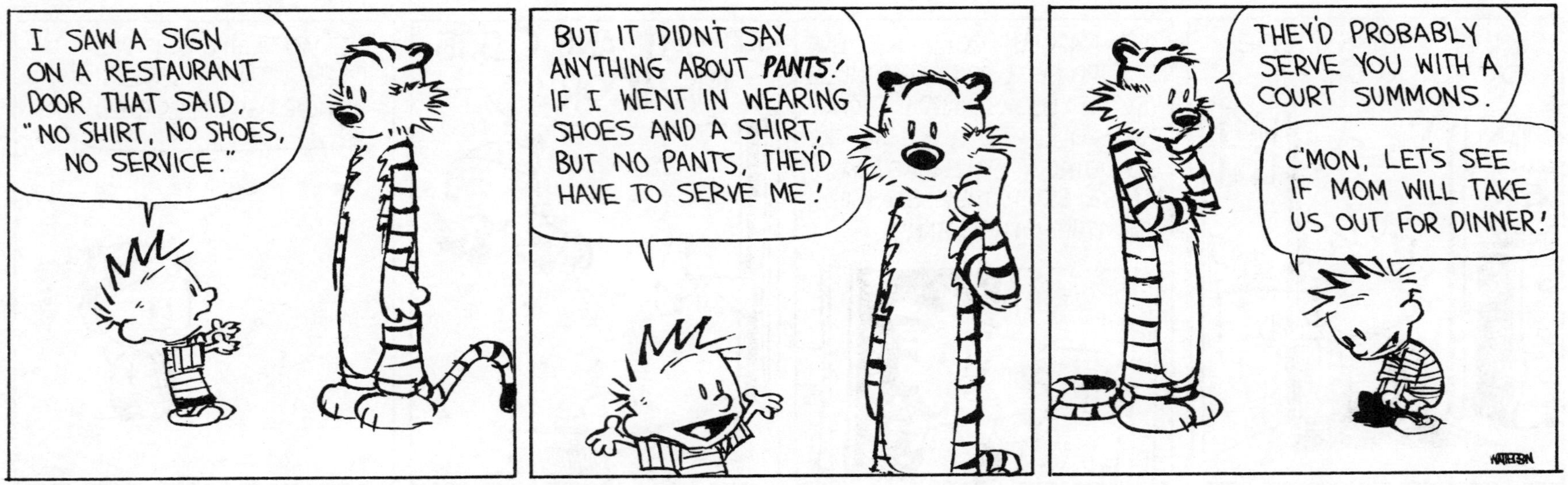
I SAW A SIGN ON A RESTAURANT DOOR THAT SAID, "NO SHIRT, NO SHOES, NO SERVICE."
BUT IT DIDN'T SAY ANYTHING ABOUT PANTS! IF I WENT IN WEARING SHOES AND A SHIRT, BUT NO PANTS, THEY'D HAVE TO SERVE ME!
THEY'D PROBABLY SERVE YOU WITH A COURT SUMMONS.
C'MON, LET'S SEE IF MOM WILL TAKE US OUT FOR DINNER!
WATTERSON

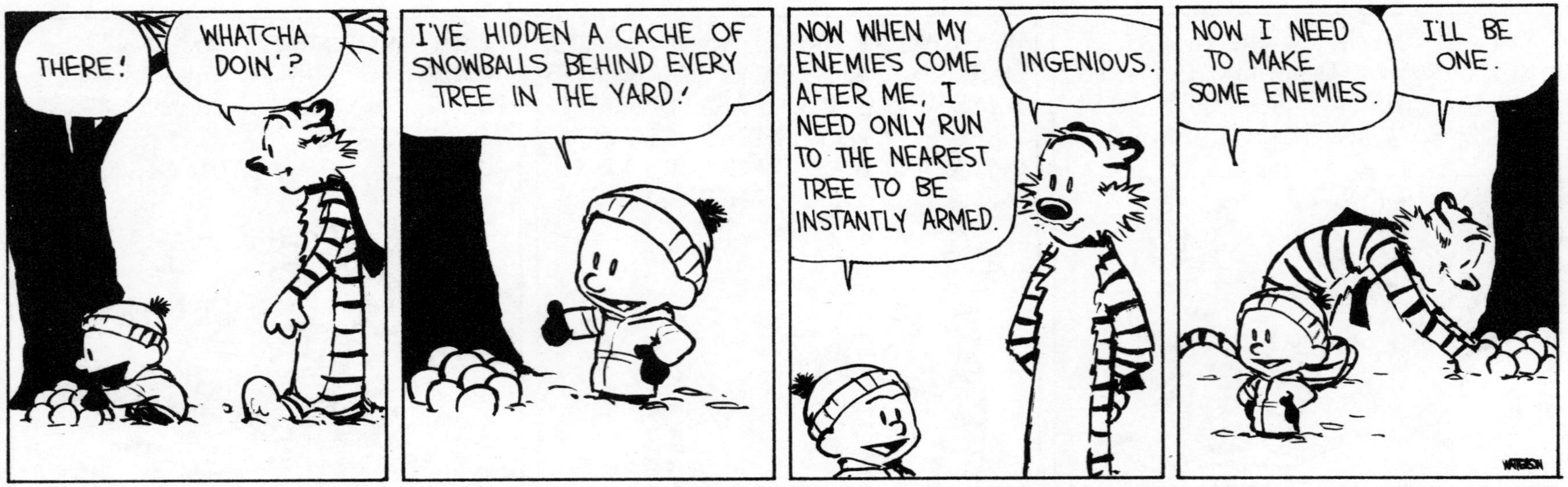
THERE!
WHATCHA DOIN'?
I'VE HIDDEN A CACHE OF SNOWBALLS BEHIND EVERY TREE IN THE YARD!
NOW WHEN MY ENEMIES COME AFTER ME, I NEED ONLY RUN TO THE NEAREST TREE TO BE INSTANTLY ARMED.
INGENIOUS.
NOW I NEED TO MAKE SOME ENEMIES.
I'LL BE ONE.
WATTERSON

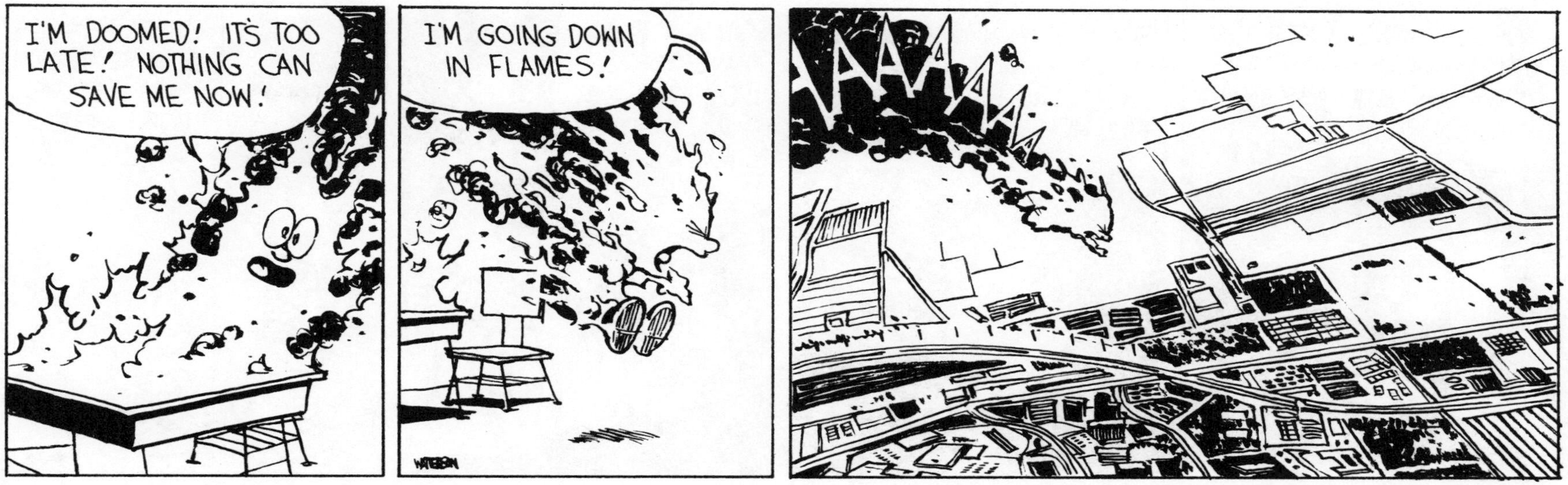
I'M DOOMED! IT'S TOO LATE! NOTHING CAN SAVE ME NOW!
I'M GOING DOWN IN FLAMES!

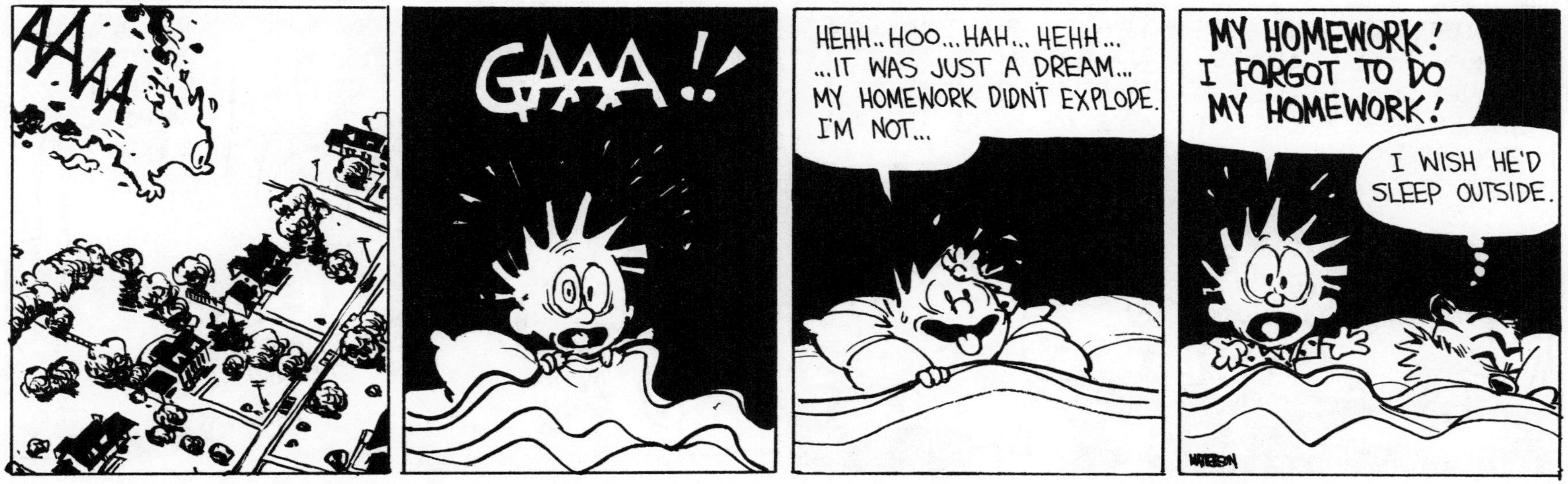
GAAA!!
HEHH.. HOO... HAH... HEHH... ...IT WAS JUST A DREAM... MY HOMEWORK DIDN'T EXPLODE. I'M NOT...
MY HOMEWORK! I FORGOT TO DO MY HOMEWORK!
I WISH HE'D SLEEP OUTSIDE.

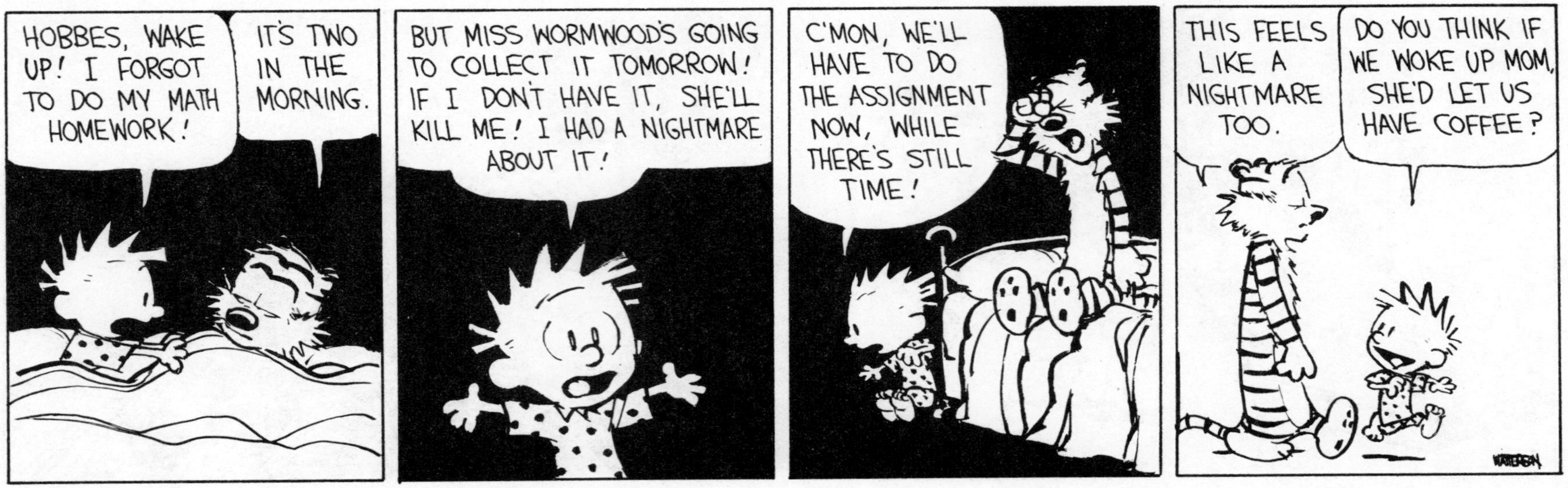
HOBBES, WAKE UP! I FORGOT TO DO MY MATH HOMEWORK!
IT'S TWO IN THE MORNING.
BUT MISS WORMWOOD'S GOING TO COLLECT IT TOMORROW! IF I DON'T HAVE IT, SHE'LL KILL ME! I HAD A NIGHTMARE ABOUT IT!
C'MON, WE'LL HAVE TO DO THE ASSIGNMENT NOW, WHILE THERE'S STILL TIME!
THIS FEELS LIKE A NIGHTMARE TOO.
DO YOU THINK IF WE WOKE UP MOM, SHE'D LET US HAVE COFFEE?

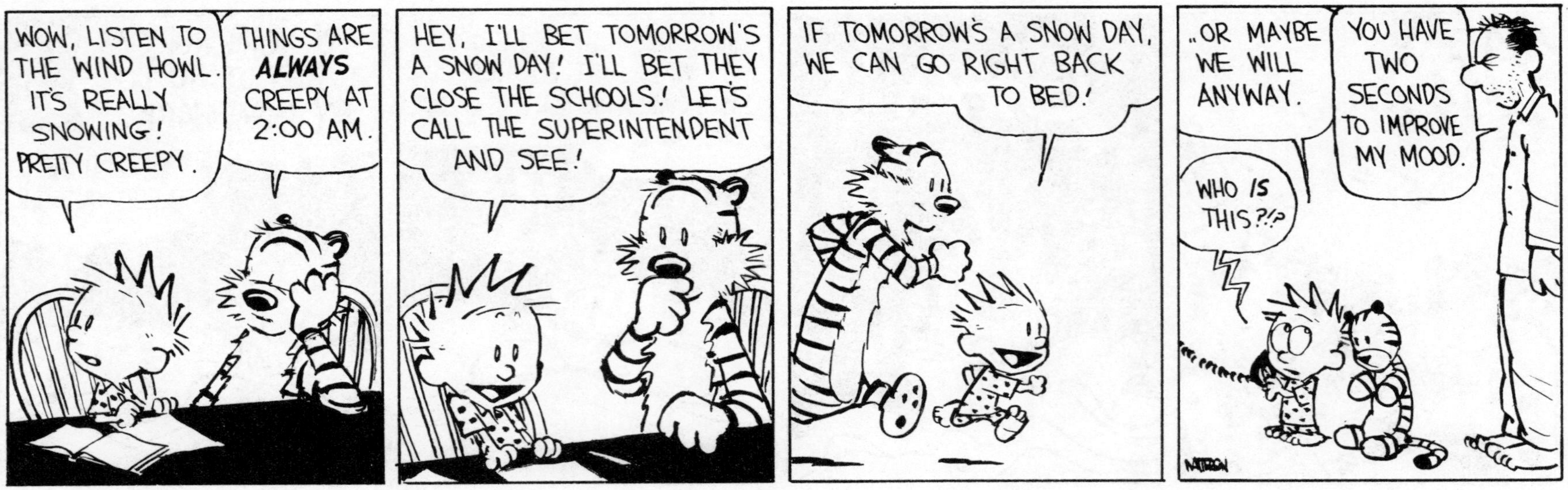
WOW, LISTEN TO THE WIND HOWL. IT'S REALLY SNOWING! PRETTY CREEPY.
THINGS ARE **ALWAYS** CREEPY AT 2:00 AM.
HEY, I'LL BET TOMORROW'S A SNOW DAY! I'LL BET THEY CLOSE THE SCHOOLS! LET'S CALL THE SUPERINTENDENT AND SEE!
IF TOMORROW'S A SNOW DAY, WE CAN GO RIGHT BACK TO BED!
..OR MAYBE WE WILL ANYWAY.
YOU HAVE TWO SECONDS TO IMPROVE MY MOOD.
WHO **IS** THIS?!?

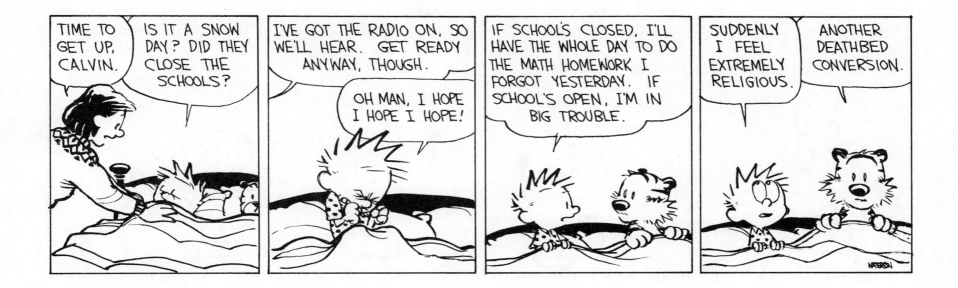

117

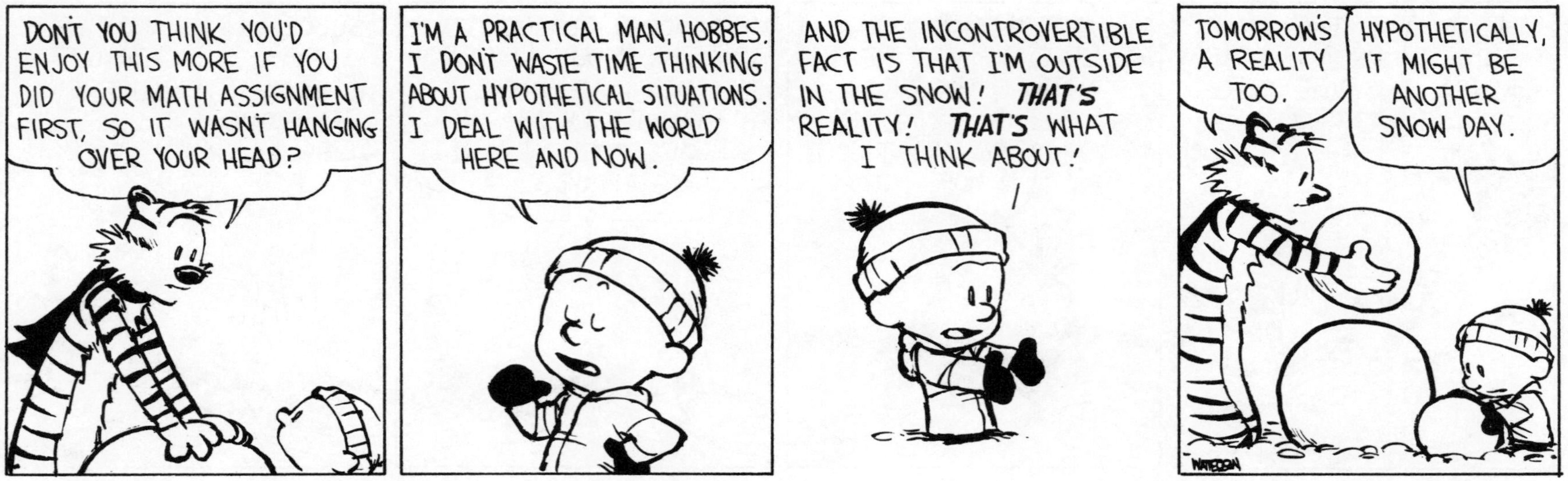
DON'T YOU THINK YOU'D ENJOY THIS MORE IF YOU DID YOUR MATH ASSIGNMENT FIRST, SO IT WASN'T HANGING OVER YOUR HEAD?
I'M A PRACTICAL MAN, HOBBES. I DON'T WASTE TIME THINKING ABOUT HYPOTHETICAL SITUATIONS. I DEAL WITH THE WORLD HERE AND NOW.
AND THE INCONTROVERTIBLE FACT IS THAT I'M OUTSIDE IN THE SNOW! THAT'S REALITY! THAT'S WHAT I THINK ABOUT!
TOMORROW'S A REALITY TOO.
HYPOTHETICALLY, IT MIGHT BE ANOTHER SNOW DAY.

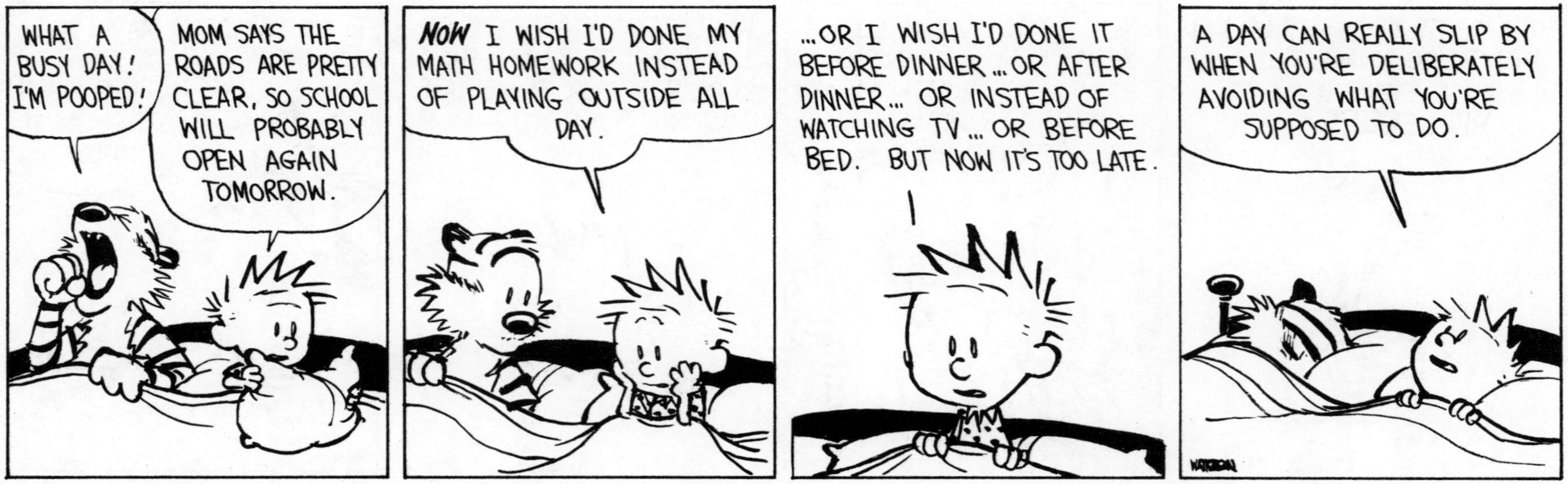
WHAT A BUSY DAY! I'M POOPED!
MOM SAYS THE ROADS ARE PRETTY CLEAR, SO SCHOOL WILL PROBABLY OPEN AGAIN TOMORROW.
NOW I WISH I'D DONE MY MATH HOMEWORK INSTEAD OF PLAYING OUTSIDE ALL DAY.
...OR I WISH I'D DONE IT BEFORE DINNER... OR AFTER DINNER... OR INSTEAD OF WATCHING TV... OR BEFORE BED. BUT NOW IT'S TOO LATE.
A DAY CAN REALLY SLIP BY WHEN YOU'RE DELIBERATELY AVOIDING WHAT YOU'RE SUPPOSED TO DO.

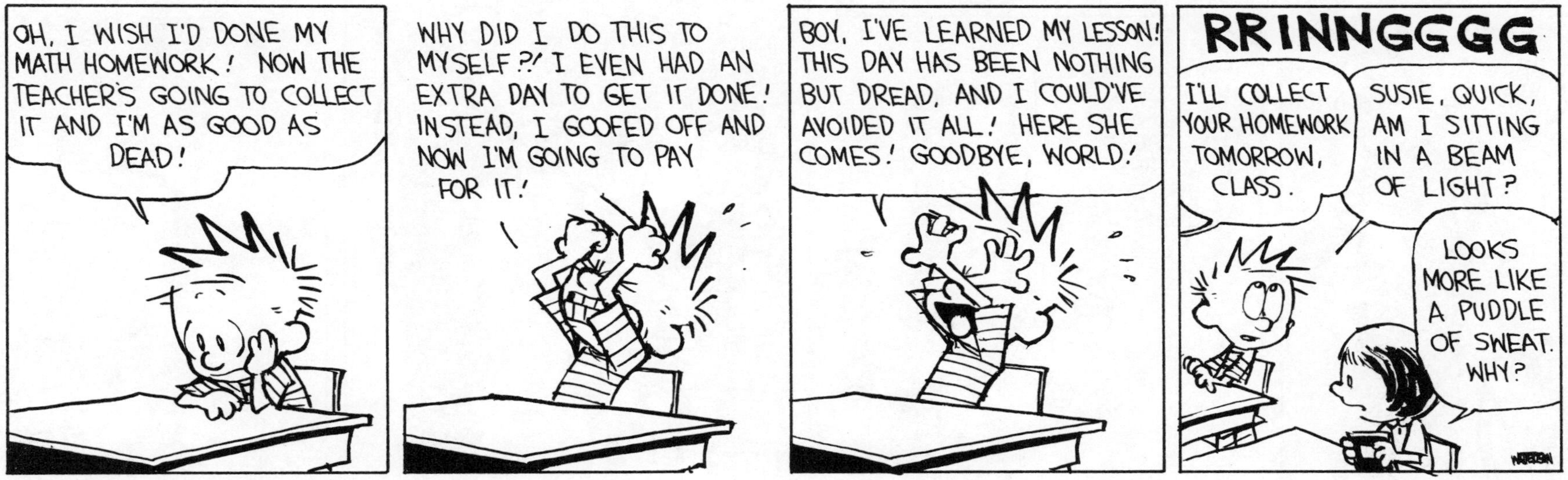
OH, I WISH I'D DONE MY MATH HOMEWORK! NOW THE TEACHER'S GOING TO COLLECT IT AND I'M AS GOOD AS DEAD!
WHY DID I DO THIS TO MYSELF?! I EVEN HAD AN EXTRA DAY TO GET IT DONE! INSTEAD, I GOOFED OFF AND NOW I'M GOING TO PAY FOR IT!
BOY, I'VE LEARNED MY LESSON! THIS DAY HAS BEEN NOTHING BUT DREAD, AND I COULD'VE AVOIDED IT ALL! HERE SHE COMES! GOODBYE, WORLD!
RRINNGGGG
I'LL COLLECT YOUR HOMEWORK TOMORROW, CLASS.
SUSIE, QUICK, AM I SITTING IN A BEAM OF LIGHT?
LOOKS MORE LIKE A PUDDLE OF SWEAT. WHY?

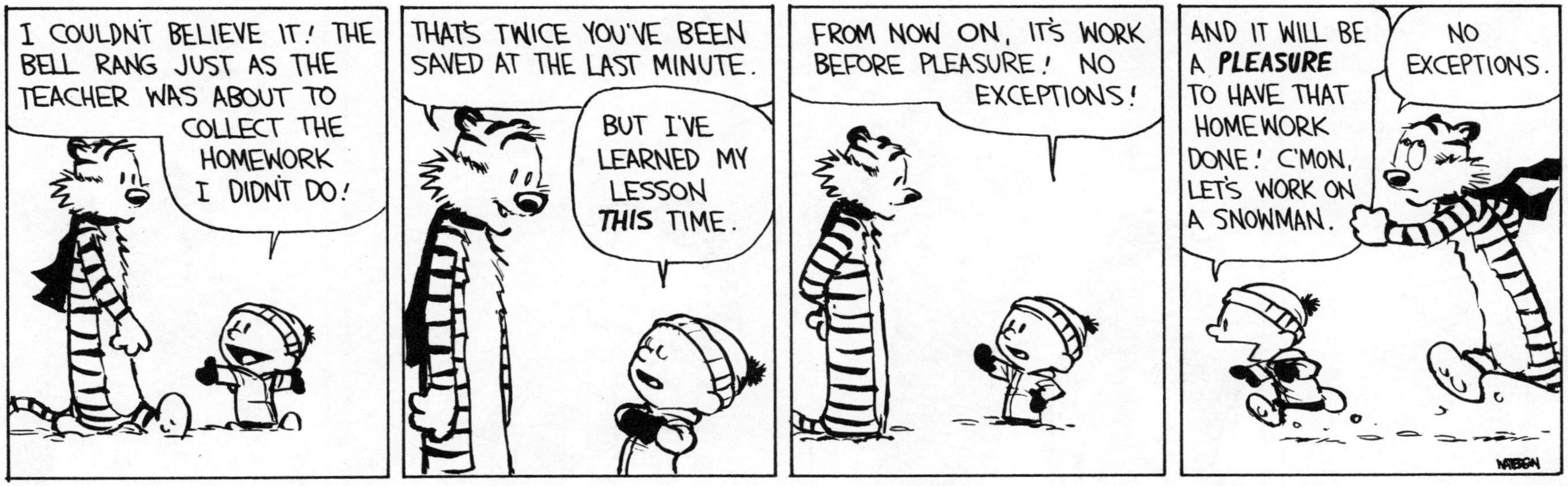
I COULDN'T BELIEVE IT! THE BELL RANG JUST AS THE TEACHER WAS ABOUT TO COLLECT THE HOMEWORK I DIDN'T DO!
THAT'S TWICE YOU'VE BEEN SAVED AT THE LAST MINUTE.
BUT I'VE LEARNED MY LESSON THIS TIME.
FROM NOW ON, IT'S WORK BEFORE PLEASURE! NO EXCEPTIONS!
AND IT WILL BE A PLEASURE TO HAVE THAT HOMEWORK DONE! C'MON, LET'S WORK ON A SNOWMAN.
NO EXCEPTIONS.

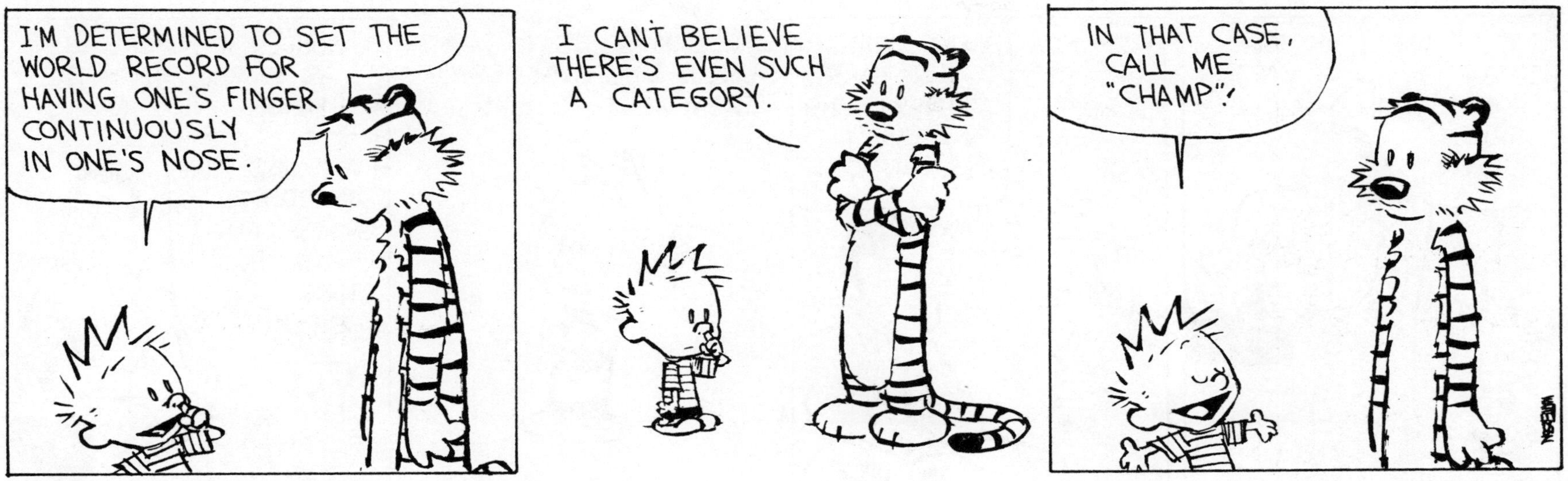
I'M DETERMINED TO SET THE WORLD RECORD FOR HAVING ONE'S FINGER CONTINUOUSLY IN ONE'S NOSE.
I CAN'T BELIEVE THERE'S EVEN SUCH A CATEGORY.
IN THAT CASE, CALL ME "CHAMP"!

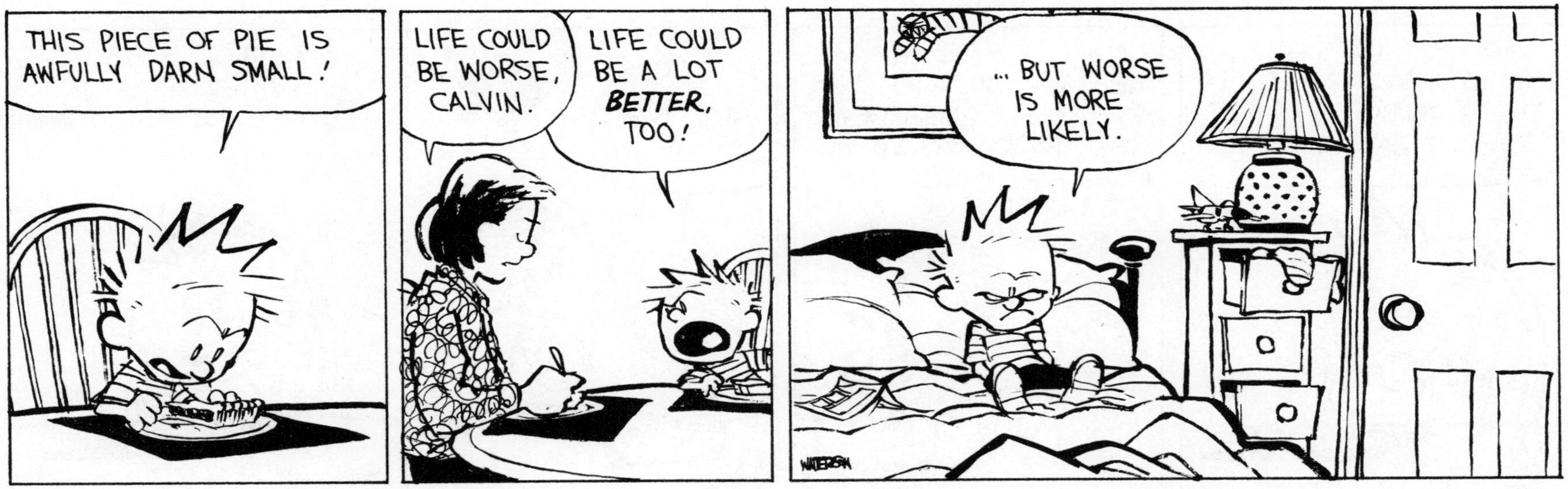
THIS PIECE OF PIE IS AWFULLY DARN SMALL!
LIFE COULD BE WORSE, CALVIN.
LIFE COULD BE A LOT **BETTER**, TOO!
...BUT WORSE IS MORE LIKELY.

122

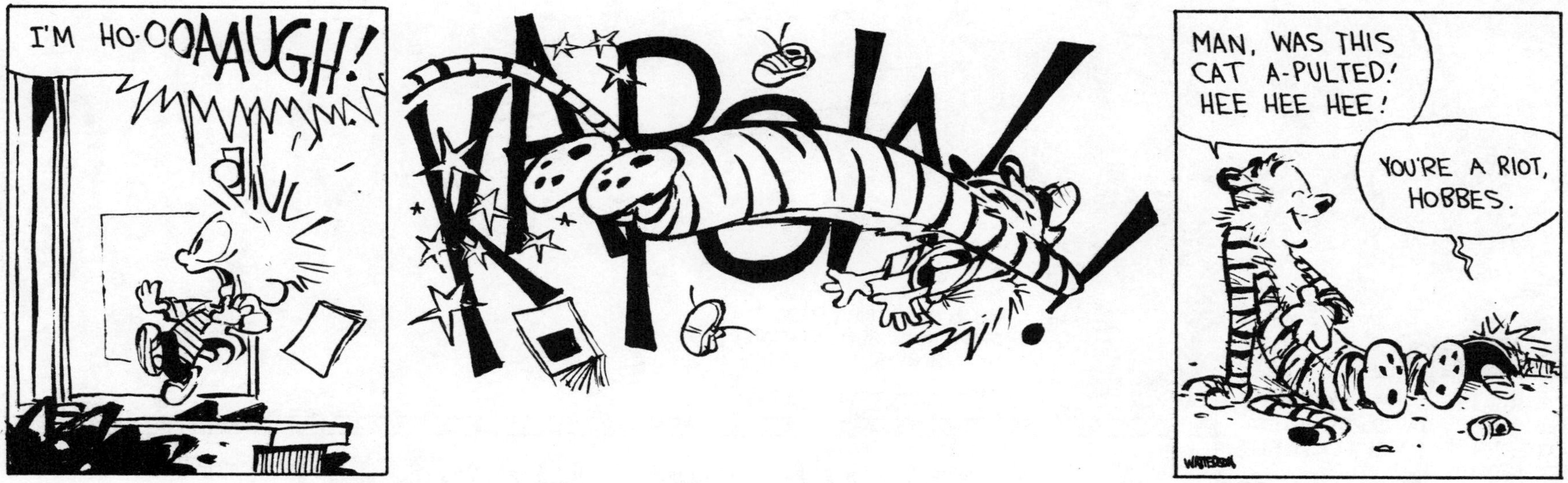
I'M HO-OOAAUGH!
KAPOW!
MAN, WAS THIS CAT A-PULTED! HEE HEE HEE!
YOU'RE A RIOT, HOBBES.

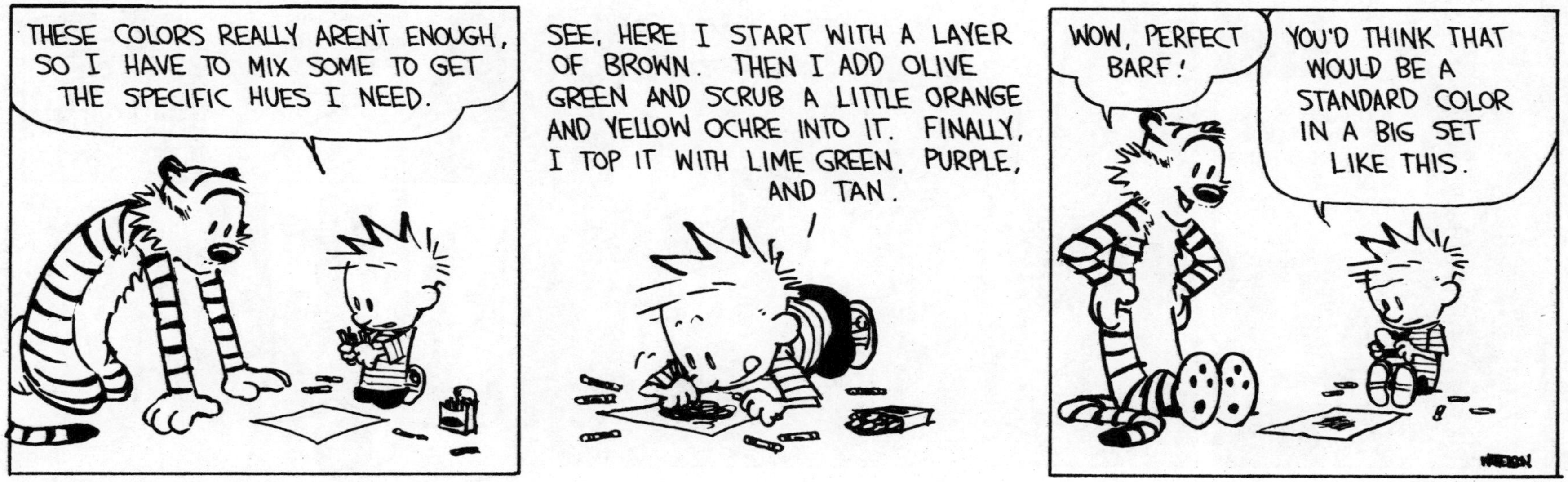
THESE COLORS REALLY AREN'T ENOUGH, SO I HAVE TO MIX SOME TO GET THE SPECIFIC HUES I NEED.
SEE, HERE I START WITH A LAYER OF BROWN. THEN I ADD OLIVE GREEN AND SCRUB A LITTLE ORANGE AND YELLOW OCHRE INTO IT. FINALLY, I TOP IT WITH LIME GREEN, PURPLE, AND TAN.
WOW, PERFECT BARF!
YOU'D THINK THAT WOULD BE A STANDARD COLOR IN A BIG SET LIKE THIS.

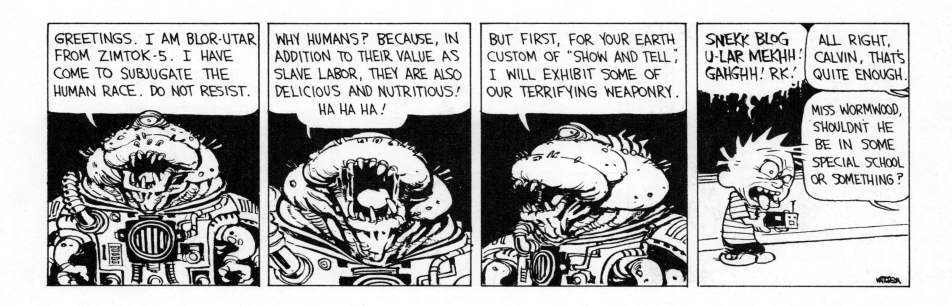

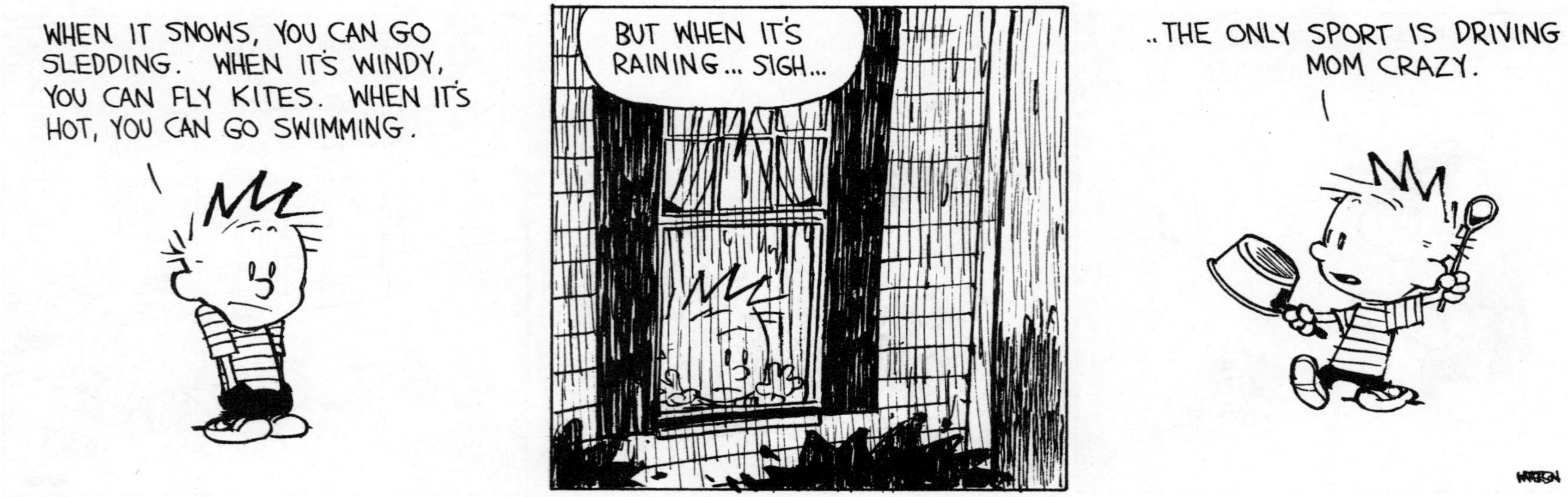
WHEN IT SNOWS, YOU CAN GO SLEDDING. WHEN IT'S WINDY, YOU CAN FLY KITES. WHEN IT'S HOT, YOU CAN GO SWIMMING.
BUT WHEN IT'S RAINING... SIGH...
..THE ONLY SPORT IS DRIVING MOM CRAZY.

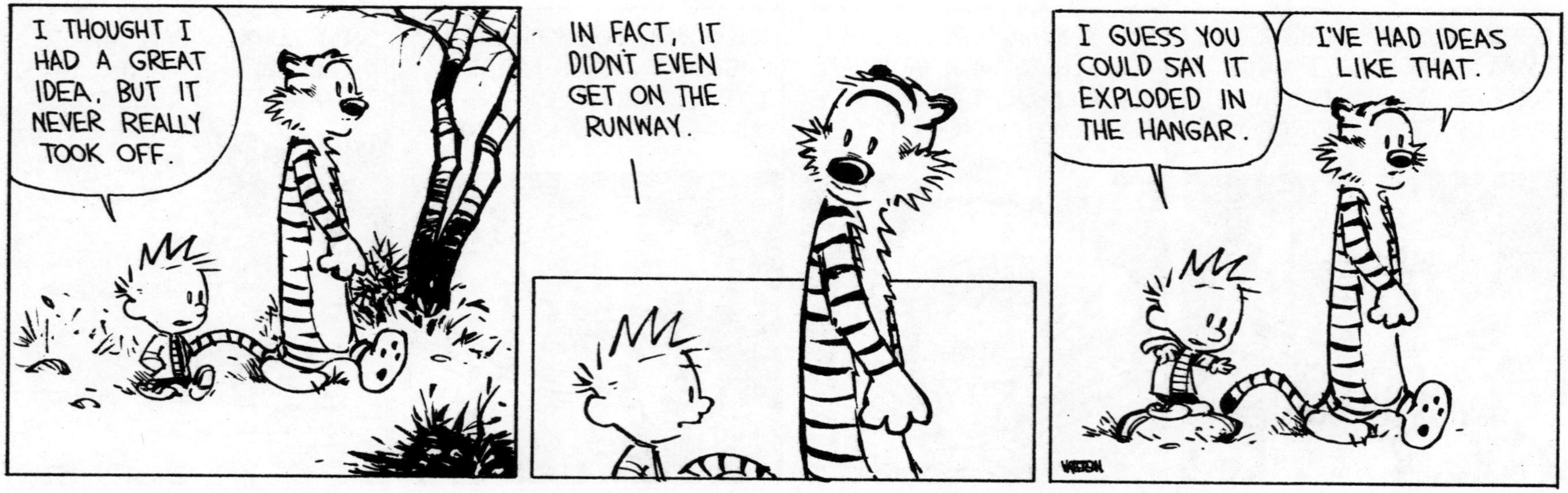
I THOUGHT I HAD A GREAT IDEA, BUT IT NEVER REALLY TOOK OFF.
IN FACT, IT DIDN'T EVEN GET ON THE RUNWAY.
I GUESS YOU COULD SAY IT EXPLODED IN THE HANGAR.
I'VE HAD IDEAS LIKE THAT.

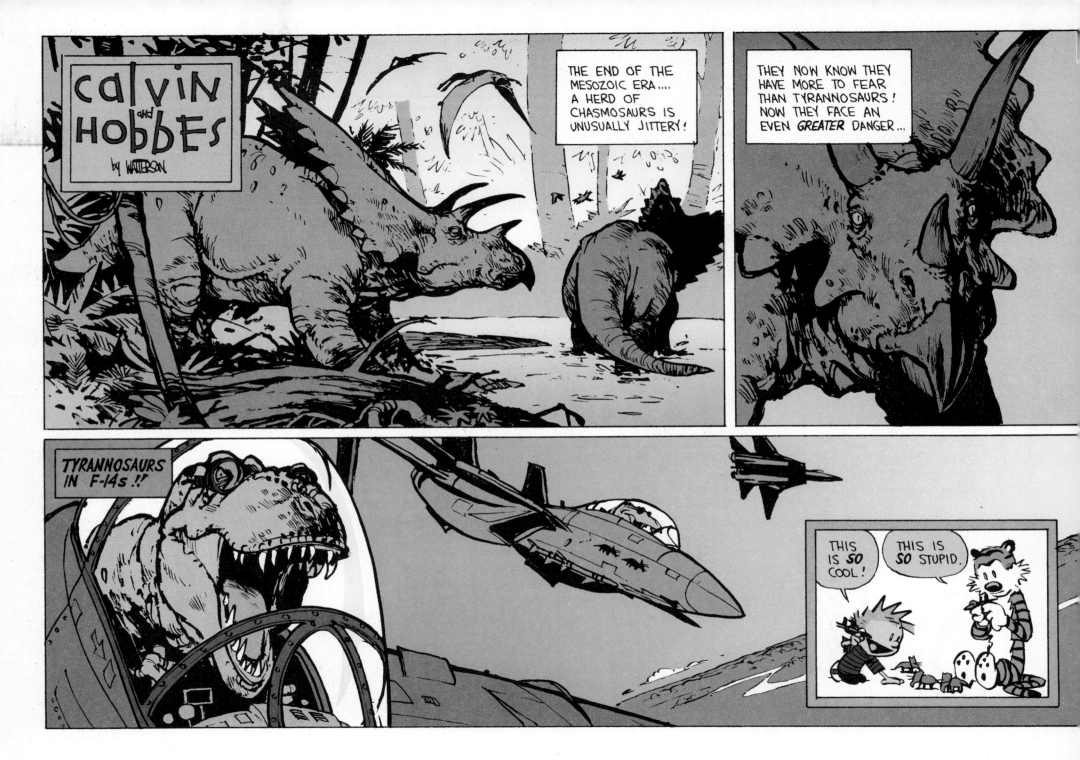

128

130

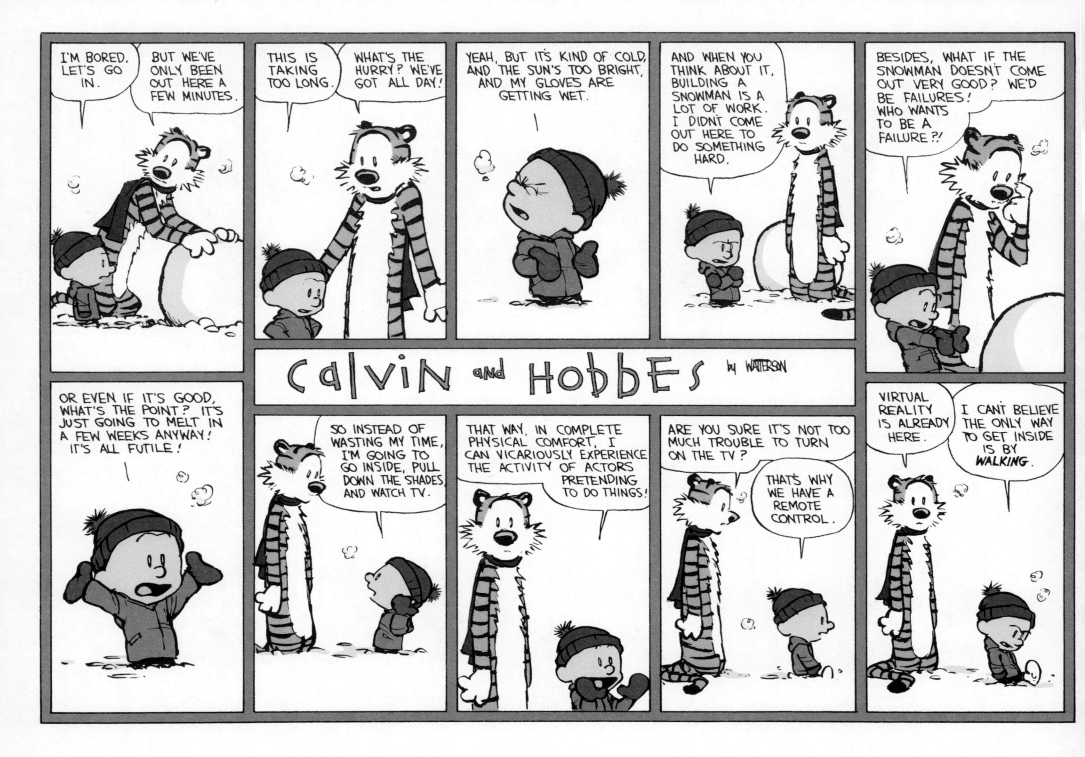

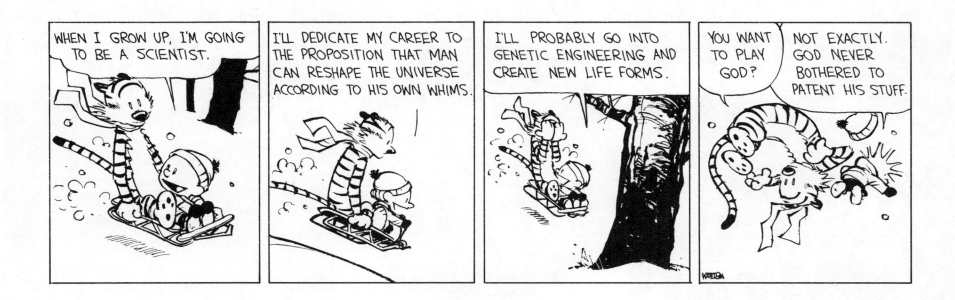

135

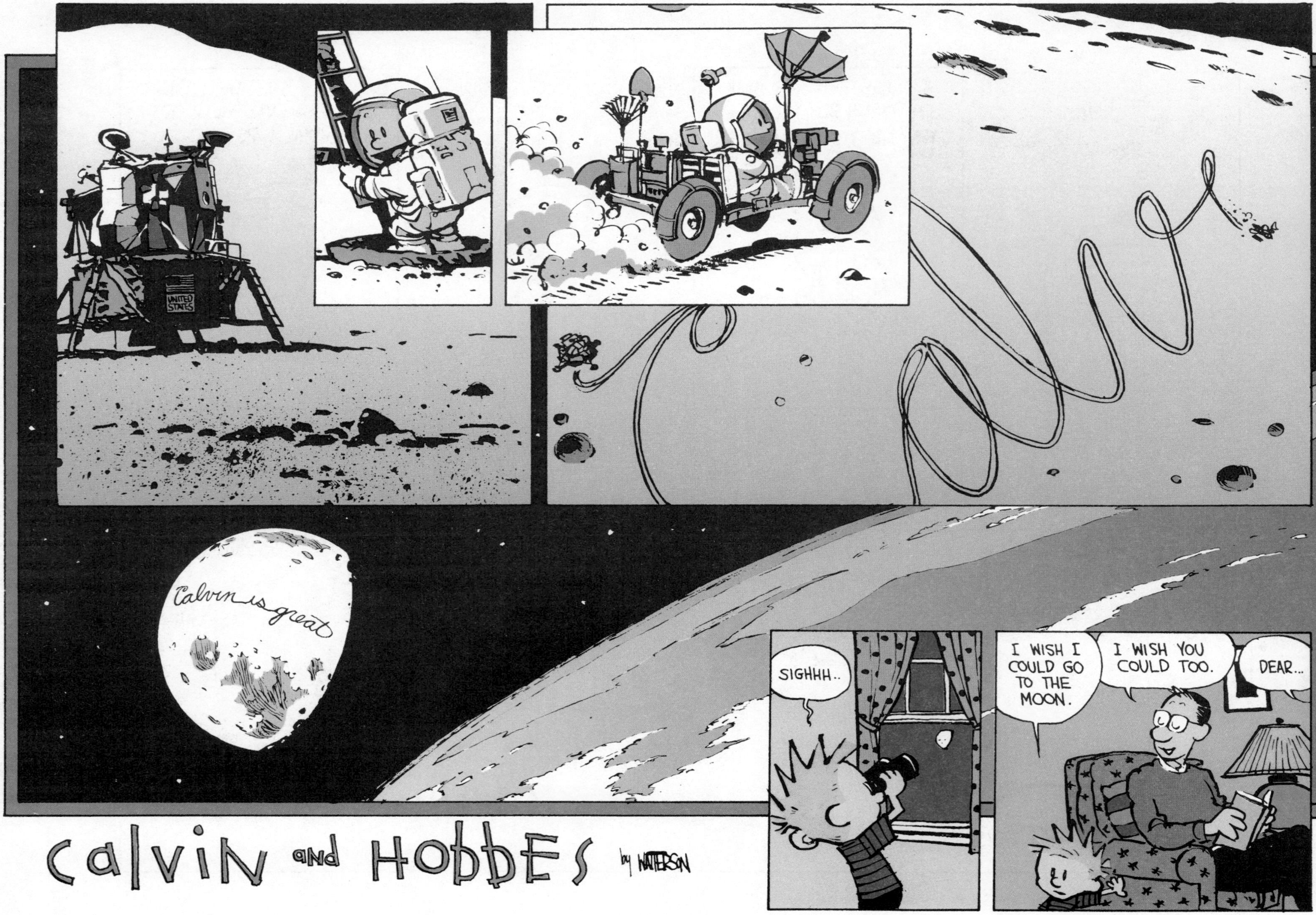
UNITED STATES
Calvin is great
SIGHHH..
I WISH I COULD GO TO THE MOON.
I WISH YOU COULD TOO.
DEAR...
Calvin and HOBBES
by WATTERSON

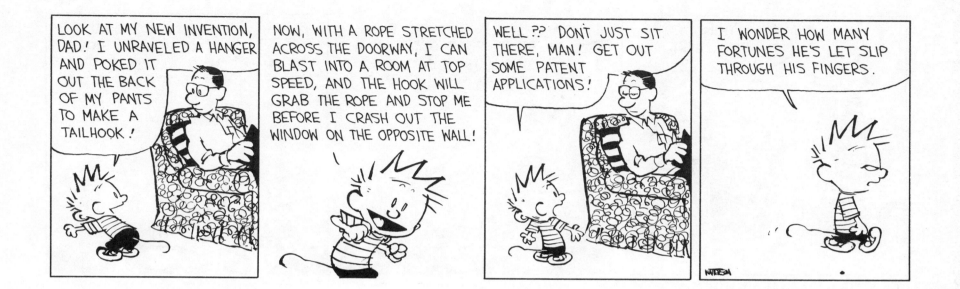

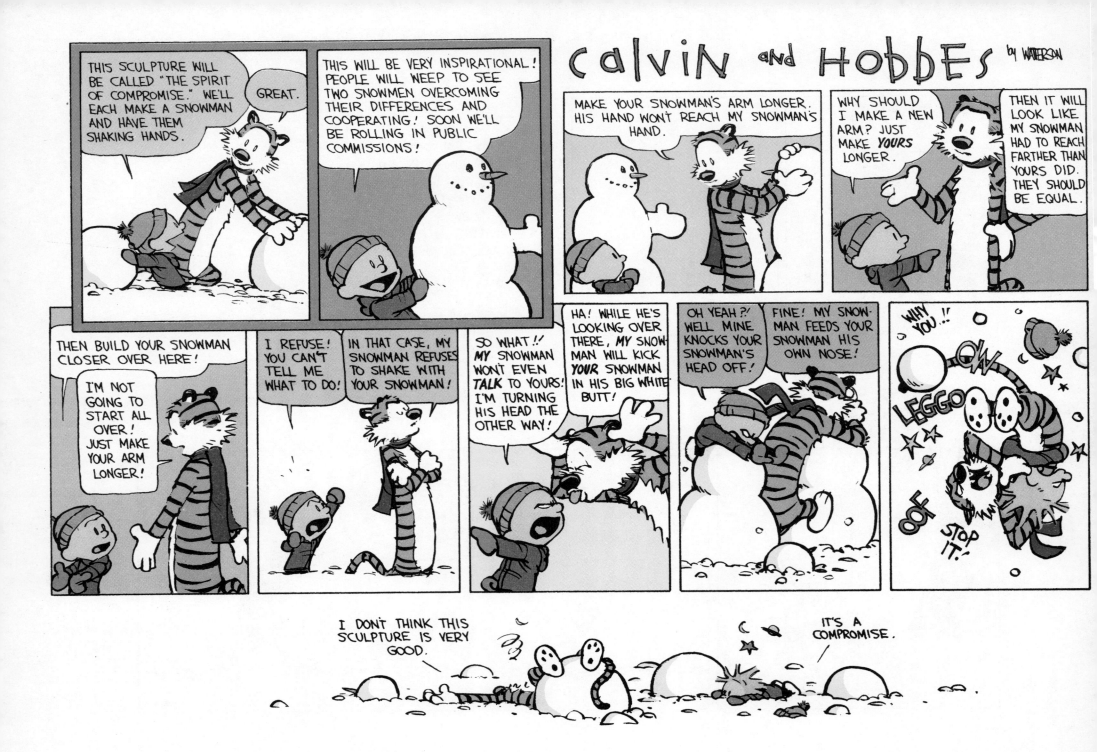

145

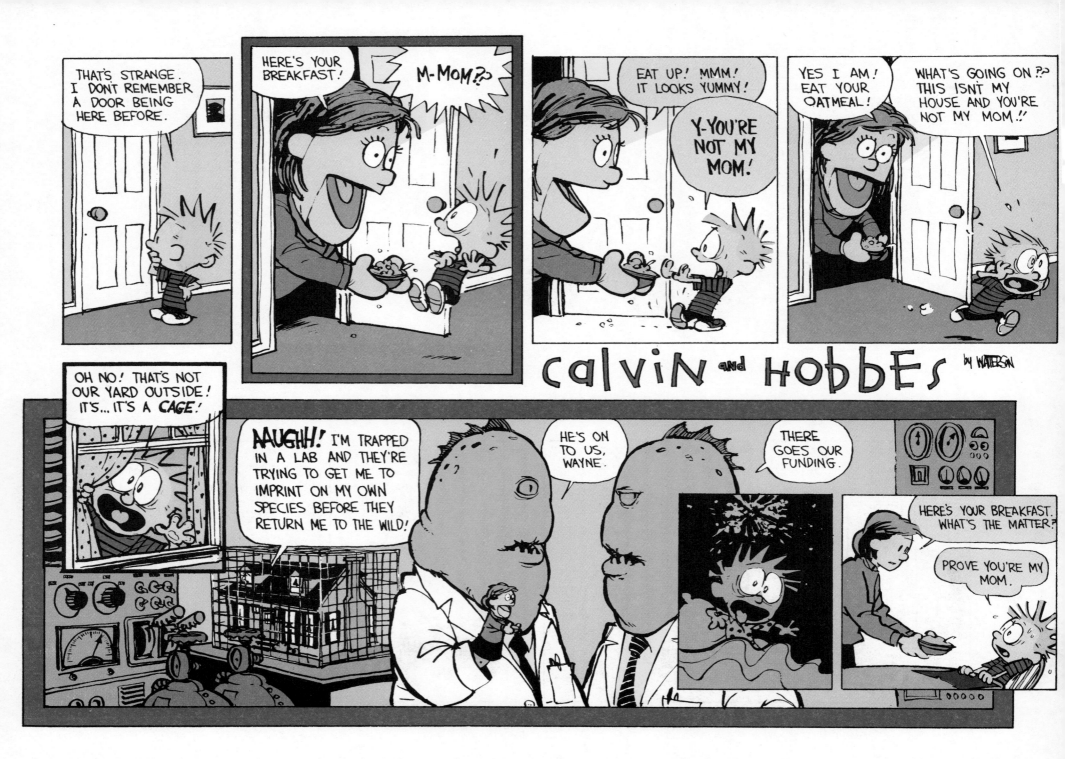

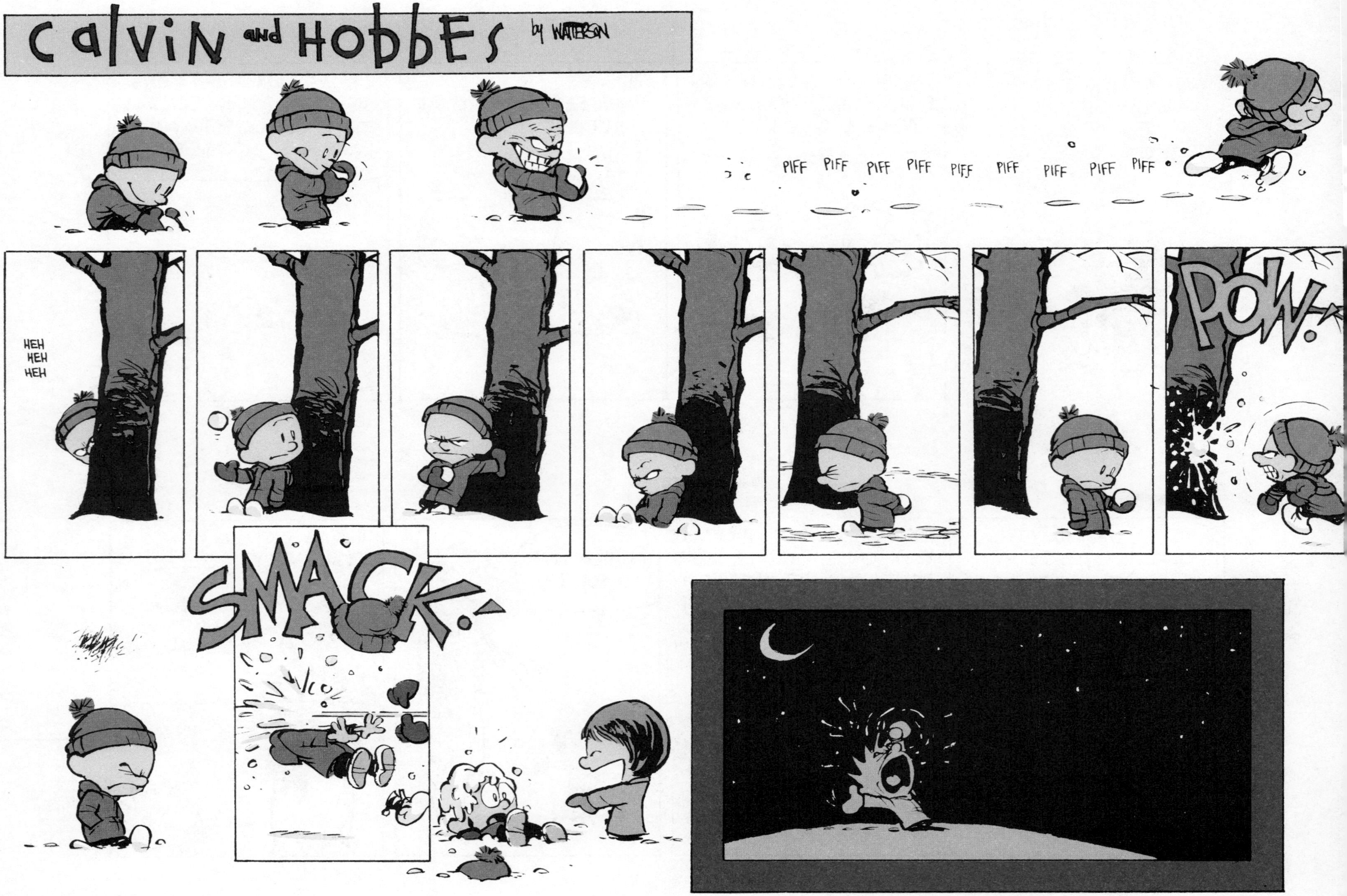
Calvin and HOBBES
by WATTERSON
PIFF PIFF PIFF PIFF PIFF PIFF PIFF PIFF PIFF
HEH HEH HEH
POW!
SMACK!

153

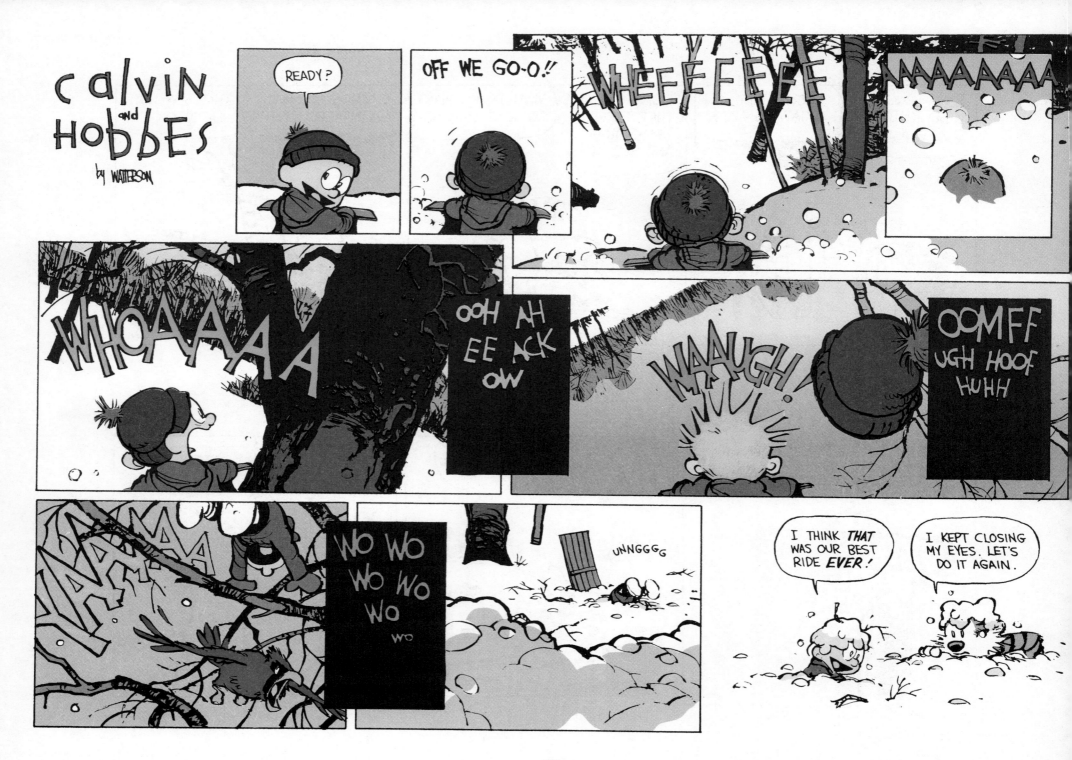

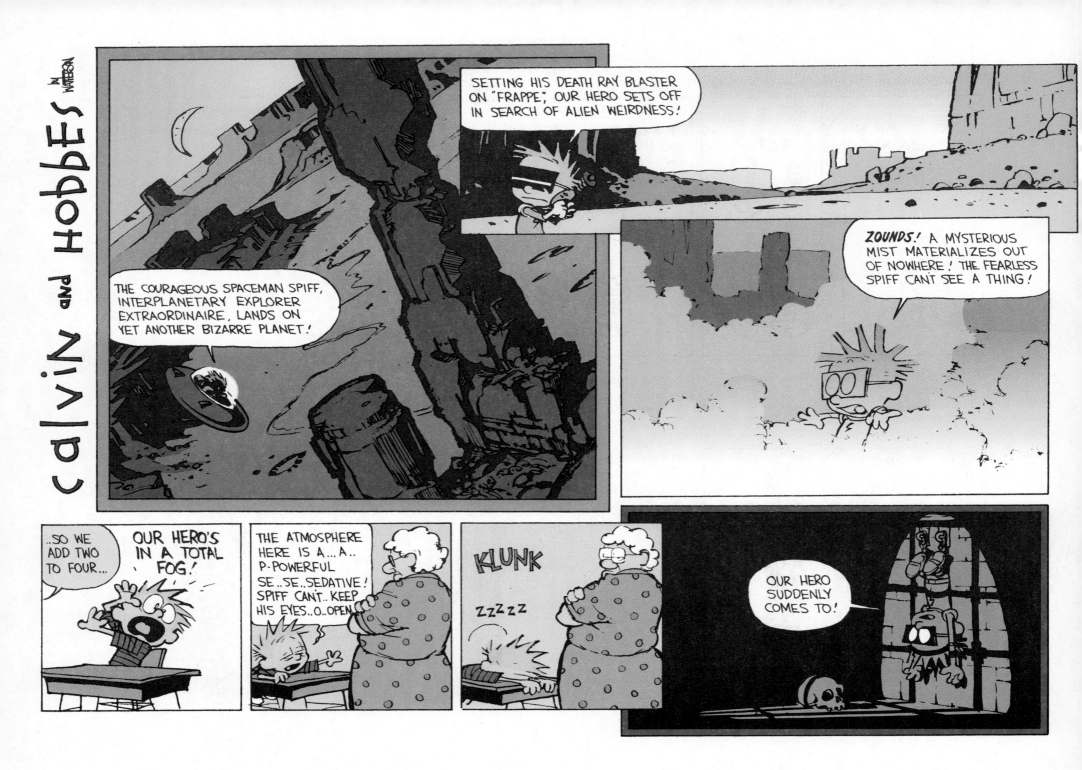

169

174

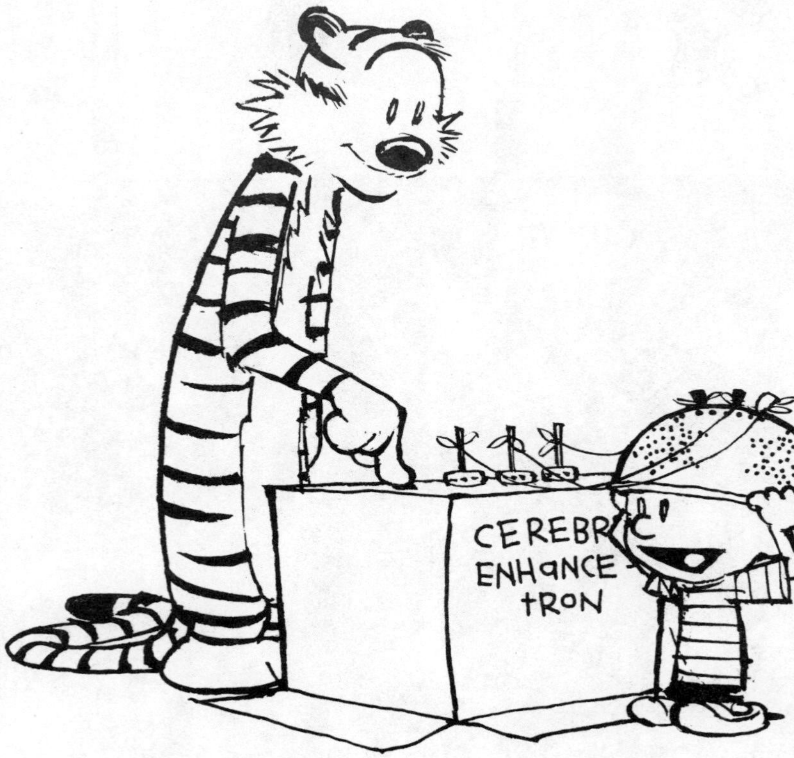
CEREBRAL
ENHANCE-
TRON